"Dear Old ROANOKE"

A Sesquicentennial Portrait, 1842–1992

Mark F. Miller

"Dear Old ROANOKE"

A Sesquicentennial Portrait, 1842–1992

MERCER UNIVERSITY PRESS

ISBN 0-86554-366-6

"Dear Old Roanoke":
A Sesquicentennial Portrait, 1842–1992

The paper used in this publication
meets the minimum requirements of American National
Standard for Information Services—Permanence of Paper
for Printed Library Materials, ANSI Z39.48-1984.

Library of Congress Cataloging-in-Publication Data

Miller, Mark F.
  ``Dear old Roanoke": a sesquicentennial portrait, 1842-1992/ by Mark F. Miller
  x + 330 pp., 8.5 x 11"
  Includes bibliographical references and index.
  ISBN 0-86554-366-6
  1. Roanoke College–History.   I. Title.

Contents

Foreword

It isn't often the author of a *centennial* history has the opportunity to greet the readers of the *sesquicentennial* history. Roanoke College is privileged to offer a few words from William Edward Eisenberg (class of 1925), author of *The First Hundred Years* and now a retired pastor living in Winchester, Virginia.

The First Hundred Years, published for Roanoke College's centennial in 1942, endeavored to relate the story of the institution's founding, its preservation during the dark days of the Civil War, and its hard-won establishment as a reputable center of learning. In point of time that has since elapsed, that volume dealt with the initial two-thirds of the record.

Another cluster of fifty years has now swiftly passed. Much has happened, and continues to happen, in the college's growth and development that surely fulfills the dreams of the founders and of those who have administered its affairs. Presidents Bittle, Dosh, Dreher, Morehead, and Smith must rejoice, I am quite sure, in the accomplishment at long last of their prophetically envisioned prayers and hopes for the school.

This third fifty-year unit of history includes the latter years of Dr. Smith's administration, the entire tenure in office of Presidents Oberly, Kendig, and Fintel, and the beginning of President Gring's.

What the record holds and what the latest story reveals is portrayed in graphic style by the author of this new volume. It brings the history of the college up to date. For all alumni and alumnae, in particular, it is a thrilling account of progress and development that will make their hearts beat with joy and pride. The espoused goal of Excellence will be seen being accomplished and achieved, even as the beacon dome of the expanded new library, dominating the entire campus, points to the fact that here is indeed a seat of learning.

God has blessed the college with gracious favor. To Him be thanksgiving and praise.

—*William Edward Eisenberg, '25*

for
Linda

Preface

This college history was designed to be seen on a table, not lost on a shelf. From the outset, this book was envisioned and planned to be a ready reminder of the remarkable story of Roanoke College. Most of all, I wanted a book that would be used and enjoyed.

I have tried to write a history that is more popular and general in nature than an "insider's account." I have attempted at every step to keep in mind the typical reader of this book—the students of Roanoke who passed through this place for four brief years yet have always kept a part of the school with them. I have hoped in every chapter to recreate a Roanoke that would be recognizable to them. This is, I trust, less a story of what went on in the boardroom and more an account of life on the back quad.

Along with the narrative of each chapter, there are two other features that are an integral part of the story: the photographs and the sketches. The photographs are a visual record of a changing campus, while the sketches—some serious, some not so serious—offer a chance to highlight an episode or character in greater detail.

Since the summer of 1985 when this project began, many people have helped and offered encouragement. I am grateful and indebted to all of these for their assistance.

Let me begin with two former students and dear friends: Carol Bernick (class of 1985) and Anne Bowles (class of 1991). After her graduation, the college hired Carol for a year to do historical research. She did an incredible job. She abstracted the trustee minutes, the faculty minutes, the Brackety-Acks, and almost every other important record group the college owns. She took research trips through Virginia, North Carolina, Maryland, and Pennsylvania, and made stops in Washington, New York, and Chicago at various repositories. She made the job of writing this history easier and better.

Anne has been my student assistant for the past four years, including the summers she spent chained to her archives desk. She has done a wonderful job in selecting most of the topics for the book's sketches as well as calendaring all of the *Collegians* and yearbooks and conducting several interviews. To my best buddies—Bernick and Bowles—a heartfelt thank you!

This project has had a publication board from the beginning. Its members have helped define and refine the nature and scope of this history. I have certainly profited from their counsel and insight. They are Clarence Caldwell, Woody Middleton, Bob Fishburn, Tex Ritter, and George Kegley.

It has been my pleasure to have had many conversations, interviews, and tours of the campus with the people who made Roanoke what it is today. Their stories and accounts enabled me to get it right. Thanks to Ray Brown, Sam Good, Tex Ritter, Clarence Caldwell, Hap Fisher, Don Sutton, Woody Middleton, William Eisenberg, and so many others. I certainly enjoyed the Elizabeth College reunions and offer a special thanks to the Seig sisters, Katharine and Martha, as well as to Gay Goodwin and Hortense Hunton.

This book has required the talents of a number of people on campus. Bob Walter of the English Department served as the manuscript's principal reader and editor and saved me from many embarrassing errors. Tex Ritter helped catch many factual errors as only Tex could.

My colleagues Dan Richardson, John Selby, and Bill Hill all provided sage advice and a receptive ear when needed. My former advisor at the University of North

Carolina, Don Higginbotham, provided some crucial assistance at a critical time. Faculty secretary Anna Gibson typed the manuscript, and Miller Hall secretary Karen Ford Harris (class of 1979) helped prepare a number of sections as well. A special thanks to the college's Audio-Visual Department—namely, Lou Graham and Mike Womack—for shooting and reproducing all of the photographic material used in this book; thanks also to the library's director, Stan Umberger, who let them do it.

Two college presidents have played important roles in bringing this book to fruition. More than anyone else, Norm Fintel was determined to see a new college history written, and he ensured that that goal was accomplished. David Gring has been most supportive of the project since he came. Judi Nelson, Director of Public Relations, has been the cheerful liaison between me and the administration during the last three years. Thanks to Frank Williams, music professor and author of the *Alma Mater Hymn,* for letting me borrow the phrase "dear old Roanoke" for the book's title. Roanoke has indeed served us well.

Numerous students have helped over the years in performing countless tasks and undertaking studies in their own right. Kathy Fairbanks, Tom Mays, Lee Scharges, and Nikki Martin went above and beyond the call.

The project has had the kind assistance of others from beyond these college walls. Robert Downey of the *Salem Times-Register* supplied a number of important photographs, as did Sara Mummert, the archivist at Gettysburg Theological Seminary in Pennsylvania. Mrs. Beverly Repass Hoch of Albuquerque, New Mexico, kindly supplied copies of the James L. Buck letters.

It has been a delight working with the people at Mercer University Press. Susan Carini and Margaret Jordan Brown, sometime managing editor and designer/production manager, respectively, have through their expertise and good humor made this book a reality.

Throughout this project, my family has never been far. My mother was always good for those phone calls and the "It'll all be fine, dear" assurances that even big boys need now and again. Thanks, Mom. My daughters, Kirsten and Casey Grey, helped the most by just being themselves. Each said, upon hearing the book would be half words and half pictures, that if I needed any help in drawing some of those pictures, I should let them know. Last, I owe an inestimable debt to the Roanoke College archivist. This project has become as much hers as it is mine. She has served as author, editor, proofreader, photo selector, typist, and general production chief in this last hectic year. Only she knows what she has meant to me. Thanks, honey.

Finally, I want to thank Dodger, my wonder dog, who took me for long walks and let me clear my head.

—*Mark F. Miller*

CHAPTER 1

"A healthy, moral neighborhood," 1842–1847

Portrait of David Bittle as a young man.

Every historian has trouble starting because it is rarely clear where any story begins. The story of Roanoke College is no exception. That story could begin in Germany in the sixteenth or seventeenth century; it could begin in the immigrant communities of southern Pennsylvania in the eighteenth century; or it could, almost certainly, begin in the rolling hills of western Maryland in the early nineteenth. However, one date stands out among the others as the moment of beginning: 19 November 1811, the birth date of David Frederick Bittle.

The world in which David Bittle grew up was still a remarkably isolated, close knit, self-contained one. Even though his father's family had immigrated to America several generations earlier (his grandfather had been born in Pennsylvania in 1759), Bittle was raised in a truly German setting—speaking only German, learning German customs and traditions, and, of course, worshiping in the Lutheran faith. As a teenager, Bittle began his study of English at a neighborhood school. As the story goes, his father joined him at home in the evenings, trying to master this new language.

Bittle's lifelong traits soon became evident while he was growing to manhood on his family's simple farm. He was industrious and determined, never content with simple answers or solutions, convinced that through hard work and dedication all was possible.

Young Bittle's life changed in 1828, with the arrival of the Reverend Abraham Reck. The new pastor of the Middletown Valley congregations was determined to foster the advance of Lutheranism, in part through the training of some of the more able, young minds. Two years before, Reck had been instrumental in the establishment of the Gettysburg Theological Seminary. Furthermore, he continued to be an ardent supporter of the Gettysburg Gymnasium, a preparatory school that in time would become Gettysburg College.

Reck had an obvious effect on the seventeen year old Bittle. Two years later, in 1830, with his pastor's encouragement and his parents' blessing, David Bittle headed north to enroll in the Gymnasium. Reck was doubtlessly influential in arranging for Bittle's financial assistance to attend the school. The American Education Society was a Lutheran aid organization that provided the resources to enable preministerial students to attend the Gymnasium before their enrollment in the seminary. Bittle never forgot his debt and the opportunity that such assistance afforded; he vowed both to repay the loan and to encourage others to take advantage of such offers, two promises that he would keep.

As a student, Bittle was not exceptionally gifted; rather, his instructors recalled him as "diligent" and "steadfast." While in the school, Bittle and a number of other boarding students formed a small club, "the Brotherhood," which spared them some of the costs of room and board. Bittle was also a member of the debating society, probably "The Philomatheans," because as we shall see, Bittle would take both group names with him to Virginia and incorporate them into his own school.

By 1832 the Gymnasium received a charter transforming it from an academy to a college: namely, Pennsylvania College (Gettysburg today). His college course of study offered a classical education: Latin and Greek, mathematics and natural sciences, mineralogy and botany, and moral and intellectual science.

A view of the campus of Pennsylvania College (today Gettysburg College) drawn in the 1830s when both David Bittle and Christopher Baughman were students. (Courtesy of Lutheran Theological Seminary, Gettysburg, Pennsylvania)

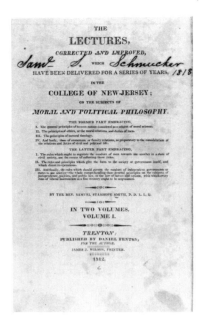

Samuel Simon Schmucker signed his copy of Reverend Samuel Stanhope Smith's Lectures, *a text he used while a student at Princeton between 1818–1820.*

Immediately upon completion of his undergraduate studies in 1835, Bittle commenced his ministerial training. Across town and upon a ridge was the Lutheran seminary in which Bittle enrolled. There he met another principal force in this formative period of his young life, the redoubtable Samuel Simon Schmucker, who was a Lutheran churchman of the first order. Schmucker's influence would cast a shadow not only over David Bittle, but over a whole generation of nineteenth-century Lutheran leaders.

Samuel Simon Schmucker, a patriarch of American Lutheranism, the founder of Gettysburg Seminary, and David Bittle's principal mentor.
(Courtesy of Lutheran Theological Seminary, Gettysburg, Pennsylvania.)

SAMUEL SIMON SCHMUCKER (1799–1873), the son of John George and Elizabeth Gross Schmucker, was born in Hagerstown, Maryland. After the family moved to York, Pennsylvania, he attended York Academy. At the age of fifteen, Samuel entered the University of Pennsylvania, where he studied for two years. Returning to York in 1816, he was placed in charge of the classical department of York Academy.

Since there was no Lutheran theological seminary in the United States at that time, Schmucker studied theology with Dr. Heinrich Helmuth at the University of Pennsylvania; with his father while in York; and at Princeton Seminary, where he spent two years (1819–1820). On 2 June 1820, he was licensed to preach by the ministerium. Later that year, he accepted a call to become pastor to four congregations in the area around New Market, Virginia. Arriving early in 1821, he stayed for six years. This was to be his only service as a congregational pastor.

Schmucker became a vital force in the Lutheran Church in America. He played an active role in the establishment of the general synod in 1820, serving as its president from 1828 until 1845. He was a prolific writer, authoring more than forty works on theological issues. Doctrinally, Schmucker began his career as a conservative Lutheran. However, by the time his career had come to a close, he had come to espouse the more liberal views of "American Lutheranism." Among his more controversial writings was, with an unknown coauthor, the *Definite Synodical Platform,* in 1855, which charged the Augsburg Confession with five errors. Such controversy led to the eventual breakup of the general synod in 1867.

Schmucker had long felt the need for a Lutheran seminary in America and used his own parsonage in New Market to that end for three years. Finally, in 1826, after much prodding from Schmucker, the general synod established Gettysburg Seminary as the first theological school of the Lutheran Church in America, electing Schmucker its first professor. He headed the seminary and served as professor of systematic theology for thirty-eight years, helping prepare more than 500 young men for the Lutheran ministry, among them David F. Bittle.

The Encyclopedia of the Lutheran Church, ed. Julius Bodensieck for the Lutheran World Federation (Minneapolis: Augsburg Publishing House, 1965). Rev. Luke Schmucker, *The Schmucker Family and the Lutheran Church in America* (n.p., 1937).

GETTYSBURG LUTHERAN THEOLOGICAL SEMINARY

"The institution having been now regularly organized, the Professor immediately commenced his lectures with great zeal and ability." Thus speaks the early record of Gettysburg Lutheran Theological Seminary, which first opened its doors for instruction on 5 September 1826.

Lutherans had long felt the need for a theological seminary in America. At the strong urging of Samuel Simon Schmucker and others, the general synod finally agreed in 1825. Of five choices, Gettysburg, Pennsylvania, was selected as the site, in part because its offer was the most generous and in part because of its convenient and central location. Schmucker was the near-unanimous choice for its professor and head. The first session met in the Adams County Academy. Eight of that year's fifteen students were present the first day to participate in the four-hour ceremony inaugurating Schmucker and marking the opening of the school. The seminary remained there until 1832, when it moved to a new site on a ridge to the west of town.

It didn't take Schmucker long to realize that the majority of his students were not academically prepared for theological work and that he had neither the time nor the energy to make up for the deficiencies. By June 1827, the Classical School was begun in the Adams County Academy, with one teacher and two students. Two years later it was renamed the Gettysburg

Gymnasium and in 1832 was chartered as Pennsylvania College (the present Gettysburg College). Its primary purpose was to prepare students to meet the academic standards of the seminary.

While the seminary program was designed to take three years, most students left after two, since the demand for Lutheran pastors was so great. By 1830 the need arose for a second professor, but for most of the 1830s that position was unfilled on a full-time basis. During David Bittle's tenure at the seminary, Charles Philip Krauth, president of Pennsylvania College (and Bittle's future brother-in-law) taught several classes. Schmucker taught by using both lecture and discussion. Many of his lectures were later published as textbooks (e.g., his *Popular Theology*). Classes focused on theology, exegesis, ancient languages, ecclesiastical history, and homiletics. German was emphasized, with many courses being taught in it. The spiritual life was cultivated as well. There were private devotions, daily devotional exercises by instructors, and weekly conferences on the more practical aspects of religion. Students were examined twice a year in the presence of the board of directors.

Abdel Ross Wentz, *History, 1826–1965*, vol. 1 of *Gettysburg Lutheran Theological Seminary* (Harrisburg PA: Evangelical Press).

LUTHERAN THEOLOGICAL SEMINARY, GETTYSBURG, PENNA.

Gettysburg, Sept. 19th 1842.

The Gettysburg Seminary where Bittle and Baughman were trained. (Courtesy Lutheran Theological Seminary, Gettysburg, Pennsylvania.)

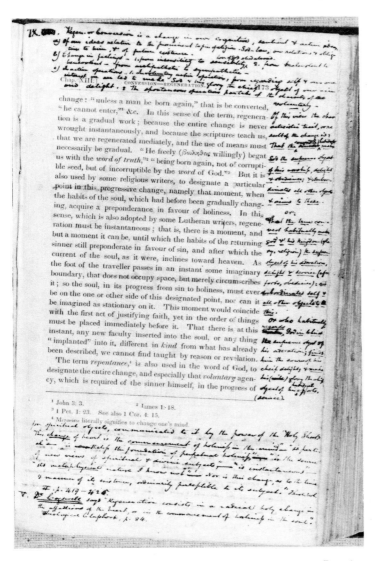

A page of one of Schmucker's published works; the notes are in David Bittle's hand, a student in the 1830s.

While in the seminary, Bittle served as a tutor and refined his skills as he prepared for his life's calling. It was also during this time that Bittle found another object of his affections, Louisa Krauth, the sister of the college's president. By 1837 Bittle completed his studies, was licensed to preach, and on 13 November, married his Louisa, a native Virginian.

Upon pulling up stakes in Pennsylvania, Bittle accepted a call from St. John's congregation in Augusta County, Virginia, near the town of Staunton. The parish was a rambling collection of several towns and villages, and featured at least three separate congregations worshiping at different sites, in an area covering 180 square miles. One of Bittle's first priorities was to establish a central location where the entire congregation might come together. According to local legend, two families started for the center— one from the northern limit of the parish and the other from the southernmost region. Where they met, the new church would be constructed. The wagons met at a place they called Mt. Tabor, and here Bittle built his church.

Earliest known photograph of David and Louisa Bittle. This daguerreotype was probably taken in a Staunton studio in the early 1840s.

The parsonage at Mt. Tabor. Bittle's classical academy first met in the parlor on the first floor.

In 1837, David F. Bittle, having just graduated from Gettysburg Theological Seminary, accepted a call to become pastor to a number of congregations in the vicinity of Staunton, Virginia. In the following year, the Reformed and Lutheran congregations that shared St. John's Church decided to separate, with the Lutherans building a new structure in a more central location. This new church was to be called Mt. Tabor.

A building committee of the church contracted with Benjamin F. Hailman to build the main church and a small session house. The contract read in part:

> That said Hailman engages to build a church on the lands of Peter Strouse, the situation of which may be pointed out by said committee. Said house is to be 50 feet long, 43 feet wide and 15 feet high of bricks, 18 inch wide from the stone to the joist, and fill to the top of the joist with bricks. Stone under church to be one foot above ground at the lowest place. The foundation to be dug solid. Said Hailman will also plaster said church. Said Hailman will also build a Session house 14 ft. long and 12 ft. wide, eight ft. high of bricks, with a sufficient stone foundation and one chimney, and plaster the same; all

to be done in a good and workmanlike manner and of good material. It is understood that said Hailman is to build 2 flues in the gable end for the purpose of conveying the smoke from the pipes.

For the aforementioned work, Hailman was to be paid "the sum of $670, current money of Virginia," in three equal installments.

The building was completed in 1839 and dedicated in May 1840. Reverend Lewis Eichelberger preached the sermon, using Luke 23:33 as his text; Reverend Phillip Krauth consecrated the church building. But it was not until 23 December 1840 that the title of the land was actually transferred from Peter and Catherine Strouse to the trustees of the church. The cost was $62.50. David Bittle served as pastor of Mt. Tabor until 1845, when he accepted a call from a parish in Middletown, Maryland. His successor was Alonzo P. Ludden. The building served the congregation until 1889, when a new building was erected across the road.

The Historical and Anniversary Committee, *Sesquicentennial History: Mount Tabor Lutheran Church, 1839–1989* (Staunton VA: McClure Co., 1989).

Bittle's church at Mt. Tabor. The structure stood until 1889 when a new, larger church was constructed across the road. Many of the bricks of the original church were salvaged and incorporated into the new edifice. (Courtesy Mt. Tabor Lutheran Church).

A letter addressed to Bittle while at Mt. Tabor.

Evidence of Baughman's association with the academy is scarce. Here is a part of a letter of recommendation he wrote for a student.

David Bittle quickly immersed himself in synod affairs. Beginning with the synod's convention of 1838, Bittle marked his presence by being elected secretary of the Education Society, a group dedicated to helping attract young men for the ministry. By the following year, Bittle was elected president of the society, underscoring his dedication to the cause; and it was also at this convention, at Zion Church in Roanoke County, that Bittle was ordained to the ministry. The Virginia Synod further appointed him its secretary for its conventions of 1841 and 1842. Bittle's impact had indeed already been felt.

It was also in 1842 that church governance was altered to reflect a growing, westward movement of the Lutheran population. A new synod was organized at Zion Church in Floyd County, and the Synod of Western Virginia came into existence. The new synod, it was hoped, could better serve the needs of the faithful in the hills and valleys south and west of the James River. Five years hence, the existence of this new synod would have a profound influence on a fledgling academy located at Mt. Tabor.

The neighborhoods around Staunton witnessed the arrival of a newcomer in the summer of 1842, another Lutheran minister, Christopher C. Baughman. His coming would prove most fortuitous. Like Bittle, he had attended the preparatory school in Gettysburg and was graduated from Pennsylvania College in 1839. It seems plausible that the two had become acquainted during their stay in the small Pennsylvania town. In any event, Baughman elected to study for the ministry privately and accepted a call to a church in Maryland in 1841. In only a year, though, Baughman's throat and general health had begun to fail. Searching perhaps for a warmer climate and a less-taxing assignment, Baughman headed south to Staunton for rest and recovery.

It did not take long for the two men to meet and begin plans and projects. The origins of a small pastor's school may have been in David Bittle's mind for some time, and with the addition of Baughman, Bittle was prepared to make his dream a reality. In the fall of 1842, with perhaps a dozen students, Bittle opened the doors of his house to begin his classical academy. His purpose was twofold. First, as a service to his parishioners, he was dedicated to the educational needs of their young sons. Second, Bittle could well remember Reverend Reck's efforts and inspiration. By opening his own school and by hoping to guide others into the ministry, he could begin to repay his debt. Bittle's congregation approved his endeavor and granted him two days a week away from his pastoral duties to devote to the school. Almost from the outset, Baughman became a formidable presence in the school's operation. Because Bittle had to attend to the continued demands of his church, Baughman served as principal and taught languages to the students; Bittle offered instruction in mathematics. The little school, as yet unnamed, continued through the winter and into the spring with little recognition and less fanfare.

When the Virginia Synod met in the spring of 1843, Bittle and Baughman were determined to argue for the support of their fledgling institution. They hoped to receive not only the acceptance of the convention but, ideally, its official sanction with the promise of financial support. They were rudely disappointed; the synod voted down their resolution on the grounds that they had not had ample time to consider the proposition. Furthermore, the convention had never before voted to endorse a school. Although stunned, Bittle and Baughman regrouped. Rallying support from among the membership, the two ministers managed to bring the whole issue back to the convention later that very afternoon.

This time, the politicking had worked. The assembly voted to embrace the resolution and appointed a committee to review the question and to recommend a course of action. The next day the committee submitted its report. It suggested that a classical academy, now referred to as the Virginia Institute, was indeed a worthy project and that the synod should look upon it as a source of future ministers as well. The committee also resolved to ask the convention to petition the newly formed Synod of Western Virginia to see if it might join in this undertaking.

Fresh from their success, the two ministers were eager to follow up their advantage. The following month, June 1843, Baughman set off to meet with the convention of Western Virginia. At Burke's Garden, Virginia, Baughman delivered his plea. He stated that "the synod had established a classical Institute and located it in the valley of Virginia, in which every advantage would be offered to young men to secure a thorough academical education."

With official backing secured, Bittle and Baughman were determined to establish a more permanent setting for the institute. Immediately they began soliciting funds from local parishioners and patrons,

A present-day photograph of the site of the Virginia Institute. Bittle's parsonage still stands today, a few yards to the right.

Benjamin Hailman, a major benefactor of the church, donated the land for the institute and served on its board and that of the college until after the Civil War.

Mrs. Benjamin Hailman.

and as the summer progressed, so did the school. An influential resident, Benjamin Hailman, donated land for the school, and numerous "friends" contributed funds for the construction. Two wooden structures were raised and readied to house classes by the fall of 1843. Hailman provided most of the materials for the structures as well as significant funding for the undertaking. Only one first-hand description of the buildings survives, that recorded by the future college's longtime professor of mathematics, Simon Carson Wells. He related that "the first building was a one-storied structure of two rooms, one used for recitation purposes, the other being intended for a library. In architecture it was severely simple, with none whatever of the graces of conveniences now aimed at in school or college buildings."

The second building was "a two-storied affair with four rooms, and was even more unpretentious, if possible, in its style and in all its appointments, than the first. In this Brotherhood, as it was called, the early students were lodged, and here they prepared themselves, their simple meals." The name of this structure was an obvious reference to the old Gymnasium at Gettysburg; to Bittle, the link was as symbolic as it was real.

In preparation for the upcoming term, Bittle and Baughman needed to spread the word about the readiness of the newly christened Virginia Institute For three consecutive weeks in July, the Staunton *Spectator and General Advisor* carried the announcement of the school's opening planned for August. The school was "situated in a healthy, moral neighborhood, near Mt. Tabor Church, Augusta County, Virginia. Its location is delightful, and easy of access, being only about two miles northeast of Middlebrook." The academy offered two 5-month sessions per year at a tuition rate of $15 per term. The ad noted that "great care has been taken to make its organization complete and efficient. With this view buildings sufficiently spacious to accommodate a large number of students will soon be completed; and the services of gentlemen well qualified to teach have been secured." Those gentlemen were, of course, listed as "Rev. C. C. Baughman, A.M., Principal; Rev. D. F. Bittle, A.M., Assistant." The

A sketch of "the Brotherhood"; this spartan structure featured classrooms downstairs and a dormitory upstairs. Roanoke's origins were humble indeed.

Earl H. Tiffany '16 was instrumental in having a number of the Institute's foundation stones identified and shipped to the campus in Salem.

Those stones were then shaped and recrafted into this memorial and dedicated in 1956. The marker stands today next to the entrance of the Alumni Gymnasium.

announcement concluded with this observation: "Particular attention will be paid to the moral character of students. They will attend service at the church on Sabbath morning and a Bible recitation in the afternoon, conducted by the Principal."

No official records survive of that fall session: no board documents or letters or notes of the instructors.

"The Debated Was Decided on the Affirmative"

On 2 September 1843, the students of the Virginia Institute met to form a debating society, which they named the Philomathean Society of Virginia Institute. Its purpose was to "promote the intellectual and moral improvement of its members and curculate [sic] a spirit of fraternal regard between them." The first question selected for debate was: "Is man pro[m]pted to the performance [sic] of any action except by self-interest?" At the following meeting, the question was debated "for some time," but there was no decision "in consequence of the Pres. participating in the debate."

The students met on a weekly basis, proposing the question for the next meeting, selecting the declaimers, and then discussing the current question. After several meetings, the society decided to have a public debate for the entertainment of the "ladies and gentlemen in the vicinity." The proposed question was: "Would it be good policy in the U. States government to emancipate and colonize the slaves of the U. States?"

Questions for debate touched on philosophical as well as social and political issues. The following are some of the questions debated in the Philomathean Society's first year. It should be noted that decisions were based on the technique of presentation, not on the "rightness" of the answer.

•"Which has the greater influence over the minds of men, woman or money?"

"After a long and sanguine debate it was decided on the affirmative."

• "Which deserves the greater praise, a statesman or a soldier?"

"After considerable debate, it was decided on the negative."

• "Which have the greater right to complain of the white population, the African or the Indian?"

Decided on the negative.

• "Which is the stronger passion, love or anger?"

Decided on the affirmative.

• "Which rests on the more firm basis, a Republican or Monarchical government?"

"After an interesting discussion, it was decided on the negative."

• "Which deserves the greater applause, Columbus for discovering America or Washington for protecting it?"

Decided on the affirmative.

• "Which has been the more to be dreaded by institutions of the U. States, Intemperance or Roman Catholicism?"

"After quite an interesting discussion, it was decided on the Negative."

From the minute book of the Philomathean Society, 1843–1850.

The only surviving record is a student ledger book, dated 2 September 1843, which was the first entry noting the charter meeting of a new student debating society. It should be no great surprise that its name was the "Philomathean Society." According to its list, there were eighteen students enrolled in some course of study that year, a successful if humble beginning.

The society served both as a debating forum as well as a setting for entertainment. The students discussed such timely topics as Texas's admission to the union and the righteousness of slavery along with debate over "the desirable traits in women."

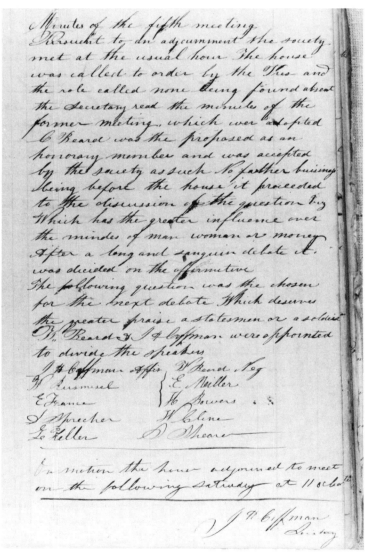

A page from the Philomathean Society minute book. This 1843 debate asked "which deserves the greater praise, a statesman or a soldier?"

After a successful first year in operation, Baughman and Bittle, with the support of several local individuals, decided that the Augusta County school should be officially licensed by the Commonwealth of Virginia. Accordingly, in the fall of 1844 Bittle drew up a petition for a charter to present to the state legislature. It was faithfully delivered to Richmond, and by 30 January 1845, the Virginia assembly and senate gave final approval to the charter request. The charter established the "Virginia Collegiate Institute" and called for a board of trustees of twenty-three members to be a self-perpetuating body and to hold legal title to all lands and property of the institute. The document stipulated that a quorum of nine be required to conduct routine business and that a majority of board members be present for the annual election of officers and the selection of instructors.

A copy of the petition to the state legislature asking for a charter as the Virginia Collegiate Institute. The 1845 request was granted.

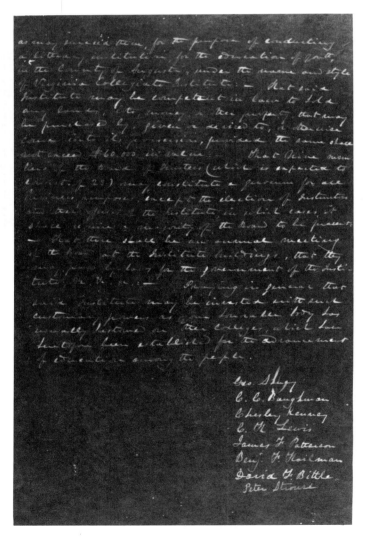

Instruction in this preparatory school revolved around the nineteenth-century notion of the recitation. With all the students gathered together, the teacher would expect them to read and recite their lessons in common. Memorization of certain passages of their languages studied, for example, was a principal means to achieve mental rigor. For the student who was unprepared, the teacher's scorn could be well observed by the fellow students.

11 April 1845: The Principal was requested to suggest a proper course of study to be published, in connection with the advertisement of the Institution, in the papers of Staunton. The Tuition for the scholastic year of 10 months was fixed at $30.00 to be paid in advance.

The Principal was authorized to sell five scholarships at sixty dollars, $60.00, each, entitling the purchaser to three year's [sic] tuition; provided that no scholarship be sold to parents or guardians.

25 July 1845: The Principal, the Rev. C. C. Baughman, was requested to have such notice of the Institution published in such papers as he might deem necessary.

31 Dec. 1846: It was thought that the Institution was not favorably located by some; whilst others were wholly opposed to its removal. The subject of its removal was agitated, and to test the sense of the Board, B. F. Hailman Esqr. offered the following res. "Res.—that Virginia Collegiate Institute be removed from its present location to the Town of Salem in the County of Roanoke Va." This resolution was very fully discussed and finally decided by a vote of *seven yeas, to five nays*. (The whole number of the members present in favor of the removal was nine—The Pres., Jacob Baylor Esqr., and Capt. R. H. Holland Sect. did not vote.)

Messrs. Geo. Shuey, R. H. Holland and Peter Strouse were appointed a committee to dispose of the property of the Institution situated in Augusta Co. (in any way thought best), and apply the proceeds to the payment of the debt now due for the Buildings, and report to the Board at its next meeting. The Pres., Jacob Baylor, was added to the above comm.

It was decided that the removal take place on or before the 1st day of June 1847. Rev. G. Scherer, M. Miller, Geo. W. Rader, Doc. J. H. Griffin, and Jno. P. Kizer, were appointed a committee to procure suitable buildings in Salem Roanoke Co. for the use of the Institution.

The Board authorized the sale of Forty Scholarships at fifty dollars each, entitling the purchaser to three year's [sic] tuition in Va. Col. Inst.—the money on all cases to be paid strictly in advance. The Board further ordered that any indigent young man, of approved piety and ability, having the Ministry [in] view, might be permitted to purchase a three year's [sic] scholarship on the terms specified above.

Excerpts from the minutes of the Board of Trustees of the Virginia Collegiate Institute, 1845–1895.

This "miniature", a customary painting of the nineteenth century, depicts Julia Bittle Pendleton, a daughter of David and Louisa Bittle. Julia was one of the first women to attend Roanoke, as a special student during the Civil War.

During this moment of triumph, tragedy struck the Bittle home. Since their arrival in Augusta County, David and Louisa had brought three children into the world: Charles Krauth, Thomas Chalmers, and Ruth Pauline. Unexpectedly in February 1845, just two weeks after receiving news of the charter, the Bittles' eldest son died. Whether the decision had been long considered or was more an instantaneous response to escape this painful memory, David Bittle resolved in any event to leave Augusta County just a month after his son's death. After eight years of labor—with a new church, a school, and countless friends—the Bittles were going home. He accepted a call from two congregations to return to Middletown, Maryland, the place where he was born. Thus, David Bittle passes out of the picture for a time, but not for good. When Bittle returned eight years later, the school he inherited had changed in every fashion: in nature and scope, in composition, and even in location.

A "Valedictory Address" from a student at the Institute in 1844. In the mid-nineteenth century, each student offered a "farewell address" upon graduation or upon leaving the institution.

The institute's trustees met first in April 1845 to conduct business and to elect officers; lacking a majority, the board had to call another meeting for July. By the summer, then, officers were duly elected: Baughman was affirmed as principal; and to replace Bittle, the trustees hired A. P. Ludden as the school's assistant.

A lone student account of life at the institute survives today. John Jacob Scherer attended the Augusta County academy and kept a diary that he would use later in life to sketch a brief autobiography. He found the school, in time, to be a helpful, supportive place; but at first, things appeared rather bleak. "Soon after I got there," Scherer recalled, "I broke a glass inkstand, and was severely reprimanded for it. I went out behind the building and wept, and longed and longed for mother."

The institute's days near Staunton were numbered. After the initial eighteen students had enrolled in 1843–1844, the figures improved to twenty-one for 1844–1845. But then the slide began. Records reveal that the student count dropped to fourteen for the

1845–1846 session and fell further to ten in 1846–1847. Clearly, something had to be done. The trustees met on the last day of the year, 1846, and voted 9 to 5 to search for greener pastures. After several years of trials and tribulations, the experiment had come to a close. The board recommended that the school move to the town of Salem, a prosperous community of 2,000 inhabitants, about 150 miles to the south. Salem seemed to afford at least two advantages. First, there was no other chartered academy in town. Second, the site was close to the dividing line between the two synods. From this more central location, it was argued, the institute might better enjoy an increase in enrollment and enhanced prospects.

Still, there were no guarantees. The decision to relocate must have been a wrenching one for the board, not to mention for Baughman and the students. With more hope than confidence, the members of the institute loaded its equipment and belongings onto a single wagon and headed south in April 1847. The memories of its Augusta County days soon began to fade as the fledgling school pinned its hopes on another community and on a faraway county named Roanoke.

A gavel made from the wood of the original Virginia Collegiate Institute building. It was presented to President H. Sherman Oberly by the D.C. Chapter of the Roanoke College Alumni Association, 14 November 1957.

CHAPTER 2

"A lively time in Salem,"
1847–1860

ROANOKE COLLEGE
SALEM, ROANOKE CO.
VIRGINIA

In the spring of 1847, few people in Salem had ever heard of the Virginia Collegiate Institute. When its wagon rolled into town, the school arrived unnoticed, unheralded, and uninvited. Christopher Baughman and the other school officials knew that timing was critical if they were to offer a summer session and thereby continue the institute's income. Within a few weeks, arrangements had been made to rent an abandoned Baptist church located just east of town, and preparations began for the upcoming term. By May, the building committee of the board of trustees secured the purchase of four acres just a block north of town, approved plans for a new building, and two days later, signed contracts to begin construction.

Nathaniel Burwell was a leading Salem citizen and the first President of the college's Board of Trustees. This student description services: "All who ever saw him remember Mr. Burwell. A gentleman of the olden times, a vision of the past and type of the old English days we so love to read about. He rode a handsome chestnut sorrel horse, with silver plated bit and stirrups that shone in their polished lustre."

BYLAWS OF THE TOWN OF SALEM

"11th. Slaves, free negroes and mulattoes shall not be permitted to gather in companies or groups in the streets or alleys of the Town on the Sabbath or at night, nor to appear drunk in the Town at any time, under the same penalty provided for the offence of appearing or being found in the town at night, without permission, after the ringing of the bell.

"12th. The owner, if known, of any animal that may die within the limits of the corporation shall immediately remove the same to such a distance without said limits, as will prevent its offensive smell from reaching any part of the Town, under the penalty of not less than One nor more than Ten Dollars for every day such dead animal shall be permitted to remain in town; and if no owner can be found, it shall be the duty of the Sergeant to cause the same to be removed forthwith, at the expense of the Town, and have it deposited at least one hundred yards from any public road.

"13th. If any person shall exhibit a stallion on any of the streets of the Town in which persons reside, he shall be subject to a fine of Five Dollars for every such offense.

"14th. No person shall be permitted to keep or confine his or her hogs, cows, or other animals in any part of his or her lots, so as to produce a nuisance, and every occupier of a house or lot who shall do so, and fail to remove such nuisance when required by the Sergeant, shall be fined Fifty cents for every 24 hours; and every owner of a privy who shall fail to keep it properly cleansed and limed so as to prevent it from being offensive to the neighborhood in which it may be located, shall forfeit and pay a fine of Fifty Cents for every day its offensiveness may continue.

"15th. A tax of Five Dollars shall be colected [sic] from every exhibition of a menagerie or circus, and a tax of of [sic] Three Dollars on all other public shows within the corporation."
Bylaws of the Town of Salem, Roanoke County, Va., June 1, 1859.

On 24 May 1847, the first session commenced in Salem on East Hill in the old church. Several students had followed the institute from Augusta, and to their ranks had come another score from the local vicinity. For the year's charges, a student could expect to pay $30 for tuition, $20 board, $8 for washing, $6 for lights and fuel, and room rent for $3, for a total of $67. Ministerial students were offered a discounted rate of $54.

The academic year included a summer term from May through September and a winter term from November to April. Five weeks of vacation separated the two sessions. During the first winter term of 1847–1848, conditions at the old church proved to be less than satisfactory. Severe cold forced the institute to seek other quarters, and space was rented in a building in town. Soon the school moved again as the local Presbyterian academy offered to share some of its space. By the beginning of the May term, 1848, the institute's own building was ready, and enrollment had climbed to a lofty thirty-four. The school's building was eminently simple—a two and a half storied square edifice with the topmost floor unfinished. The center section of today's Administration Building, this building lacked its future wings, the third story, and the porches that would soon be added. On the main floor were two recitation rooms and the "Long Room," which served as a multipurpose space: the chapel, the library, the laboratory, and a place for convocations. Upstairs were the student rooms, and in the basement, Principal Baughman and his family took up residence.

Soon the campus began to take shape. By 1849, under Baughman's supervision, students planted trees in the front of the campus; and after clearing additional ground, a fence was constructed across the front of the property. Baughman was eager to add to the physical plant as well. The principal shortly thereafter purchased an additional four-acre tract (today's Back Quad where the Student Center now stands) and built a separate residence for himself and his family. Apparently, living in the basement was not all that it was cracked up to be! In Baughman's vacated quarters, the students were allowed to establish their "Mess

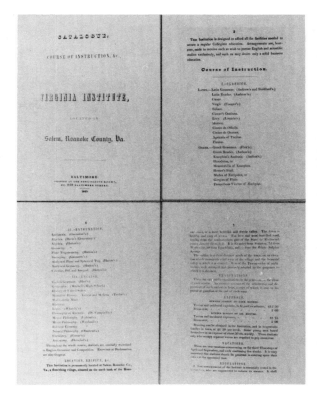

An early catalog of the school soon after its move to Salem, "a flourishing village—situated . . . in a most beautiful and fertile valley."

The original Administration Building, as drawn by Guy A. Ritter, Jr.

The Reverend John B. Griffin, a former Virginia Collegiate Institute student, saw service in the Civil War as a chaplin.

Samuel Griffin, another former Institute student, fought in the Civil War as a major.

Charles Griffin, the third brother to have attended the Institute, rose to the rank of Captain during the war.

Club," which served as a place to take meals and to socialize. The main building also had porches added, front and back; and a student, Festus Hickerson, was contracted to finish the interior of the top floor. Each room had a small fireplace or stove, and it was the students' responsibility to maintain their own wood supply. Cords of stacked wood would have been a common sight behind the Administration Building throughout the nineteenth century. In 1851 the institute added a small two-story frame structure behind the main building; this was known as "Grub House," the place students ate their meals. Upstairs, the school's steward, the official charged with the supervision and upkeep of the grounds, resided with his family.

Early on, the trustees established six basic rules that governed student conduct at the institute. First, the board made it clear to the students that their instructors' word was law. Second, good moral character was requisite. Third, strict recreational hours were established: 8-9 A.M., 12-2 P.M., and 5-8 P.M. in winter—5-9 P.M. in summer. Further, the students must have permission to leave the campus except during recreational hours. Fourth, the school required prayer every morning and afternoon, plus service and Bible recitation on Sunday. Fifth, any damage would be charged to the individual in question; if the culprit could not be apprehended, the fine would be charged to the entire student community. Last, with an eye on the pocketbook, the trustees admonished the students to be sure that their accounts were paid on time.

The Philomathean Society had made the journey south from Augusta County as well. In Salem, the student club prospered until 1850 when several of the group's leaders reasoned that if the school had two organizations instead of just one, much could be facilitated. After all, the principal function of the society was to debate, and the students had grown weary of debating each other. Two clubs, they argued, would promote rivalry and competition, and instill in the students a keener sense of loyalty and dedication. Accordingly, the students divided themselves and voted into existence two new societies: the Ciceronians and Demostheneans. Few present that cold January day could have sensed the significance of their actions; nevertheless, the two groups born on that occasion would dominate both the intellectual and social life of the student body for well into the next century.

It was during the 1851–1852 session that the institute decided to refashion its calendar and to adopt the now more familiar September to June schedule. July and August were set aside as vacation months—a needed respite for both students and faculty. The curriculum of the early 1850s reflected the classical educational approach of the times. Latin and Greek were required of all students, as were mathematics and English; other courses included history, geography, philosophy, political economy, chemistry, astronomy, grammar, rhetoric, and logic.

Financially, the school struggled to survive through these first difficult years. The balance sheet rarely offered good news, so it came as no great surprise to learn in 1849 that Baughman's assistant, John Herbst, had decided to try his luck in the gold fields of California. One reason in his decision to head west was doubtlessly the fact that after two years on the faculty, Herbst had not collected a single cent of his salary! Brighter days would come.

Despite its economic hardships, the institute still planned to press ahead with a program of physical expansion. The board approved the erection of new wings to the main building, with the construction to commerce when the funds had been raised. The west wing, accordingly, was finished in 1852, and the east wing followed, complete with cornerstone and formal dedication ceremony by 1854. The original structure was beginning to take on the dimensions and stature of an impressive campus centerpiece.

Discussions concerning the transformation of the institute into a college were first formally recorded in 1850. In that year, the board of trustees examined the issue of granting degrees—a power withheld by the state in its charter of 1845—and also studied the financial advantages of incorporation as a college. Even though the conversations were of a preliminary nature, the issues were still hotly debated, and the board was divided over the issue. Ultimately, a majority felt that Virginia had a surplus of colleges but few quality preparatory schools, and the board decided to remain an institute. Throughout the controversy, several board members resigned, while others appeared openly factious. The wounds of 1850 would never entirely heal; rather, the question would fester beneath the surface for two more years. Principal Baughman apparently played the issue as

Expansion underway. The west wing is added in 1852.

Two years later, the east wing was completed and with the cornerstone affixed, the building was formally dedicated in the fall of 1854.

delicately as he could; certainly he was no major proponent of college status, but his precise role or inclination is not entirely evident.

By fall 1852, the issue had come to a head once again. This time the initial catalyst was not so much the board but more the Virginia Synod. Meeting coincidentally at Mt. Tabor church in October, the synod passed a resolution encouraging the institute's board to take the appropriate steps to secure a college charter. To underscore its seriousness, the synod further suggested that future financial support— namely, the synod's contribution to the administration building's expansion—might indeed depend upon the board's charter plans. This not-too-veiled threat would soon find its mark.

Next, action fell to the students of the school. In November, the students gathered together and wrote a petition encouraging both Baughman and the board to consider the college application. It is clear at least from one surviving account that Baughman was less than thrilled over the prospects of another showdown. If the principal had hoped to keep the issue under wraps, the students promptly proceeded to blow the lid off the whole affair. By December, the students had even threatened mass defection if the institute did not respond to their wishes. Baughman's response must have been measured; it was again evident that he did not favor the proposed transformation. Perhaps Baughman was an ardent realist. After all, for a fledgling academy that was barely established in the first place and hardly solvent, to consider declaring itself a candidate for a bona fide college must have taken a good imagination. Baughman must have known that the resources to operate a legitimate college—the physical apparatus, the financial foundation, and a trained faculty—were all lacking. The proposition must have struck him more as whimsy than rational.

Nevertheless, the board met on 22 January 1853 and decided to proceed: it passed a resolution calling for a petition to be presented to the General Assembly requesting a charter for college status. However grudgingly, Baughman set off for the state capital. By February, Baughman had resigned himself to the proposition; and if not quite the outspoken enthusiast,

John A. McCauley, Roanoke County's representative to the Virginia House of Delegates, played an influential role in helping the school receive its college charter in 1853.

he dutifully became the cause's chief spokesman in Richmond. Through his labors, a bill was introduced into the senate on the last day of February.

The board had earlier considered names for the proposed college. Several titles were offered. First, perhaps, was "Virginia College," but this was soon eliminated as being too presumptuous. Next under discussion was the name "Madison College," but because of the existence of another school by that name in New York state, the board felt another choice would avoid the obvious confusion. "Wartburg College" was offered as another choice, but that name was rejected because it reflected too much Lutheran ecclesiasticism. Ultimately, the name "Roanoke" was presented as an appropriate reference to the region— to the valley and the river that flows through it. It met with "immediate approval" and was duly inscribed on the memorial sent to the state assembly.

"An Act to establish the Roanoke College in the county of Roanoke" was passed by the Senate on March 10 and shortly thereafter by the House of Delegates on 14 March 1853. Roanoke College was born, and back home in Salem the students celebrated with a bonfire.

Events of the spring of 1853 are still shrouded in mystery and Christopher Baughman is at the center. Precisely what happened between the celebrations of March and the board meeting of June will never be learned. What is clear, however, is that when the plans were being formulated for the establishment of the new college, Baughman was not included. Perhaps because of his initial reluctance or general indifference, Baughman must have strained his relations with the board. When the time came to select leadership for the new college, Baughman's name was never considered. After a decade of careful direction and dedication— in taking over a fledgling academy, in supervising the transfer to Salem, and finally in securing a college charter—the end came abruptly. By term's end in May, Baughman had departed. Repeated efforts on the part of the board to receive reports from the principal detailing different issues and financial questions went unanswered. Baughman had severed all ties.

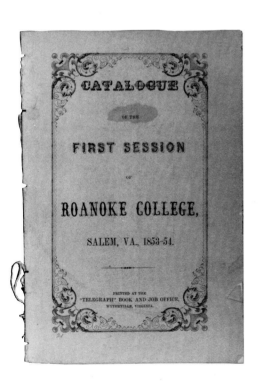

The cover page of the fledgling college's premier catalog.

The annual expenses from the first year; the comprehensive fee has escalated a bit from the advertised $111.25 to the $15,000 of 1992!

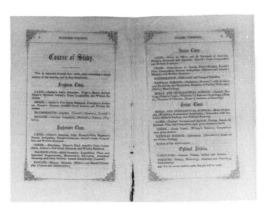

The proscribed course of study. Latin and Greek were required into the 1890s.

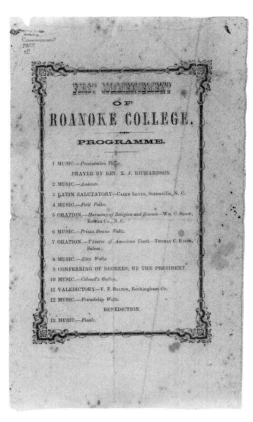

The college's first commencement was held in June 1855; the program featured fine entertainment and stirring presentations. Doubtless, the audience was impressed by all four graduates.

If there was anyone who might pick up the pieces, it was David Bittle. Although he had been away from the school since 1845, Bittle had remained very active in the field of education. In 1849 he had published a 111-page tract entitled "A Plea for Female Education" and had played a key role in the establishment of two academies for women in Maryland. Bittle, with his election to the presidency in June 1853, was ready for a new challenge—and the little college in Salem would certainly be that. Bittle inherited a burdensome debt, a modest physical plant, a faculty of two (plus one tutor), and a student body of thirty-eight, of whom only sixteen were enrolled in the college course of study.

David Bittle's text of his commencement address to the "first class of graduates."

Bittle was formally inaugurated in March 1854. His address was well received, and he concluded with this observation: "The well educated young man must have a pure moral character, based upon the faith, power, and obligations of Christianity—he must be an original thinker—a clear systematic reasoner—and a tasteful, chaste writer." One student has left the only eyewitness account: "Oh, we had quite a lively time in Salem. The students, Proffs, board of trustees marched in procession through the streets of town to the Presbyterian church, where Mr. Bittle was regularly installed President of R. College. The building was handsomely illuminated that night, and the students brought out the cannon and fired three rounds in honor of the new administration."

Bittle's two priorities were clear. He needed to raise revenues and also to attract more students. For the first cause, Bittle increasingly spent his time away from the Salem campus, and fund-raising did increase dramatically. Still, there was never enough money. For the second cause, Bittle supervised the publication of a pamphlet: "An Appeal to the German Population of Virginia and Adjacent States." The statement stressed that the college was not a theological institution but a literary one. The little publication must have helped in part because by the second year of the college's operation, enrollment had ballooned to eighty.

Compared to Baughman's conservative management approach, Bittle was almost reckless. With his immediate success in mind, Bittle was determined to forge ahead. He soon committed the school to a major construction program. The east wing of the main building was finished in 1854; Grub House was enlarged in 1855; and in the following year, Bittle announced a campaign to build two matching halls on either side of the main building. By any measure, Bittle's design was more than ambitious.

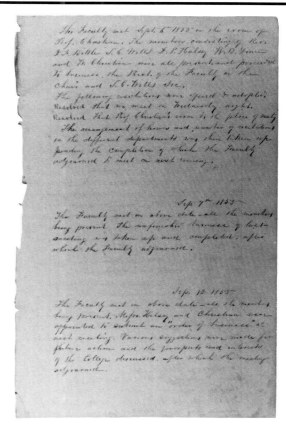

A copy of the first page of the faculty meeting minute book. In a momentous first decision, the faculty agreed to meet on Wednesday evenings.

The President's brother, Daniel, served the college first as a professor of ancient languages and literature from 1854–1858. He returned briefly after the Civil War to act as the school's financial agent before he moved to North Carolina to become a college president in his own right.

Daniel Bittle's devoted wife, Susan E. Bigelow Bittle.

Confident that student enrollment would continue to improve, Bittle embarked on personnel moves as well. To his embattled faculty, he added William B. Yonce as principal of the preparatory department and assistant professor of ancient languages in 1854. The next year, Bittle's brother Daniel was hired as professor of belles lettres and as financial agent, and also in 1855, William Christian became the first instructor of modern languages. By 1856 Bittle established a chair of natural sciences and hired Henry Osborne to fill it.

BOARDING AT PROFESSOR OSBORNE'S

"In looking over the *Christian Observer* one day, my eye fell on an advertisement of Roanoke College, with directions to write for further particulars to Prof. O———. . . . The notice seemed to attract me, and I read it over several times. The next day it came to my mind again, so I determined to write to the Professor in regard to the institution, and thus began a correspondence between him and myself, which resulted in my determining to try what Roanoke College would do for me, and in my accepting the Professor's invitation to take board with him— as he termed it—'to make one of his little family.'

"The Professor was tall and straight, quick and restless—the embodiment of a skeleton with a skin shrunk to it, which want of flesh was easily accounted for afterwards, as I found he rarely ate anything—he never thought of it, or could not take the time from carrying out some new idea; he was as full of science and theories 'as an egg is full of meat.'. . . [He was] as goodhearted a fellow as ever lived, kind and courteous, but as little fit to keep boarders as I was to fill his chair as Professor of natural sciences.

"For a little while we got on finely; he had laid in a barrel of flour, a sack of coffee, and some other articles. In a short time the other articles gave out, and we were then reduced to the first two articles of food. Days elapsed—nothing else came in. . . . So we came to try apples in all forms—we had baked apples, stewed apples, fried apples, apple pies. For breakfast we had apples and coffee, for dinner, coffee, apples and apple pie. For supper apples and coffee. At last, after this had been running on for weeks it became a serious question with us, if feeding on apples so con-

stantly might not result in cholera, for some of us were possessed with very curious feelings at times. . . . The boldest of us, the ever-ready A. spoke up: 'Professor, don't you think where people are restricted to one diet for a long time, they are apt to get the scurvy? for instance, where people eat apples as long as we have been doing of late!' [The professor's response was] 'Well, now, I declare, I hadn't noticed it, but I don't believe we have had any meat for a good while . . . but I will send for it, and have it over at once.'

"The beef came [and] for a while we reveled in roast beef, but, alas! the salt began to strike in—each day she got salter and salter, harder and harder; each day we took a smaller and smaller piece! At length it became, as it were, petrified with salt. . . . One day . . . the Professor [asked] 'Well, A, what will you be helped to?' [A answered] 'I will take a piece of that Lot's wife there, sir,' pointing to the beef. [To which the professor added] 'Now, this meat, I remember, has been getting very salt lately. . . . I will get up some poultry to-morrow.' And sure enough he did. The barrel of beef was rolled into a house in the yard, and there she stayed. Several years after I left College I visited Salem for a few days, and on my enquiring after that beef, I was assured that there it sat where we had left it, in as perfect a state of preservation as it was on the day we le[f]t it there."

From an article in the *Roanoke Collegian*, January 1875, recounting life at the college during the 1850s.

Bittle's fund-raising met with continued success, and by 1857 West Hall, later to be known as Miller Hall, took its place astride the main building. Construction of the matching hall was delayed, in part, by controversy regarding the naming of the buildings. It would take college officials a few years to extricate themselves from that misunderstanding, and by then the Civil War would intervene. The companion piece, Trout Hall, would not be built for a decade.

Michael Miller, a member of the Board of Trustees, donated one thousand dollars in 1857 to help underwrite the cost of the new west hall—soon named Miller Hall in his honor.

Mathematics professor Henry Osborne painted this picture of the college's anticipated front range of buildings in 1856 as a fund raising project. It is the earliest rendering of the college campus. Miller Hall, on the left, appeared a year later but a decade would pass before Trout Hall would match it to the right.

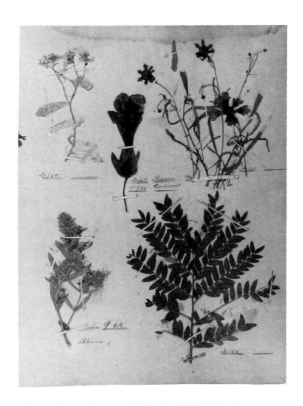

A page from a botany lab book, 1858, belonging to freshman W.C. Wire of Loudon County, VA.

Student life on campus saw developments as well. Along with the two debating societies, which sponsored forensic exercises and essay contests, students had begun a number of little clubs and activities. The Arboricultural Society consisted of students who helped to tend the college grounds; the Society of Inquiry of Missions encouraged other students to consider the ministry as their life's work. President Bittle and the faculty were surely delighted to witness the debut of a campus chapter of the Sons of Temperance. Student accounts from the period often comment on the relative isolation of the school, the "boring" life that Salem afforded, the problem of goats wandering through the campus, poor food, and persistent faculty attempts to cut the candle ration. (It seemed that students were using their candles for purposes other than study!) One last campus group would foreshadow the tumult that was to come. Innocently enough, Professor Arthur Grabowsky, who had been trained in the Polish Army, organized a student military group in 1859 known as the Roanoke College Musketeer Guard. Little did the students imagine that two short years later, playing soldier would turn painfully real.

This turn of the century photograph is of James P. Houtz, a Roanoke freshman in the fall of 1858. He served as a captain during the Civil War and returned to graduate after the war. He enjoyed a career as a prominent Salem attorney.

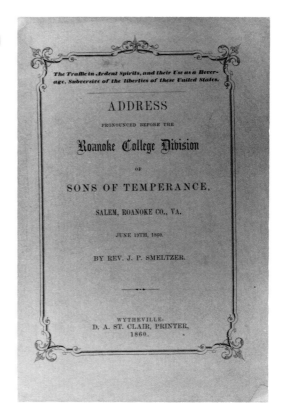

The Traffic in Ardent Spirits, and their Use as a Beverage, Subversive of the liberties of these United States.

ADDRESS

PRONOUNCED BEFORE THE

Roanoke College Division

OF

SONS OF TEMPERANCE,

SALEM, ROANOKE CO., VA.

JUNE 19TH, 1860.

BY REV. J. P. SMELTZER.

WYTHEVILLE:
D. A. ST. CLAIR, PRINTER,
1860.

To protect the "liberties of these United States", Reverend Smeltzer addressed the college chapter of the Sons of Temperance in 1860.

CHAPTER 3

"Sometimes we have milk for supper," 1861–1865

A photograph, a carte-de-visite, of David Bittle taken during the 1860s.

Louisa Bittle during the Civil War. This type of photography, imprinting an image on a card, was made popular by the soldiers wishing to have the image of a loved one with them as they marched off to battle.

Roanoke College watched with a keen eye as the Union dissolved through the winter and spring of 1860–1861. With Lincoln's election in November, South Carolina had led the move to secession before Christmas. By February, the Confederacy had been born in Montgomery, Alabama, and by April, attention focused on a small, unfinished fort in the harbor of Charleston, South Carolina. With Sumter's fall and Lincoln's subsequent call to arms, Virginia followed suit and joined the southern cause.

Excitement on campus ran high. For the young students, the thrill of a good fight and a war that threatened to be over quickly offered a ready diversion from the demands of the end of the term. By early June, the campus was nearly deserted—only seventeen students remained out of the more than one hundred who had enrolled that semester. Commencement activities were canceled, but the faculty and trustees were determined to keep the institution operating. No one could have foreseen the length and toll of the war at that point. There was a reasonable chance, or so the newspapers said, that all might be settled by fall. The faculty also felt that by keeping the college open, they could at least prevent the acts of vandalism that were bound to occur.

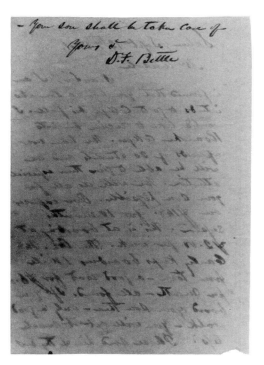

A letter from Bittle to a prospective student's father, assuring the parent that "your son shall be taken care of."

"The students of '61 will remember the irregularity and confusion produced in the College by the approaching war. In consequence of this, the usual discipline was somewhat relaxed. . . . It was during the last month of this session that the circumstances of our first demerit occurred in the extreme northwest room of the College, second floor. This room was occupied by . . . Bob. His most intimate associate was . . . called little P. The spirit of evil suggested to Bob that, as his room was retired, the Faculty a little careless, and especially as the boarding-house table was not groaning under either variety or delicacies, that he should have a supper in his room and invite little P. and ourself to contribute to the material and share the feast. We . . . employed as much strategy as possible in getting biscuits, butter, pepper, salt, &c., from our boarding tables, as necessary parts of the supper. During the day several of the steward's chickens were waylaid and two of us went to the river for fish . . . we acknowledge catching some frogs. Everything was prepared and taken to [the] room before night. . . . [W]e impatiently waited for ten o'clock and the Tutor's round. Dr. B., either through his predominant kindness of heart, or, through suspicion, relieved the Tutor that night and visited the rooms himself, but found all in order. After he had gone and the lights in the building had been extinguished, preparations for cooking the supper were commenced, and soon a mess . . . was steaming on the table. But alas . . . the delicious morsels were stopped half way to the mouth as a gentle tapping was heard at the door. Who could it be? The suspense was relieved by the voice of Dr. B. asking 'Who is in here?' No reply was given and the tapping and enquiry were renewed. Then very quietly chicken, fish, frog, &c., &c., were thrust under the bed and little P. followed them. We took refuge beneath some clothes and Bob, opening the door, said as demurely as possible 'Walk in Dr.' After so polite an invitation he did walk in, and according to his custom, asked no questions, but went to investigating things for himself. The first object that attracted his attention was a boot projecting from under the bed. He seized the boot and pulled it out, little P's leg followed and then little P. himself. 'What are you doing in here, Jimmy?' 'I was studying Greek with Bob.' But the Dr. thought that the time of night, the posture and place were not very favorably [sic] for prosecuting the study of Greek. . . . [T]hen he examined the mass of clothing and we were revealed in all our helplessness. After gazing at us very steadily for a moment . . . the silence was broken by the question, 'Are you studying Greek too?' We said nothing, we had nothing to say, little P. retired to his room, we to outer darkness. The Dr. did not trouble the supper, he didn't like frog. We satisfied ourself of his going home this time by following him till he entered his door.

"The supper was then brought to light again, though in a miscellaneous condition and eaten with much enjoyment. On the next Thursday evening, in the week's report, our first demerit was read out. Though expected, it came with that crushing weight which attends the first of every calamity—having passed the first six consecutive years as a student with no demerits. This occurred within thirty days of the final examination.

"It stands to-day on the Faculty's books, but if we had the power we would erase it."

From the *Roanoke Collegian*, May 1875.

To get into the fight, most college students boarded trains and headed home to enlist in units that were forming in all corners of the nation. For the students who were from the local area, several options existed. The Salem Flying Artillery, a prewar group organized by college trustee Abraham Hupp, attracted a number of students as did the Roanoke Grays, a company organized in May 1861. The following month, the Dixie Grays started for the front with several college men in their ranks. For those too young to be accepted into regular units, county boys formed the Roanoke Young Guard to drill and train, hoping that one day soon they could take their place beside the other units in the fight. Prominent in the Young Guard were several students in the college's preparatory division, including William Hubbard, who served as the group's secretary. The boys drilled every Saturday on the courthouse green through the summer before the little band broke up.

GENERAL REMARKS.

The College maintained its regular sessions during the whole of the war with an average of more than 100 students. Its present prospects are very flattering to its friends. The institution never before had as many students enrolled in the Catalogue, but by reference to their class standings it appears that but few comparatively are in the higher classes. This is accounted for from the fact that during the last four years we had no graduates nor regular College classes, most of our students being boys under 18 years of age.

A page from the college catalog, noting the school's "present prospects are very flattering to its friends."

Abraham Hupp was a college trustee and the organizer of the Salem Flying Artillery. Hupp became ill and died in 1863.

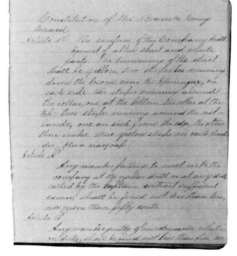

The constitution of the Roanoke Young Guard, a group of college boys not of draft age who trained during the summer of 1861.

A hand stitched Confederate flag with twelve stars. The design suggests late 1861 and could possibly have been a flag flown over the Administration Building.

THE ROANOKE YOUNG GUARD

"SATURDAY, JUNE 8th, 1861

"Persuant to adjournment the company convened June 8th, when Messrs. Peter Capt., Johnston, Adj. & Secy., Hatcher Sr. withdrew from the company. These gentlemen immediately set off for the seat of war, there to take an active part in driving back the Userper's minions, lead by the renegade Scott. May success attend them and the fair Goddess of Lyberty enshrine their banner with the laurels of Victory is the earnest prayer of friends at home. On motion Mr. B. P. Dyerley was elected captain, W. G. Register Adjutant, S. White Orderly Sargeant. After a parade the Company broke ranks to meet 2 P.M.

"SATURDAY, JUNE 29th, 1861

"The company met at 1 1/2 P.M. The weather being very inclement—the attendance was sparce. Several pugilistic exhibitions marked the proceedings, showing that the neccessary [sic] strict military surveilance did not reign. After the regular parade, no business on file, the company was dismissed to meet on 4th of July, extra drill.

"THURSDAY, JULY 4th, 1861

"As bright Aurora gilded the azure blue vault of heaven with his beams of brightest hue not a cloud could be seen to deck the azure dome. . . . To carry ones thoughts to bygone years, and rest awhile on memory's page and paint the scenes of Yorktown and kindled anew the fires of lyberty, unimpared, the 'Young Guard' assembled for parade. Subsequent to a 'field' drill, the company marched through Salem, at intervals firing a salute—in honor of the great day. While the last germ of republican lyberty in the U.S. was fraught with decay from improper culture, the C.S. were nourishing the tender bud, just sprung into existence, destined ere many years to yield an ample fruition. So make it be.

"SATURDAY, JULY 13, 1861

"Pursuant to adjournment the Company assembled in Co[urt] H[ouse] square, where after a drill in the manual of arms we repaired to the College grounds. . . . The Court Martial being in session a number of delinquents were arranged before its tribunal to await the decission [sic] of its majesty. Several had their purses curtailed of a dime or so.

"SATURDAY, JULY 20th, 1861

"There were no meetings of the company posterior to July the 20th 1861, at which time there was a *minor* parade. The Company then disbanded, and from the remnants of which number a Young Guard was formed composed of youths fourteen and eighteen. The Juveniles organized August 10th 1861. Thus it passeth away.
"Wm. E. Hubbard R. Sec'y"

Excerpts from the minute book of the Roanoke Young Guard,

By the fall of 1861, David Bittle's report to the synod reflected the worsening state of war. "All our students," the president explained, "capable of bearing arms are in the military service of the Confederacy, consequently our present session opened with only twenty students instead of one hundred and twenty as we had expected." Still, the school planned to continue. Recognizing the futility of maintaining the college curriculum, the faculty refocused its efforts to concentrate on the preparatory division.

In an even more dramatic move, the school agreed to admit women in order to see itself through the emergency. The female students— instructed separately, of course—attended over the next two years until the school felt more confident that it would survive without them. Women students would not return to the college until the late 1880s, again conditionally.

On behalf of the school, Bittle made numerous trips to the Confederate capitol in Richmond. One of his first trips took place in the fall of 1861, when he met with the secretary of war to secure an agreement regarding the college's right to stay open. For the embattled Confederacy, manpower was a foremost concern, making it a fine line between support for the cause and the pursuit of higher education. Most schools across the South had closed long before, but because of Roanoke's rather remote location, Bittle felt his case was defensible. The secretary agreed; students could stay in attendance at the college and complete the term during which they turned eighteen. In return for this concession, Bittle agreed to form a college company; the students were to be drilled and trained to serve as a home guard unit and to assist local authorities if the county was threatened. Professor George Holland, a college graduate and wounded veteran of the conflict, was charged with the responsibility for getting the boys into some kind of military order. As events would have it, Holland would have two years to get them ready.

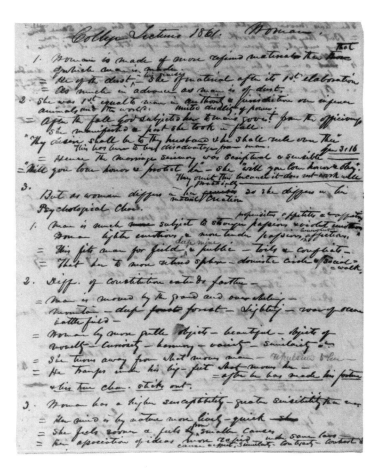

David Eittle's lecture notes from 1861 regarding his presentation on "Women."

George Holland, wounded in the war, returned to Roanoke as a professor and commander of the college company.

Pauline Bittle Holland, daughter of David and Louisa and wife to George, departed Salem in 1867 with her husband and moved to South Carolina where he became president of Newberry College.

The historian sometimes has the pleasure of seeing two seemingly unrelated things suddenly link up to give a fuller picture of a person or event. Such was the case with David Cloyd McGavock, a student during the 1861–1862 session. The following are excerpts from a letter from McGavock to his uncle, probably Gordon Cloyd of Horse Shoe. The letter, dated 5 March 1862, was written on stationery bearing the seal of the Ciceronian Literary Society. By June, McGavock was serving in the Confederate army; he was killed two years later.

"Dear Uncle, I take this opportunity to write you a few lines as I am at leisure. . . . I suppose you are glad that the Militia is ordered out, so as to get rid of some of those scamps around you. A good many students are leaving here on account of the draft and our school will be considerably reduced. I begin to think I am *so large* and *strong* that I ought to be in the army *fighting like a Turk*. . . . I have nothing more to tell you but I will give you a list of my studies. I am studying latin Greek French algebra geometry grammar History Rhetoric latin prose, composition and speaking. I wish you would send some money about $10.00, and when you write to me tell me what is going on your farm and in the country. Your attached nephew, Cloyd McGavock"

Several hours after the above letter had been edited, the following story was found while looking for a totally unrelated article.

"On one occasion, a strong gale of wind carried away about one-fourth of the tin roof of the Ciceronian Hall, and in its flight it carried the tops of two chimneys of the west wing of the main building with it. Some of the students narrowly escaped with their lives from the falling bricks. Now, what was to be done? No mechanics at home; they were all in the army, and no material to work upon if they had been at home. The fall rains commenced and the plastering of the Ciceronian Hall was about to come down. The rooms of the three-story building were liable to be drenched with rain. The treasurer of the Faculty [Prof. Yonce] was always wide awake, with his pockets so full of Confederate money that he could hardly sit down. He heard of some plank in the country, managed by virtue of his abundance of Confederate to have them conveyed to the College, and with the aid of the students, he had the building temporarily covered. I will always remember two students particularly active in this work. Amidst the pouring rain Cloyd McGavock, who was afterwards killed in the army, and young Gordon Kent, were on the roof laying down the plank which others were pulling up with ropes, under the superintendence of Prof. Yonce. The building and its furniture were saved."

Now, if there was only a picture.

Letter from the David Cloyd McGavock Papers, Special Collections Department, Virginia Polytechnic Institute and State University; story from the *Roanoke Collegian*, November 1875

ROANOKE COLLEGE.

—:0:—

THIS Institution will open its next Session 1st of September, 1862. It is located in the Valley of the Roanoke on the Va. and Tenn. R. R., in a healthy, quiet and fertile section of Virginia, in Salem, a village of 1000 inhabitants, free from the invasion of the enemy.

EXPENSES FOR A SESSION OF 10 MONTHS.

Boarding,	$84 00
Tuition,	35 00
Room-rent,	5 00
Washing,	10 00
Fuel and light,	10 00
Incidental,	4 00
Total,	148 00

Half of the tuition and one-fourth of boarding in advance. Should it be necessary, from the high price of provisions, a small advance may be demanded on the single item of board. Modern Languages included in the above charges. No Extra Charges but for the Hebrew Language under Prof. Cammann.

Any number of boys will be accommodated, instructed and superintended by the Faculty.

REV. D. F. BITTLE, D. D.,
President of Roanoke College.

Salem, Roanoke Co., Va., July 19, 1862.

The school must stay open. This advertisement ran in numerous publications in 1862. Note that Salem was a "quiet" village, "free from the invasion of the enemy."

The war had not reached Salem by 1862, but the college had paid a dear price in other ways. Bittle recounted to the board in the fall of 1862 that "former students stand high in the divisions of the army. Many of them have been honored with responsible offices, on account of their competency and good character. . . . About fifteen of the gallant boys are dead; they have either been killed in battle or died of disease in camps. Perhaps more than double the above number have been wounded and now bear the marks of their bravery and patriotism."

"During the Session of 1864–65, at Roanoke College, I had command of the company of reserves, known as the College Company, composed of students from 16 to 18 years of age. This company was called out on a number of occasions, and had great longing for an engagement with the enemy, but in the good providence of God no such longing was gratified. At the surrender at Appomatox, in 1865, this company was in Lynchburg, in hearing of the last cannonading of the great struggle. On Sunday evening of April 10th, 1865, all the troops in Lynchburg, including our disappointed young comrades, were disbanded and told to go home. This company, of about 40 boys and young men, were kept in line, and in twenty-four hours from their dismissal from service, were at Beaufort's, having counted crossties for forty miles.

"An incident of this retreat from Lynchburg is worth being preserved. At Beaufort's, on the east of the mountain, these irrepressible young soldiers found two large dirt cars standing on the track. The proposition to push these heavy cars up to the top of the mountain and ride down on the other side met with instant approval. Well do I remember my feelings, as we prepared to get into those cars, for the uncertain ride down the steep grade. It was night and dark. Whether the enemy had been before us and destroyed the track, whether there were any obstructions on the track was unknown, and by those boys unthought of. Discipline was gone; orders were useless; only one was given and that was that their Captain should say who should go in the first car. There were no brakes to the cars. The students were divided into two equal parties; into the first were put those who were either better prepared to die, or who could best be spared by their parents and friends; into the second the rest, who were ordered to remain on the top of the mountain until they felt sure the first car had safely made, what their Captain believed was, a dangerous descent. Getting into the foremost car, the order was given to let go; down we went with increasing velocity, the other car coming closely behind ours. Wild, hilarious boys those were, and utterly regardless of the danger that their Captain felt was imminent and real. But the cars kept the track and the ride was completed without accident."

To the memory of Rev. George W. Holland, Ph.D., D.D. (Charleston SC: Book Presses, Lucas & Richardson Co., [1896?]).

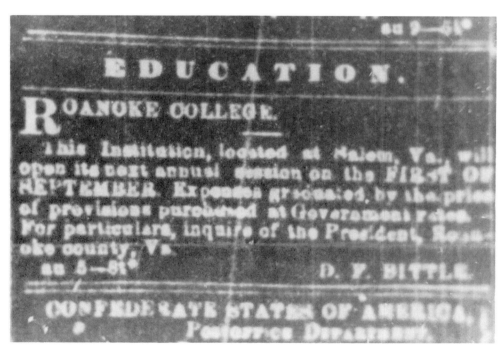

Even as the Federal noose tightened around Richmond in 1864, Bittle made sure that the college's name remained in front of the newspaper readership in the Confederate capitol.

As the intensity of the war increased by the spring of 1863, the college was drawn even closer to the conflict. Bittle apparently made several visits to minister to the troops along the front lines, and several students kept in touch with their mentor despite the ravages of war. One student, James W. Dixon, wrote Bittle from the woods of Chancellorsville, the site of Robert E. Lee's great battle and Stonewall Jackson's untimely death. Dixon was appalled by northern morals: "I found not one among the Yankees who had the least bit of respect for the Diety or for any of his laws or morals. Some of them under the most excruciating pain would use the most wicked expressions." Dixon added, after reading confiscated northern letters, that the missives were "a mass of obscenity" lacking all "litterary teste."

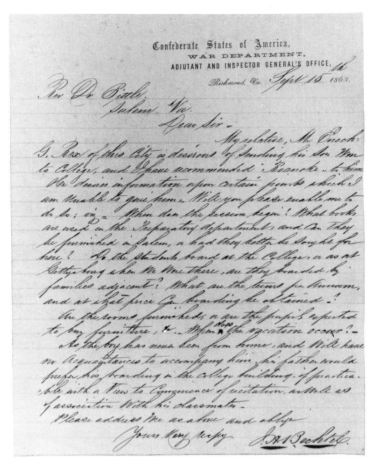

A letter from a Confederate official, writing to a friend, asking Bittle for information about the college and the boarding arrangements.

A few of the bullets, fragments, and buttons recovered on the campus.

In response to increased casualties in central Virginia, the college was visited by a Confederate officer and surgeon who explained to Bittle that there were plans to turn the college into a hospital to treat the wounded. At once, Bittle embarked for Richmond in an attempt to forestall the occupation. Again, the president was successful, but he was doubtless disheartened to find upon his return a college that had been ransacked by marauding Confederate troops. They had occupied the buildings for a day and a half and had managed to destroy or to carry off a good deal of equipment and supplies.

Salem faced its first true threat in December 1863. Union General William Averell approached with four regiments of mounted infantry, an artillery battery, and a battalion of cavalry. His orders called for him to destroy the railroad at Salem and also to confiscate the military supplies that were stored in town. In an attempt to locate Averell before he attacked, a scouting party was arranged and headed by Thomas Chapman, a former Roanoke student. It is likely that some other boys from the school were also involved in the late-night escapade. Unfortunately, the Federals discovered the boys before the scouts found them. Chapman was killed, and the rest of the little band were captured. The troops entered the town without opposition, and Averell promptly seized the stores and destroyed the railroad lines through town.

The token defense offered by the college company was swiftly handled by Averell as well. He ordered the boys rounded up and marched north to Mason's Cove, where they bivouacked for the night. More frightened than dangerous, the students awaited their fate. In the morning, Averell inspected his captives and sent them back to their campus with the advice: "You go to your books and study your best."

By the early months of 1864, the Confederate congress was pulling out all the stops. By law, all volunteer militia companies were now pressed into regular military service. The college company was promptly sworn in as Company E, First Regiment, Virginia Reserves; but again, Bittle was able to intercede. Somehow, he convinced Confederate authorities that the boys should be left to their studies. They would, however, be readily available to respond to emergencies.

Soon, the college company would get another chance. The boys were ordered north of town to Hanging Rock to watch for another suspected Federal attack. The youthful enthusiasm of the students was still in evidence: "The college was all life. Everybody wanted a chance at the Yankees. They rubbed up their guns, blacked their boots, tied up blankets, gathered haversacks and provisions, looked brave, shook hands with their friends, and the smaller ones were kissed by the ladies." To the students' disappointment (and

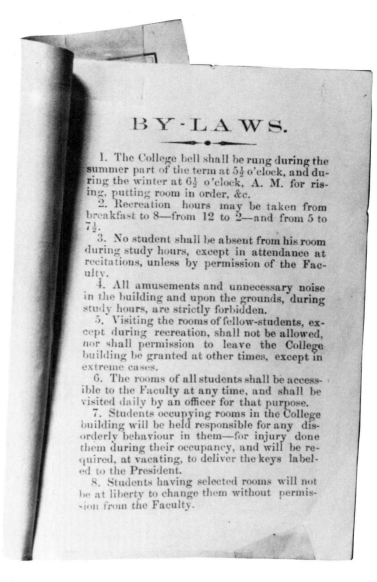

The 1861 Catalog featured these By-Laws to insure better student performance.

Long before the days of published yearbooks, students kept scrapbooks and autograph books. This page taken from a student's memory book from 1861 implores the owner to "Remember me. Yours truly, W.C.W."

A page of faculty minutes during the war. The routine seems little affected by the war around them.

to their good fortune), the Yankee advance never materialized. After several days, they marched back to the campus "without losing a man . . . dirty, brave, but not well disciplined for study."

The students had hardly settled into their normal routine before the alarm sounded again, during an unusually cold spell in the spring of 1864. The Federals, reports detailed, were marching to attack the Confederate salt works in southwestern Virginia. The students rallied to the call. Two weeks later, no Yankees had been spotted, no shots fired. The students returned discouraged, with several of them suffering from exposure. Some of the luster of war was wearing thin.

The students were spared the largest military operation of the war to affect Salem and the vicinity in late March 1864. The term had come to a close just a few days before, so the campus was largely deserted as Union General David Hunter fled into town from the east, being hotly pursued by Confederates. Hunter had been crushed in his assault on Lynchburg and was in full retreat in his attempt to reach safety in West Virginia. The Confederates managed to catch his rear guard as he turned into the mountains just north of Salem. The battle of Hanging Rock was the result. By Civil War standards, the engagement was hardly more than a skirmish, but the impact on the college was real enough. For the dozens of wounded soldiers, the Administration Building served as a hospital for the next several weeks.

Bittle and his skeleton staff scraped and scratched their way into another session for 1864–1865. The college was forced to grow much of its own food, and Bittle himself even went on a cattle drive to return with beef for the college community—much to the delight of the students. A letter from November 1864 recounts one student's impressions of hard times: things were "right bad here now we get nothing but bread and butter for breakfast [and] supper as a general thing. Sometimes we have milk for supper; but very little of it. Some of the boys swear that the butter can stand alone, but I don't think its [sic] over twenty years old."

David Bittle was determined to make one last trip to Richmond. With the Confederacy's fate appearing more and more gloomy, Bittle was fearful that the college might get stuck holding more than a thousand dollars of Confederate money— certain to be deemed worthless with the Federal victory. To avoid that possibility, Bittle set off for Richmond to buy books for the library. His ingenious plan, though, was soon foiled. In the disarray of the Confederate capitol, the mass exodus had begun, and the roads leading west were jammed with citizens looking to get out of harm's way. The college president never had a chance. Deflected and disappointed, Bittle turned around and returned to Salem. Bittle later reported to the board that the "sum perished in my hands."

The college company was pressed into service on one more occasion, in the spring of 1865 during the final days of the Confederacy. The boys were ordered east to Lynchburg to await further word. As the Federal noose tightened around Richmond, Lee's army was forced to take flight to the west. Lee's desperate attempt to escape came up short. Just fifteen miles east of Lynchburg, the Federals tracked him down at Appomattox. Again, the college company was spared the full brunt of war. With Lee's surrender, the boys were dismissed, and Professor Holland and his little band made their way back to Salem.

With the collapse of the Confederate government, the future seemed anything but certain. Bittle and the faculty decided to dismiss the students in April instead of waiting until the end of the term. The college president was one of three town officials designated to surrender Salem to Union troops, and he did so on 4 April 1865. The southern world had fallen.

John Trout served for twenty years as a college trustee, from 1862 to 1882, and was President of the Board for fifteen of those years. His principal gift resulted in the construction of the building in 1867 that still bears his name—Trout Hall.

Robert E. Lee sent this note of appreciation to the Ciceronian Society upon the occasion of his election as an honorary member in the fall of 1865. He also sent a photograph of himself which hung in their parlor into the twentieth century.

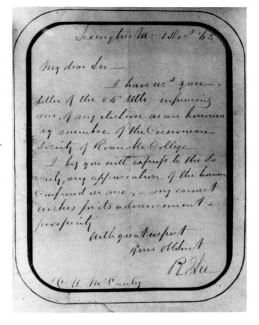

CHAPTER 4

"A useful
and practical institution,"
1865–1876

ROANOKE COLLEGE,
SALEM, VIRGINIA.

As the cataclysm of war subsided, the college and its environs began to emerge from the relative safety of southwestern Virginia. Even though the town had been visited by numerous Federal columns, Salem was saved the enormous death and destruction that befell the Virginia communities to the east and north. The college too had tasted war but had managed to survive and, more remarkably, to remain open throughout. Few schools in the South could boast of that by war's end. The security of Salem had served the college well.

Still, there were scars. In human terms, the college had paid a staggering price. Of the student body that welcomed the war in the spring of 1861, few would ever return to complete their studies. Indeed, only 15 of the 118 were graduated. The war had claimed many lives; however, of those who did survive, many were apparently prevented from returning—either because they were disillusioned, disheartened, or too hardened by war to imagine returning to campus to take up that life again. The college would have to go on without them.

In June 1865, the board of trustees met for the first time since the war began. Bittle's report brought them up to date with college affairs that had transpired during the interval. The president noted that the school had operated without many frills—even graduation ceremonies had been suspended. On a more positive note, Bittle was pleased to announce that the state of college indebtedness had actually improved during the war from $11,500 in 1860 to $3,500 currently. Bittle could still work miracles! His last item, however, brought the board back to earth by invoking some of the mundane charges of running a college: "The porches, roofs, chimney, etc., of the buildings need immediate attention for repairs, as soon as practicable."

David Bittle's "Clergyman's Ticket," good for a fifty percent discount on railroad travel.

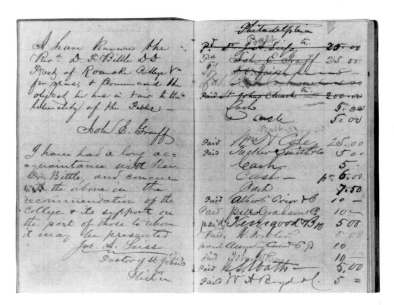

Pages from one of Bittle's trip account books. The personal testimonials on the left were a common nineteenth century feature to authenticate the person's credentials. Bittle's collections are recorded on the right.

The board received the report from Bittle and rededicated itself to the business of operating a college. Heading the list of priorities were financial considerations. First, the board reappointed Daniel Bittle, the president's brother, as financial agent. If the school were going to prosper, much of the burden would rest on the young Bittle. Brother Daniel did well; his fund raising provided critical income for the school in the next several years, and his decision to search for patrons in "Baltimore and certain of the northern cities" did much to prepare the way for future campaigns later in the century.

The second decision the board reached was, doubtless, less than exciting news for the faculty. To prepare for harder times ahead, the board voted to abolish fixed faculty salaries. Instead, the board announced that the college would be run on "a self-sustaining basis"; the revenues generated by tuition and gifts would be pooled, and then expenses would be met. The remainder, if any, would then be paid to the faculty on a pro-rata basis as salary. Needless to say, the faculty hoped for brighter days as well.

By the fall of 1865, prospects had improved. Despite the uncertainty of the times and the shadows of Reconstruction looming on the horizon, the college still managed to attract 145 young men, although most were enrolled in the preparatory division. The college muster included only two seniors, two juniors, four sophomores, and twenty-one freshmen. The college also welcomed back its most senior faculty member, Simon Carson Wells, who had joined the army in 1861.

This 1872 photo is of J.J. Moorman, M.D. He served the college from the 1860s to the 1880s as physician, lecturer on Physiology and Hygiene, trustee, and finally as President of the Board from 1882–1885.

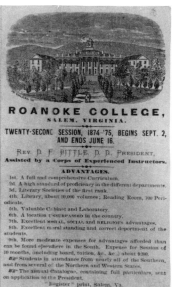

An 1874 advertisement from the college with Bittle and his "corps of instructors."

Enoch Rex was the Steward of the college from 1868 to 1877. He and his wife maintained the Grub House—serving meals and boarding students—and oversaw the general upkeep of the college grounds.

Mrs. Caroline Rex assisted her husband with the Grub House. The Collegian *recorded this account in 1875: "The College Boarding house, kept by Enoch G. Rex, is quite popular with the students this session. The boarders number about one fourth of the whole number in attendance. Mr. R is very attentive to the wants of his boarders—feeding them well whilst in health and bestowing upon them no little care and anxiety when sick. It is the most convenient boarding house in connection with the Institution."*

"[I] WILL STAND UP TO IT MANFULLY"

John Rice Hudson was a member of the class of 1861. In 1866, he became principal of the Preparatory Department, a post he held until 1871. Additionally, he served as adjunct professor of Greek for one year. The following are excerpts from letters to his brother, Isaac Hudson, written in 1866 and 1867.

Roanoke College, Oct 10th 1866

Dear Brother

I received yours & sister's letter the other day and was truly glad to hear from you all. . . . I am getting on finely with my classes. Have a nice set of young men here this session, 145 students, and I have been very successful so far in making them friends and still demanding the respect due me. All treat me kindly and don't seem to feel a disposition to try to trouble me with any mischief as is frequently the case with boys. We have some very fine young men here from all bastions of the state. . . . There is quite an interesting meeting going on in College Church conducted by Dr. Bittle and there is considerable interest among the students.

Your affectionate Brother
Jno Rice Hudson

Roanoke College, June 6th 1867

Dear Brother

It has been some time since I wrote to you. I have been intending to do so but different things have caused delay. We are busily engaged in closing up the studies preparatory to examinations which commence Monday morning, and will continue all week. I dread the weeks work but as it is the last from this session will stand up to it manfully and try and get home and rest for awhile. I am tired and really need some recreation, for my duties here have been confining and hard, but my health has been very good during the session and is yet.

Will you be down here at Commencement. Phillip Jr. is to be here to deliver the address to the Alumni. The Societies succeeded at last in getting a man to address them, Col. Mumford son of Geo. W. Mumford of Richmond is to deliver the address. . . . Dr. Bittle is anxious for you to attend the exercises.

Your affectionate Brother
John R. Hudson

William Rex, a son of Enoch and Caroline, entered Roanoke in the Preparatory Division in 1864. His brother Benjamin followed the next year, and in time, his parents moved from the ruins of Richmond to Salem. Both brothers entered the college program but never took degrees.

By the spring of 1866, David Bittle was convinced that the worst was over and that it was time again to go on the offensive. At the board meeting, Bittle proposed that the long-intended eastern hall—the companion piece to Miller Hall—be undertaken. Grudgingly, the board approved, and construction began immediately. In a year, Trout Hall was the result, and it became home to the chapel on the first floor and the boy's school on the second floor. The top floor served as the formal parlor for the Demosthenean Society. The Ciceronians could now have the third floor of Miller Hall all to themselves.

Bittle was never a big believer in process. He typically ran the school as if it were his own personal academy. There was a board, to be sure, but with care it could be manipulated and when it could not, Bittle often became "forgetful" about decisions and details. Bittle was never unlawful. He just believed in getting things done, and sometimes, procedures and regulations went out the window. No doubt the experience of the Civil War had convinced Bittle that he could run the institution with or without a board. The readjustment that came after the war was natural enough.

In 1867, Bittle alone approved the reopening of the boys' school, much to the consternation of the board. He was rarely accountable, likewise, for funds solicited and expenses met. Bittle saw no conflict, for example, in accepting donations for a building project and yet applying the funds to an existing debt in some other account. The thought of having all the funds in hand before a building project was begun was probably an idea that Bittle never considered. Before the mortar was set on the bricks in Trout Hall, Bittle was back at the drawing board. In 1868, he proposed two new structures: a library-museum building and the college's first dormitory. But Bittle had gone too far too fast; the board balked at his recommendation and asked the president to cool his heels. More than forty years would pass before the college finally opened its first dormitory.

Bittle's actions had so frightened the board that he inadvertently triggered a series of measures designed to rein him in. The board demanded for the first time that Bittle submit a written, itemized budget report. The trustees also hired the Reverend John F. Campbell to serve as financial manager. Campbell attempted to standardize current financial practices: he supervised the college's treasurer, hired an attorney to protect interests, and improved the college's accounting system.

Unofficially, the board might have had one other charge in mind for Campbell—namely to keep an eye on the president. It is not altogether clear whether Campbell succeeded in watching Bittle; what is clear is that by 1871 the board was still not satisfied that it had the kind of control it wished. Accordingly, it authorized an executive committee to insure greater

Bittle posed for this photograph in the mid-1870s.

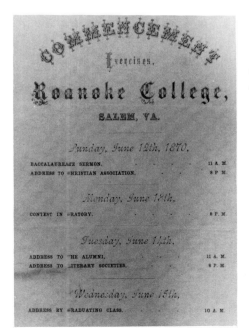

A Commencement Program from 1870.

An 1875 "recruitment flier" for Roanoke College.

Roanoke College envelopes from the mid-1870s. Winthrow McClintic graduated in 1879 and later moved to West Virginia. He never returned to Salem until 1928—in time for the college's "Diamond Jubilee."

supervision over the institution. At last, Bittle was in check; a new accommodation had finally been achieved between the president and the trustees.

That Roanoke College should be a liberal arts institution was never written in stone. Indeed, for David Bittle, Roanoke's educational mission was as open to interpretation and as subject to review as any other policy. As blithely as he raised and spent money, Bittle was equally content to experiment with the college's basic mission. On four different occasions between the end of the Civil War and 1872, Bittle and the board flirted with opportunities that would have transformed Roanoke into a very different institution.

The commotion of the Civil War had hardly died down before the college was prepared to make its first move. The passage of the Morrill Act in 1862 by the Congress of the United States was an event not unnoticed by David Bittle. Bittle reasoned that this bill establishing the land-grant state college system in the North might soon be in force in the South as a Reconstruction measure. Bittle hoped to maneuver the college into an advantageous position should that eventuality occur. The board was sold on the measure and in the summer of 1865 established the Chair of Agriculture and Mining. The Reverend John B. Davis was hired to begin the program.

As Bittle waited for developments on that score, he was prepared to explore other options. In 1870, the federal government was awarding funding to schools that would offer a program in military training. To that end, the college promptly hired Major J. H. Whittlesey as professor of military tactics to conduct instruction. But soon, funding seemed in jeopardy, and the board apparently lost interest. The program was discontinued after only a short time.

Undaunted by that setback, Bittle began another project by 1871. Long a supporter of compulsory primary education and knowing that the state legislature was considering such a bill, Bittle asked the board to establish a Normal Department for the training of teachers. Professor Luther Holland was hired to head the program, and Bittle himself was listed as "Lecturer on the Art of Teaching." Again, there was no luck; the legislature failed to offer any assistance, and even a special appeal to the Peabody Fund, a national endowment for the support of teaching programs, proved unsuccessful.

The fourth opportunity also surfaced in 1871. The state announced its intention either to establish an agricultural and mechanical college or to attach that program to an existing school. At last, Bittle hoped, the college's investment in the agricultural and mining chair of 1865 would pay off. Professor Davis was sent to Richmond to present the college's case, but disappointment was again the result. The assembly decided in 1872 that creating a new college was the proper course of action, so an agricultural and mechanical college was begun in Blacksburg—today's Virginia Tech.

The duties of a nineteenth-century professor were comprehensive indeed. Apart from the expected instructional responsibilities, the professors were charged with all aspects of operating the college. The faculty were the very heart of the institution—they were, in every sense, the true stewards of the school. The professors supervised all aspects of the students' lives, directed their physical exercises, watched them in chapel, supervised their meals, comforted them when they were sick, directed their chores in tending the grounds and, of course, disciplined them when they erred.

That last responsibility took an inordinate amount of time. In their weekly meetings, the faculty spent almost half of its time concerned with student offenses. The list of indiscretions is long and ingenious— humorous today but no doubt causing great consternation at the time. Along with the routine offenses, the record recounts "attending a circus at night; engaging in a calathump; exploding firecrackers in the halls; horn blowing; rock-rolling in the main building; and visiting the billiard saloon at the Duval House." Boys will be boys.

Henry Gray, M.D., taught anatomy and physiology and served as the school physician between 1867 and 1869.

A carte-de-visite of the Class of 1874.

ONE ON DR. BITTLE

"You've often heard mention of our famous old President, Dr. Bittle. The Doctor was really a studen-conferee [sic], and many of the alumni will remember some of the pranks they got in, only to find Dr. Bittle in the midst of it with them.

"There was in Salem in the days of long ago, a horse-drawn taxi, known as Ballad's Bus, and quite an antique it was. It was a great drawing card to students with malicious intent, and it's [sic] owner never knew where he was going to find it, after he left it out of nights.

"It was a hilarious Hallowe'en that united the students, Dr. Bittle, and Ballad's Bus. The boys were out looking for what they might to find to increase their joy in the night of spooks, when one of them spied the Bus, standing peacefully parked in an alley. It was a real inspiration; they would haul it down to the river, take it out to mid-stream, and leave it there. So off they went hauling the big old Bus down Main Street to Union, and down Union to the River. Then they all shed their shoes and stockings, and waded out in the cold and rocky river bed, pulling their trophy with them. They got it settled, turned to shore, and had just finished putting on their shoes, when the voice of Dr. Bittle came out of the stranded Bus, 'Well boys I certainly did enjoy my ride down, you can come and pull me back now.'

"The boys did, and it was a harder job to pull that old wagon back up the hill than it was to pull it down. They got it back to its place and Dr. Bittle climbed down, thanked them all, and went to his home.

"That was one bunch of Hallowe'en celebrators that turned in early that night; they had had enough."

The Brackety-Ack, 2 May 1934.

Examinations played a major part in the educational programming of the college. Each course typically demanded an entrance exam, a midterm, and a final examination. After two years of instruction and in order to be admitted to the junior class, a student had to pass a biennial exam; likewise after following a course of study of four years, all students were required to pass a comprehensive exam to be a candidate for the bachelor's degree. The college, like most schools of the time, also bestowed masters degrees upon any alumnus of "good moral character" who had spent time since graduation pursuing scholarly endeavors. Additionally, between 1853 and 1876, the college awarded twelve doctor of divinity degrees.

Student activities and organizations began to spring up in the postwar period. Academically, numerous groups were born, and several key organizations came back to life after their suspension during the war years. The two most important reinstatements were of the Ciceronian and Demosthenean societies. The 1870s and 1880s would in many ways represent the golden age of these groups with their debates, contests, and formal programs.

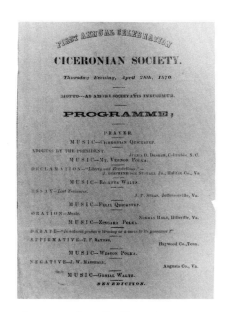

Library rules from 1869; "proper decorum" was a must.

A program from the Ciceronians, replete with quicksteps and polkas.

James Lafayette Buck (1846–1920) came to Roanoke College in 1871 from Wythe County, Virginia. He was a member of the Demosthenean Literary Society and boarded at the Goldman Mess Club. At the commencement exercises in 1875, Buck's senior address was "Influence of Difficulties," which is sometimes reflected in his letters to his friend, Isaac N. Huddle. Buck later became a Lutheran minister.

May 1873. "This evening our medals in our Literary Society were awarded. I am sorry to say that I was sadly disappointed in that Rufus [Brown] did not get justice. He was really due the first debaters medal But from a spirit of Secret fraternities he got neither the first nor the second. It can not be denied by any member of the Society that he is not the best orator and as good a debater. But it was that prejudice of Secrete Societies. He does not belong to any atal and is opposed to them and the majority of the students belong to Secrete Societies. . . . This morning brings the good news that Rufus has taken 3rd honor in his class. But sorry on the other hand to say that my friend [Vastine] Stickly failed. . . . He studied Theology last year and a part of the time this year and has been preaching frequently But I believed lacked it of making the minimum on mathematics. . . . Rufus is down in the Faculty Everybody will be if they pass all the class except Stickly. . . . I will add a word today Rufus has a petition to present to the Faculty tomorrow. Prof. Yonce encourages it, Davis also. I hope my friend may come out all right yet."[Stickly graduated that year—ED.]

1 October 1873: "I find it much harder than I expected. I may think it harder than it really is on account of not being well But others complain equally as much as I do if not more. . . . All the Junior class are complaining at the heavy course. We spend 24 hours in the recitation rooms per week. So you see we have very little time for study. They give us such long lessons too making it most awfully rigid. I am not liking my studies so very well this year except Mental Philosophy. We have some over one hundred and thirty students here now."

9 October 1873: "Dr. Bittle tells us we must be men of one idea. Select our profession and make everything tend toward that end. I believe in that doctrine strong, but whether I shall ever reach the point in life at which I am aiming is difficult to tell. . . . There were three boys sent away from this college for drinking and not studying."

21 January 1874: "I got no box of provision myself but my friends all did that remained at college and I only went to my boarding house twice from Christmas day til the next Tuesday. We had oysters, turkey, chicken and all kinds of cake. I gained a few pounds."

2 April 1875: "April made some fools here. The boys as usual sent a few rats to Crabtree for new catalogues. The catalogues for this year are not out yet. The students it is said are lazier than they ever were or there is less studying going on at least. It seems to be contagious too. I am inclined that way myself. There is one case of fever in college. Prof. Dreher's brother. He is not low though night sick. Well, you ought to have seen me eating chicken ham cake &c &c at Easter. I almost made myself sick. Yours truly J. L. Buck"

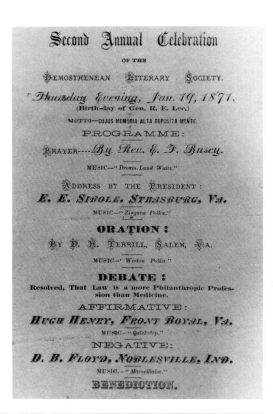

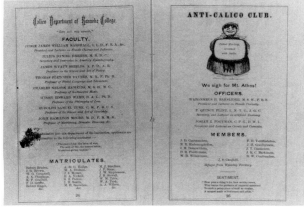

The students published "The Microcosm" for several years in the late 1860s and early 1870s. The publication offered some serious pieces but was more famous for its efforts at lampooning faculty and students alike.

Bittle himself helped found the Historical Society in 1875. Its stated purpose was to promote the study of history through the collection of books and materials devoted to Virginia history. Other students helped to establish the Mineralogical Society and would, in time, collect more than 10,000 specimens from around the world. Students with a literary bent published the school's first yearbook, the *Microcosm,* in 1870, and five years later, the college issued the *Collegian,* a multipurpose journal that would be published into the 1960s. The *Collegian* served as a college newsletter, a student and faculty literary magazine, and an alumni organ. It was also in the 1870s that the college's alumni formed their first association and organized several chapters to continue their ties to the college. One last organization needs to be mentioned: the YMCA. Even before the war, Roanoke had one of the earliest chapters of the YMCA on record in the nation, and after the conflict, the YMCA returned to occupy an important place in the life of the campus.

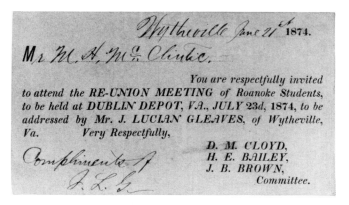

A post card detailing the time and place of one of the earliest alumni gatherings.

If the academic organizations flowered after the Civil War, social clubs positively flourished. The list of groups, official and unofficial, would run into the dozens. Most were formed around a passing issue or a small band of students, and as time progressed, the clubs faded quickly into oblivion. The rage of the decade between 1865–1875 was secret societies—some famous on campus and others so secret that any record has long since been lost. None was more important than the Black Badge Society, a prewar group that survived into the 1870s. Boarding houses, much like Bittle's Brotherhood, formed obvious associations as did home residences: there were numerous Virginia county clubs, plus the West Virginia Club, the Tar Heel Club, and more.

A natural outgrowth of the secret societies was the evolution of Greek fraternities. For the college faculty, the thought of a secret student *anything* was reason enough for the faculty to quash the secret organizations and to give their grudging support to the establishment of Greek orders. Numerous fraternities came and went during the period, but the one that did stay and is still present today is Sigma Chi, begun in 1872.

December, 1931

THE PHI GAMMA DELTA   235

A CHAPTER GROUP MORE THAN SIXTY YEARS AGO

❧ *Is this the oldest existing picture of a Phi Gamma Delta Chapter? It is Beta Deuteron at Roanoke College — probably in 1867 or 1868. The amazing thing is that one of the men in the group is still living. He is William P. Reese, '68, who has identified all of the brothers in the group as follows:*
❧ *Standing: William P. Reese, '68; James W. Shields, '70; Richard Farr, '69; John G. Brown, '70; Thomas L. Sanderson, '68; John D. Carnahan, '70.*
❧ *Seated: John H. Barb, '69; Charles N. Hawkins, '70; Henry Withers, '69; McKim H. Wells, '69; George L. Brown, '68; George E. Nelson, '69.*

The brothers of Beta Deuteron chapter of Phi Gamma Delta fraternity taken in 1867 or 1868. After the "Black Badge Society," they were the second oldest fraternity on campus lasting until 1905. (Courtesy Phi Gamma Delta)

MEAL-PLAN OPTIONS

During the nineteenth century, several boarding options were available to Roanoke students. They could eat on campus in Grub Hall where "excellent fare" was served by the steward for about $10 per month and where dining was under the supervision of "some officer or instructor of the College." A second alternative was to board at the home of one of the professors or some nearby family. That cost was estimated to run about $12 to $14 per month. A third option was chosen by a "considerable number of students"—the boarding club. By pooling their resources and dining in a group, the students could eat for about $6 to $8 per month, thus enabling "young men of limited means to reduce the ordinary expenses of attending College." Lewis G. Pedigo (Class of 1876), who became a physician and lived in the valley, later recalled the club to which he belonged, the Goldman Mess Club. The club was located in a brick building about a block from campus on Clay Street. It was later used as a morgue by a local funeral home.

"The title of the club was derived from the name of the widow lady who owned the house and cooked and served the meals.... We chose Silas Stickley, of Shenandoah County, as caterer, and he made all of the arrangements and handled the funds. Stickley was later director of weights and measures of the state of California, and no doubt received valuable training for his future position as caterer in the Goldman Mess Club.

"Other members of the society included Luther Smith, father of Dr. Charles J. Smith, president head of Roanoke College; his brother, W. J. Smith; James L. Buck, of Wythe County, and his roommate; and Ralph Morehead, for years treasurer of Pulaski, Virginia.

"[We] were able to secure board at the Goldman Club for six dollars and fifty cents per month, while the regular commons price at Roanoke was ten dollars. The commons then was run by a man named Rex, who had managed a Confederate powder magazine during the Civil War.

"However, the total cost of the year for the members of the Goldman Mess Club was considerably above the toll for college students, for the lads soon became addicted to ice-cream and spent all of their funds in the parlor of a Mr. Wolfenden in Salem."

Winthrow McClintic at his graduation. Forty-nine years later, the Brackety-Ack *described him as follows: "When he appeared at the college a week ago, Mr. McClintic was attired in a hunting costume and wore high top boots. He wears his beard in the same manner as older men did at the time of his youth—long, reaching to about his waist, and cut to tapper [sic] to a point."*

A carte de visite of David Bittle's last class, the graduates of 1876.

David Bittle was an ardent supporter of physical fitness and athletics; the president certainly believed in the expression "sound mind, sound body." To the typical educator of the nineteenth century, the college curriculum involved a much stronger balance between physical conditioning and academic course work. In today's scheme of things, a student is possibly required to take a couple of physical education courses. To the students of Bittle's Roanoke, much of their time was devoted to their physical well-being, which was defined broadly; there were courses in physical education, but that was only the beginning. The students were required to perform myriad tasks about the campus. Chopping wood, caring for the farm animals, tending crops, gardening, and "cleaning" fields all made for better students. Sports and athletics had their place too. Bittle supported the playing of games and encouraged the students to form teams and to compete on a regular basis. Much to the students' chagrin, Bittle drew the line at intercollegiate competition. That level of involvement was excessive, the president concluded; the true object was simple competition, along with training, dedication, sacrifice, and teamwork. All of that could most appropriately be conducted on an intramural basis. The students often complained, but the president would never budge.

Accepting their fate, the students made the most of it. Any number of ball sports appeared and disappeared. Rugby was a popular game that was played in earnest as early as the 1850s. Baseball debuted soon after the war, and the two most famous teams were the Tuscaroras and the Pelhams. Another team that appeared briefly, and was of dubious ferocity, was the Roanoke Daisies.

The relationship between the Lutheran Church and the college was one that was never carefully codified or, over time, clearly understood. Bittle continued to attend the annual synod meetings, yet he reported to them more out of courtesy than actual demand. In 1867, the synod admitted that the college "has no formal church connection, but religious exercises are strictly attended, yet not denominational." Church support of the college fluctuated over the period, both in terms of student recruitment and of financial contributions. Bittle complained that the "church does not send us as many students as the population under her control would indicate she could afford." The president also summed up the synod's contribution once as "small money." The closest the college would come to church control occurred in 1872, and then it was for reasons that were less than honorable. In light of Reconstruction measures being considered in Washington, the board contemplated ceding the college property to the church to evade "a bill requiring all state institutions to admit all persons irrespective of race, color, or sex to their halls, from which calamity," Bittle hoped, "all Church institutions, being controlled by Church and not the state, would be saved." This civil rights act was not immediately passed by Congress, and the crisis passed without board action.

The campus as it appeared circa 1870, from a painting by Guy A. Ritter, Jr.

CHAPTER 5

"None but scholars,"
1876–1880

ROANOKE COLLEGE,
SALEM, VIRGINIA.

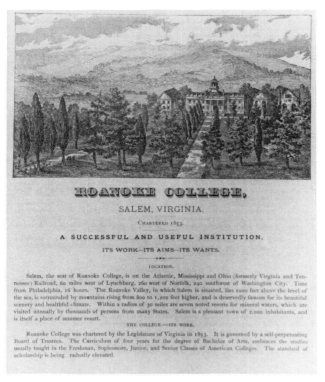

The "successful and useful institution"—a recruitment circular circa 1877.

A formal studio photograph of David Bittle taken probably in 1875—the last surviving photo of the college's first president.

The summer of 1876 was an exciting time; tens of thousands of Americans flocked to Philadelphia to witness the Centennial Exposition and to marvel at the fruits of the industrial age. For the nation, the celebration of the Declaration of Independence brought renewed feelings of patriotism and nationalism and, for the first time, helped to heal the wounds of a frightful war fought more than a decade earlier.

Salem and the college did their share of celebrating too during the summer, but as the fall arrived, the joy would soon turn to sorrow. On 25 September, David Bittle died. Although he had mentioned some heart palpitations in the past year, Bittle had paid them little attention; even before, he had taken steps to curtail his burdensome schedule. He had dispensed with most of his church duties at College Lutheran as well as many administrative and financial details with the school. Still, his schedule was exhausting. On the day of his death, he was on his appointed rounds until past 9:00 P.M. He returned to the Faculty Room on the main floor of Miller Hall to relax and visit with his collegues. He had hardly gotten settled in his chair when he was stricken. Bittle was only sixty-four.

The Roanoke Collegian.

VOL. III.   SALEM, VIRGINIA, OCTOBER, 1876.   NO. 2.

The Collegian *is masked in black borders announcing the passing of Bittle—"Our Loss—Our Legacy—Our Duty."*

The passing of David Bittle was a major shock to both the college and the community. The flood of tributes came rapidly to Salem to recognize Bittle's contributions and accomplishments. It had been almost thirty-five years since he had begun his little parson's school, and in that time, Bittle had never been far from the center. Plans were already being made to commemorate the twenty-fifth anniversary of the college's chartering in 1853. Bittle must have been proud of all that he had achieved. But in a conversation he had the day before he died, Bittle still lamented: "I am troubled about my successor here. They may get a man who will allow the collections I have made in a life-time to be scattered in a few years." It was difficult, even for Bittle, to separate the institution from the man; they had become synonymous.

Only a few hours after Bittle's burial on the crest of the ridge in East Hill, the trustees took up the process of selecting his successor. They reached their decision almost immediately, electing Dr. Stephen A. Repass

VOL. III.

OUR LOSS---OUR LEGACY---OUR DUTY.

"Death loves a shining mark—a signal blow,
A blow which, while it executes, alarms,
And startles thousands by a single fall."

Our leader has been taken! Our friend and father has been called away! Death found a shining mark; the blow fell; the founder of Roanoke College is dead! Truly thousands have been startled by a single fall! For "a mighty one has fallen."

Roanoke College mourns for him who watched over her infancy with the tenderest solicitude, who infused into the feebleness of her early years the vigor of healthful growth and development, and who lived to see her attain maternal dignity and pride, with children all over the land to "rise up and call her blessed."

We mourn the loss to our *Alma Mater*—to ourselves. Each feels that he has lost a friend, "true and tried"—a father, in interest and sympathy. That long procession of sorrowing hearts that followed his remains to their resting place in the Salem Cemetery was only a small part of the great company of mourners. Wherever he lived, wherever he was known, wherever his students have wandered—there were the mourners. His great heart went out in love to all; and just as the sea sends forth from its own bosom the rains which return to it again, so that love returned to him. Throughout the country there were streams of affection flowing back to that heart of boundless love. Living for others and not for self—giving his life for the good of his fellowman, and devoting all to the service of Christ—he has realized, in the realms of bliss, that it is "more blessed to *give* than to receive."

This is our legacy, the example of his grand, noble, devoted life. It is, if we profit by it, far more valuable than the legacy of millions of earthly treasure. As I pause to think of how little worth are the vanities for which men give

Professor William B. Yonce served with distinction on the faculty from 1853 until his death in 1895. This photo of the language and literature professor was taken in 1886.

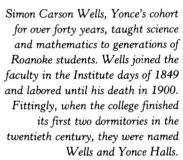

Simon Carson Wells, Yonce's cohort for over forty years, taught science and mathematics to generations of Roanoke students. Wells joined the faculty in the Institute days of 1849 and labored until his death in 1900. Fittingly, when the college finished its first two dormitories in the twentieth century, they were named Wells and Yonce Halls.

Reverend Thomas Bittle was David Bittle's son, who like his uncle Daniel, served as the college's financial agent for a time and also held the rank of professor of languages.

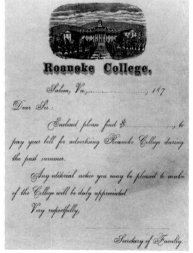

Advertising in newspapers and journals was so common that the college had a special form prepared by the 1870s.

president. Repass was no stranger to the college. He was graduated from Roanoke in 1866 (the sole graduate that year, in fact), and after his ministerial training at the Lutheran Seminary in Philadelphia, he had returned to Salem in 1869 to become the pastor of College Lutheran Church.

In 1872, the Lutheran seminary in South Carolina was relocated to Salem and took up space in the basement of Miller Hall. There resulted no institutional relationship between the college and the seminary; rather, the two coexisted side by side. The seminary was attracted to Salem by the relative prosperity of the college; and when the seminary reopened, Dr. Repass became the sole professor in residence. Repass spent the fall contemplating his future, and by December, he made his decision: he elected to stay with the seminary and forgo the college's offer.

As the trustees went back to the drawing board in January 1877, college affairs had to continue. Shortly after Bittle's death, the board had asked Professor Wells to serve as chairman of the faculty and to oversee college operations for the academic sessions ahead—until a successor could be found. Wells took on the assignment with gusto, seizing the opportunity by urging the "recasting of the course of study" and by supporting more rigorous graduation requirements. The faculty concurred, and by June, the trustees offered their assistance as well—not a bad record for a temporary administration. On a stickier topic, the board was left with the unenviable task of trying to sort out the college's financial affairs after Bittle's untimely death. Even though the board had struggled for a decade to keep a closer eye on the president's operations—and had formed an executive committee five years earlier expressly to shadow Bittle—the late president had remained elusive. After his death, numerous bills, loans, and other debts totaling several thousand dollars came to light—all privately arranged by Bittle. The board grudgingly honored most of those, but balked when it was belatedly presented with yet another charge: a contract for $1,500 for a collection of shells!

ROANOKE'S FIRST HISTORY

Long before anyone could envision a sesquicentennial history, and long before William Eisenberg could complete *The First Hundred Years* in 1942, one man could be credited with the careful preservation and telling of Roanoke's beginnings. That author was Simon Carson Wells.

Professor Wells was in a keen position to view the college's formation. Not only was Wells here longer than anyone in the nineteenth century (1849–1900), he also served as secretary to the Board of Trustees. For more than half a century, it could be argued that nothing happened with regard to college affairs that he did not know about.

Wells's history appeared serially beginning with the very first issue of the *Collegian* in 1875. His monthly installments were eagerly anticipated and widely appreciated. The college was preparing to celebrate its first real anniversary, the Quarto-Centennial in 1878, and Wells's contribution was designed to help provide the background and context for the "modern" Roanoke. The college's subsequent histories have tried to do nothing more.

THE SKATING POND

"Thursday evening at Chapel exercises, Prof. Holland announced to the students that the Faculty had decided upon Friday, the 15th instant, as the day for work upon the College skating pond. Of course the announcement was greeted with appropriate demonstrations of approval.

"Dr. Wells had already surveyed the site for the pond and the position of the levees was staked out and all that was required was an ample force of hands to complete the job.

"Picks, shovels, carts, plows, wheelbarrows, and oxen were in demand and Friday presented an active scene in that portion of the college grounds. The site chosen is on the ground lately purchased by the college, which is bounded by a moderate stream, affording an ample supply of water for the pond.

"The work is not yet completed, as it is a pretty large undertaking, but those interested in the sport of skating will soon press the job to completion. We congratulate the authorities and the students on so valuable an accession to the college possessions.

[A month later the following paragraph appeared:]

"The skating-club of the college have offered a prize for the best skater in college. Now when an aspiring youth sees about six million stars and slides thirty-five feet on his ear, and finally lands up to his eyes in mud, ice and water, he can console himself that he is striving for honor!"

Excerpts from the *Roanoke Collegian*, November 1878 and December 1878.

The selection of a new president continued through the spring of 1877, and on the 24th of March, the board elected the Reverend Thomas W. Dosh, D.D., of Salisbury, North Carolina, as president. Over the next several weeks, Dosh accepted the post and prepared to make his way to Salem in time for the June commencement and also for his inauguration. In his speech, the new president reminded his audience that "there must be no shams nor counterfeits. We shall allow none but scholars to go forth with the seal of our commendation. Diligent application, thorough attainment, and honorable deportment must be the invariable antecedents to graduation if we would be true of our trust."

After a year of some confusion and indecision, the college trustees finally elected Thomas Dosh as the College's second president in the spring of 1877.

The Commencement program for the class of 1877; the week's activities also included the inauguration of President Dosh.

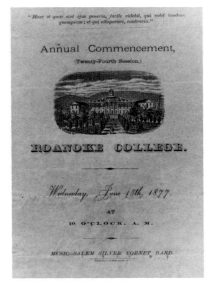

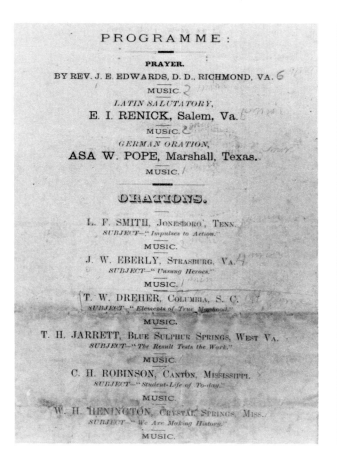

PROGRAMME:

PRAYER.
BY REV. J. E. EDWARDS, D. D., RICHMOND, VA.
MUSIC.
LATIN SALUTATORY,
E. I. RENICK, Salem, Va.
MUSIC.
GERMAN ORATION,
ASA W. POPE, Marshall, Texas.
MUSIC.

ORATIONS.

L. F. SMITH, Jonesboro', Tenn.
SUBJECT—"Impulses to Action."
MUSIC.

J. W. EBERLY, Strasburg, Va.
SUBJECT—"Unsung Heroes."
MUSIC.

T. W. DREHER, Columbia, S. C.
SUBJECT—"Elements of True Manhood."
MUSIC.

T. H. JARRETT, Blue Sulphur Springs, West Va.
SUBJECT—"The Result Tests the Work."
MUSIC.

C. H. ROBINSON, Canton, Mississippi.
SUBJECT—"Student-Life of To-day."
MUSIC.

W. H. HENINGTON, Crystal Springs, Miss.
SUBJECT—"We Are Making History."
MUSIC.

Program page of the 1877 commencement.

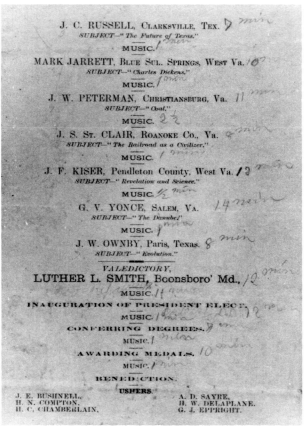

J. C. RUSSELL, Clarksville, Tex.
SUBJECT—"The Future of Texas."
MUSIC.

MARK JARRETT, Blue Sul. Springs, West Va.
SUBJECT—"Charles Dickens."
MUSIC.

J. W. PETERMAN, Christiansburg, Va.
SUBJECT—"Coal."
MUSIC.

J. S. St. CLAIR, Roanoke Co., Va.
SUBJECT—"The Railroad as a Civilizer."
MUSIC.

J. F. KISER, Pendleton County, West Va.
SUBJECT—"Revelation and Science."
MUSIC.

G. V. YONCE, Salem, Va.
SUBJECT—"The Danube."
MUSIC.

J. W. OWNBY, Paris, Texas.
SUBJECT—"Evolution."

VALEDICTORY,
LUTHER L. SMITH, Boonsboro' Md.,
MUSIC.
INAUGURATION OF PRESIDENT ELECT.
MUSIC.
CONFERRING DEGREES.
MUSIC.
AWARDING MEDALS.
MUSIC.
BENEDICTION.

USHERS

J. E. BUSHNELL,   A. D. SAYRE,
H. N. COMPTON,   B. W. DELAPLANE,
H. C. CHAMBERLAIN,   G. J. EPPRIGHT.

The balance of speakers for the commencement; notice the penciled marginalia recording the length of each presentation kept doubtless by a not-so-receptive member of the audience.

The members of the class of 1877.

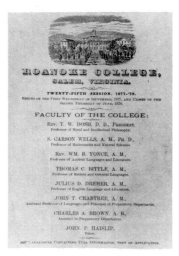

ROANOKE COLLEGE,
SALEM, VIRGINIA.

TWENTY-FIFTH SESSION. 1877-'78.
BEGINS ON THE FIRST WEDNESDAY IN SEPTEMBER, 1877, AND CLOSES ON THE
SECOND THURSDAY OF JUNE, 1878.

FACULTY OF THE COLLEGE:

REV. T. W. DOSH, D. D., PRESIDENT,
Professor of Moral and Intellectual Philosophy.

S. CARSON WELLS, A. M., Ph. D.,
Professor of Mathematics and Natural Science.

REV. WM. R. YONCE, A. M.,
Professor of Ancient Languages and Literature.

THOMAS C. BITTLE, A. M.,
Professor of Modern and Oriental Languages.

JULIUS D. DREHER, A. M.,
Professor of English Language and Literature.

JOHN T. CRABTREE, A. M.,
Assistant Professor of Languages and Principal of Preparatory Department.

CHARLES A. BROWN, A. B.,
Assistant in Preparatory Department.

JOHN P. HAISLIP,
Tutor.

CATALOGUE CONTAINING FULL INFORMATION, SENT ON APPLICATION.

The catalog title page of the college's twenty-fifth session, and Dosh's only as president.

Receipts the Reverend Dosh collected for the Theological Seminary in Salem.

Little did the returning students realize that hot June afternoon how serious their new president was; when Dosh announced that "the business of a student is to study," he was not speaking in figurative terms. With the beginning of the fall session, Dosh instituted his "no nonsense" approach. Within a couple of months, he had the student body in an uproar. His crackdown on student behavior reached the breaking point when he began forcing students to tattle on other students. At that, the students presented an appeal to the board of trustees, and the board actually asked Dosh to rethink his position. College life improved slightly into the spring of 1878, but relations between the students and the president remained rather prickly.

Dosh must have had some second thoughts about his decision to come to the Salem school. Coming from the relative security of his pulpit in Salisbury, the new president soon discovered that running herd on a bunch of rebellious students was anything but satisfying. It is little wonder, then, that when the seminary approved a second professorship in May and offered it to Dosh, the college president leapt at the chance. In the midst of the college's "Quarto-Centennial" celebration in June, Thomas Dosh announced his resignation.

News of Dosh's departure would not dampen spirits for the college's first general reunion in the twenty-five years since its 1853 chartering. A full week's activities had been planned by the college's financial agent, Julius D. Dreher, and Salem had never witnessed a spectacle quite like this before. Special trains carried alumni and friends back to the college, and the gatherings covered all of the campus and much of the town. Japanese lanterns adorned the college grounds each evening, and the United States Marine Band—with the personal compliments of President Rutherford B. Hayes— entertained the masses during the various events. Programs, speeches, the commencement of the class of 1878, dinners, and the laying of the cornerstone of Bittle Memorial Hall all highlighted the week. The festivities were capped off with a final grand banquet at the Duval House—a fine meal to be sure, replete with no fewer than twelve after-dinner speeches!

The faculty closely monitored student attendance. Here is a weekly delinquent roll from December 1878.

"THE INDISPENSABLE INTERLUDE"

That title was used by William Eisenberg in *The First Hundred Years* to characterize the one-year administration of Thomas Dosh. Why was it indispensable? Here is Reverend Eisenberg's account:

> The valedictorian of the Class of 1877 was a young man from Boonsboro, MD, named Luther Leigh Smith. After graduation he studied at the Theological Seminary in Salem—that is for part of his time. At Dr. Dosh's home he became acquainted with Miss Virginia Brown, the sister of Mrs. Dosh. Soon after entering upon the work of his first parish at Mt. Tabor Church in Augusta County, [he married] Miss Brown [and she] became Mrs. Smith. There amid surroundings hallowed by the first fruits of David Bittle's labors, and in the very shadow of Virginia Institute, Charles Jacob Smith, fifth president of the college, was born. Measured, therefore, in the light of the administrations of Dr. Dreher and Dr. Smith, the one-year presidency of Dr. Dosh becomes an indispensable factor in influencing half a century of Roanoke's future history.

"I had been at college only about a week and consequently rested under all the painful approbrium of being a 'rat.' Having decided to take the 'full course,' I had of course, to join the first calathump. A wedding party were to return to Salem on the 8 P.M. train. They were going to have a reception, and the students had decided to give them one, too.

"Well, about forty of us started for the depot. You talk about the United States Marine Band with its variety of tunes and instruments but that is nothing to the diversity which was in our calathump. . . . When the train arrived bringing the expected couple, we executed a Grand Overture on the full band. During the performance the wedding party got into their conveyances and started for town. We were about to start too, when the single word 'Faculty' was whispered around and consternation spread throughout our ranks. I have often seen the Faculty miraculously multiply on such occasions but never did I see so many professors as were presented to my distorted fancy on that memorable night. There was as near as I can recollect, about forty-two Dr. Bittles, thirty-some Professor Wellses and other professors in proportion, while the tutors and instructors were without number. There was one in every fence corner, two or more in the shadow of every building, some seemed to have wings and were perched in every tree and hid in every bush.

"By and by we found our way in small squads to the college campus. . . . The college was now all lighted up and . . . we could see three of the faculty on picket duty on the front porch with note books in hand grading the boys as they came in. . . . I told Crawford we would come in back of the Ciceronian Hall and slip in the back door and run as for dear life up the steps. . . . We tiptoed easily around to the foot of the stairs.—I made one spring, then another and another and I was up. . . . I was now on the landing above and I heard the Prof. coming after me. The long passage was before me; I must fly and I did. . . . I rushed in [my room door] and *closed it softly.* By this time the Prof. was on the upper landing too. They say he looked one way and then the other. As soon as I was in my room I heard a rousing shout go up from a group of boys who were standing on the second floor, I knew I had won.

"The next morning I learned that they had caught every one, who was on the calathump and given each five demerits apiece, except me."

The Oxford English Dictionary defines "callithump" as "a noisy, boisterous parade."

Excerpts from the *Roanoke Collegian*, February 1879.

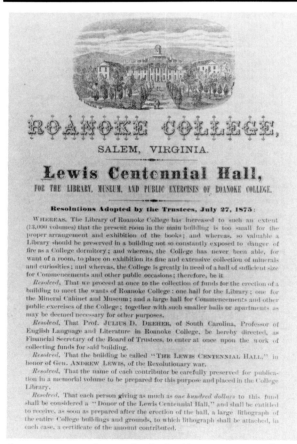

An announcement for a major fund-raising campaign involving Lewis Centennial Hall. The complex would feature a library, a museum, and a sizeable auditorium. Only the library would be built, and renamed after Bittle's death, as Bittle Memorial Hall.

The new building that the college was just undertaking enjoyed a marvelous history even before it was formally begun. In a sense, the structure was ten years old before a single brick was laid. David Bittle first proposed the building in 1868 as a set of two structures: a library and a student dormitory. The board had turned down the request, but Bittle, undaunted, only shelved his plans; he never scrapped them. A couple of years later and hoping to test new water, Bittle ventured forth with a modified plan: a library-museum building complete with a ninety foot tower to support an observatory and the rest of the college's scientific apparatus. The complex was to be named Andrew Lewis Centennial Hall, to honor Salem's most famous son and Revolutionary War hero. The year 1874 would mark the one hundredth anniversary of General Lewis's battle at Point Pleasant along the banks of the Ohio River. Bittle reasoned that merging college interests and town desires could only portend great things. Accordingly, the board approved a modified plan for Lewis Hall the following year (1874). Surely, the town faithful would embrace the plan to honor one of their own.

I, William McCauley, Clerk of the County Court of Roanoke County do certify that the real property of the Roanoke College is assessed at Forty-five Thousand Dollars; and that since the said assessment was made, a lot of five acres has been added to the College grounds, and a new brick Library Building, large and finely furnished, has been erected.

The above does not include the Library of the College said to contain Sixteen Thousand Volumes, or the Mineral Cabinet said to contain Eleven Thousand Specimens; or any other personal property to the College.

Under the laws of Virginia, the College is not required to pay any taxes whatever.

I, do further certify that there is no lien or encumbrance of any kind on the College property, except a Deed of Trust, which secures a loan of Three Thousand Five Hundred Dollars due (as I am informed) to a Miss Elizabeth Stoner, of Bennington Centre, Vermont, and I further certify that that [sic] there are no suits of any kind against the College.

And I do still further certify that I have this day examined the following Insurance Policies, owned by the said College and now in the possession of the Treasurer of the Trustees of the College:

1-One policy of Twelve Thousand Four Hundred Dollars, issued July 28th, 1879: and expires July 28th, 1884: wi[th] the Virginia Fire and Marine Insurance Company, of Richmond.

2-One policy of One Thousand Six Hundred Dollars, issued at the same time and for the same period and by the same company, above mentioned.

3-One policy of Three Thousand Dollars, issued June 4th, 1879, and expires June 4th, 1884; wi[th] the Lynchburg Fire Insurance Company, of Lynchburg, Virginia.

4-One policy of Five Thousand Dollars, issued November 16th, 1877 and expires November 16th, 1882.

The above four policies are issued to cover losses upon the Main College Building, East and West Buildings (disconnected from Main Building) The Library Building and contents (disconnected from other buildings); and the Stewards residence and Dining Hall.

In witness whereof I herein to set my hand and affix the seal of said County Court at Salem, this 15th day of September 1879.

Wm. McCauley, Clerk of Cts.
County Court of Roanoke County.

The new complex was truly massive in scale: three buildings in the shape of a giant inverted U—one flank to be the library, the matching side to be a museum, and the connecting piece in the rear to be a 1,500-seat assembly hall. The buildings would stretch from Trout Hall to High Street and face the front lawn. Bittle had been delighted by the prospects: a spacious library, a museum to display (at last) his favored mineral collection, and a cavernous meeting room that could offer virtually everyone in town a seat. At first, fund raising progressed well, but it soon became apparent—even to Bittle— that the project simply overtaxed the meager resources of both college and community. The anniversary date came and went with little fanfare. By the summer of 1876, the campaign was moving at a snail's pace.

Thorton Whaling, a student in 1879.

An oil study lamp used by John Sutton Fray, a student in the class of 1877.

When Bittle died the following September, fund raising had come to a standstill. It was only natural for the board to take the action that it did: to honor its fallen leader and to reinstill the hope of raising additional monies, the board announced that the new building would be named Bittle Memorial Hall. The friends of the college were pleased, yet one has to wonder about the effect the name change had on the population of Salem, many of whom had contributed in good faith to honor General Lewis. Privately, feelings and relations had been hurt.

When the cornerstone was set in June 1878, the college still lacked considerable funds. Already the decision had been made to scrap two-thirds of the complex. The museum would never be built, and Bittle's dream to have a grand assembly hall for town and gown passed with him. The building that remained was opened a year and a half later, in October 1879, and Bittle Memorial Hall served as the college library for the next eighty-three years.

Through the summer of 1878, to the casual observer the state of the college could not have appeared all that good. Since the death of David Bittle, disarray had characterized the college's governance. With the receivership of Professor Wells and the aborted presidency of Dosh, the college lacked the permanence and vision that it so demanded. Its prospects for success appeared as bleak in late summer 1878 as perhaps at any moment in the college's history, before or since.

At the age of thirty-two, Julius Daniel Dreher walked upon the stage.

For students everywhere, the moment of reckoning! A report card from 1880. Nineteenth-century grades were always numerical averages; letter grades did not appear until the next century.

The class of 1880.

CHAPTER 6

<u>"Animated</u>
<u>by the modern spirit,"</u>
<u>1880–1888</u>

Julius Daniel Dreher, Roanoke's third president, captured in an 1886 photograph.

Like the college, Julius Dreher had survived the Civil War. As a teenager, Dreher had marched off to war from his native South Carolina. When he returned home, Dreher came back a man—mature, sober, and perhaps scarred by the images and memories of that horrible war. There is little evidence that Dreher enjoyed talking about his wartime experiences and even less that he wrote about those years. Indeed, the war could have had an indelible effect on Dreher and his subsequent career; to prevent such madness for future generations, the key was enlightenment and learning. The answer was education.

To that end, Dreher first had to pursue his own course of study. He spent several years attending private schools near his Columbia home, and in the fall of 1869, Dreher headed north to Salem to enroll at Roanoke as a twenty-three-year-old junior. He made his mark immediately with the faculty; they found in Dreher a brilliant, industrious, and dedicated student. Even by the summer of 1870, Bittle had tapped Dreher to make a recruiting trip through the South. Bittle was convinced that the college's reputation could only be enhanced by increased exposure through the region. Moreover, given the dislocation caused by the recent war, Bittle reasoned that earlier educational ties between certain southern regions and northern colleges had been definitely

altered or severed outright. The college had nothing to lose, Bittle argued, in investigating the possibilities. Little did the college president realize that as the student representative headed south that summer, the school's demographic profile would be altered dramatically into the next century. Dreher's initial visit into the Deep South would portend great things.

Upon his graduation in 1871, Dreher had a job waiting; Bittle made sure of that. The college appointed the recent graduate principal of the Preparatory Department, adjunct professor of Greek, librarian, and secretary of the faculty. By the opening of the session of 1872, Dreher had been promoted to assistant professor of ancient languages and instructor in English language and literature. While teaching continued as Dreher's main avocation, his time was increasingly taken up by administrative duties. Soon Dreher was handling all of the college's correspondence, soliciting funds from selected benefactors, and aggressively pursuing prospective students through the mails.

By 1874, Dreher's responsibilities as an administrator became preeminent. Given Bittle's declining health and activities, and the fact that the college business of attracting students and collecting funds was deemed so important, Dreher was given license to spend more and more of his time away from Salem. His first extended expedition came with the conclusion of the fall 1874 semester. He later recalled his trek: "I left Salem, December 8, and returned May 31, having traveled a total distance of over 7,000 miles, without a single accident, and with only two unimportant delays. I saw much, learned much, enjoyed much."

To support further his activities, Dreher helped to establish in 1875 the college's first publication, the *Collegian.* It functioned as a campus newsletter, a literary journal, an alumni clearinghouse, and significantly for Dreher, both as a worthy recruitment tool for new students and as a vehicle for keeping possible donors in touch with the college.

Dreher became a more and more valuable asset to the college as the decade progressed. As financial agent, he had become Bittle's right arm. It was perhaps only because of Dreher's tender age (he had just turned thirty) at the untimely death of the college's founder that he didn't succeed Bittle directly. Dreher was given responsibility, for example, for the college's Quarto-Centennial celebration, which was to take place in the summer of 1878. With his unparalleled planning and execution, the festivities proved most impressive, and coupled with Dosh's resignation, Dreher was positioned for the appointment. Before, it had taken the board almost a year to replace Bittle; this time, a successor was announced in little more than a month.

Dreher accepted the presidency with all of the intensity, vigor, and pride that one could imagine. Already, it was difficult to separate the college from the man. Through the next twenty-five years, Dreher would dedicate himself to little else, refusing even to marry until after his tenure at Roanoke was over. His commitment was total. Dreher made Bittle's final written words to him prophetic; leaving on another fund-raising trip, Dreher received this note from the old doctor: "God bless you in your undertaking: begin with faith in the Lord, and if things do not go as you think, let not faith falter." Dreher had no intention of failing.

To honor David Bittle, Dreher planned his inauguration for 25 September 1879, the third anniversary of the founder's death. It would also coincide with the dedication and opening of the new library, Bittle Memorial Hall. Alas, construction delays caused the celebration to slip past the intended date, so to preserve the joint event, the inauguration was postponed until 17 October 1879.

The assembled crowd was treated in the morning to the dedication of the new library. The ledger book, which all guests dutifully signed, survives today as a reminder of the day's commemoration. Professor Carson Wells offered a tribute to David Bittle, and upon its conclusion, Dr. Charles Porterfield Krauth, president of the Lutheran Theological Seminary in Philadelphia, presented an address on "The Library." The benediction was offered by Reverend W. E. Hubbert. The day's events continued throughout the afternoon, and at 8 P.M., Julius Dreher was formally installed as the college's third president. His inaugural address "Education as a Preparation for Useful Living" served the audience well in its interest to understand better this president—one of the youngest in the country—and his vision of the new Roanoke.

The guest register for the dedication of the new library. The volume was used through the centennial celebration in 1942, and again at the dedication of the Fintel Library in 1991.

A student diploma from the 1880s. Along with the president's signature the diploma was signed by each faculty member, all five of them!

A. E. Peery graduated in 1882 and represents the earliest photograph of a cap and gown at a Roanoke commencement.

Dreher's message attempted to bridge the gap between the reflective world of the academy and the daily challenges and crises of life beyond its walls. "The popular idea that education is acquired only during the period spent in schools is too narrow. . . . By education, we understand not merely the acquisition of sufficient knowledge for the discharge of the ordinary affairs of life; but also such a discipline and drawing out of the intellectual powers, training of the moral character, and cultivation of the religious affections, as shall best fit a man for the faithful and efficient performance of his duties to his country and humanity, to himself and his God."

Dreher discussed the "objects" of education—"discipline and knowledge"—the advantages of liberal culture, and perhaps with an eye cast on the Civil War, cautioned his audience that "no amount of mere intellectual culture, without moral elevation, can save nations and individuals from vice and ruin." He concluded his remarks with this statement: "It is the business of a college, therefore, to teach the duty, dignity, usefulness, and happiness of labor. . . . Let our colleges, in all their teachings, impress this motto: Learn much to do much."

Despite the administrative changes and shakeups of the late 1870s, student life on campus continued as ever—much work, much play, and a general confidence that all would work out in the end. A great deal of campus enthusiasm was generated by the increased dedication to organized sports. Bittle's earlier insistence upon intramural competition passed with him, for by the very next spring, one of Roanoke's baseball clubs had challenged a team from the Agricultural and Mechanical College (Virginia Tech) to a two-game series. The teams split the pair with Roanoke winning the final game 27-20. Even the lack of formal competition—or equipment—could not stop the students. The *Collegian* recorded this account: "The young gentlemen who remained at college during the vacation express themselves as being delighted with Salem as a summer resort, and say they spent the time pleasantly. Among other healthful sports indulged in was base ball playing. They organized the 'Dirty Sock Club.' " Baseball would continue to flourish on into the next century.

Students busied themselves with a variety of other sporting activities: fencing, hiking, and archery, to name a few. A new sport debuted in the 1870s: "Foot ball is at present the most popular game with Roanoke students. They are very fond of it, although it is a regular ankle-peeler of a play." By 1878, the college attempted to accommodate the increased activity by purchasing the adjoining property along Market Street. This site would indeed serve the students and college well as the athletic field and later as stadium until the construction of the science complex in the late 1960s.

The earliest known photograph of an entire Roanoke student body including the college men, the prep school boys, and the faculty (in the center with the top hats). The photo was taken in 1886 in front of the Administration Building.

Several students agitated for a gymnastics club as well. Their petition resulted in a formal request to the faculty to consider the building of a "proper gymnasium." After due consideration, the faculty turned down the students' request because of "the diversion from studies it would cause." A few years later, the second floor of Trout Hall would be renovated to provide a place for "gymnastic exercise." An actual gymnasium would not be built until 1910.

The campus itself was the recipient of constant attention. Whether through specific "Campus Day" activities or as a general expectation, the students were required to maintain the yards, paths, gardens, and shrubs of the school. The following notice was typical. "On Thursday and Friday the 20th and 21st of this month, the students cleaned up the campus. They deserve much praise for the manner in which they performed their work, displaying in it no little taste. We can say, and truthfully too, that our campus is the prettiest in the State of Virginia. Much of its beauty is due to the care and attention the students have bestowed upon it, and they should be its true guardians and not permit it to be marred in any way."

Roanoke College.

CLASS OF '87

REQUEST YOUR PRESENCE AT THE

Commencement Exercises.

Wednesday, June 15, 1887.

A commencement invitation from 1887.

The students were frequently mobilized to repair the campus fences that stretched across the front quad and along High Street, and they often complained about the continual flooding of their "playground" in front of Trout and Bittle halls. The students were no doubt delighted when the faculty declared a holiday in November 1878 and the entire student body descended the hill behind the campus and created a skating pond from the little creek that traversed the athletic field.

ROANOKE COLLEGE,

Salem, Va., , 188....

━━━◆━━━

I hereby certify that I was present throughout regular church service in Salem on each Sunday during the quarter ending yesterday; and that I also attended Sunday-school regularly during the quarter.

Students were required to sign this pledge regarding church attendance; a mandatory daily chapel service was also demanded.

An elaborate Demosthenean Society invitation; the palmettos might have been added in deference to Dreher and his South Carolina roots.

Coal stoves were installed in the principal rooms on campus by 1879; telephones also debuted that year, and Salem's first water system brought that commodity to the school gates as well. The *Collegian* reported that in town "lamp posts have been erected along the streets, and now the darkness of the night is driven away by the steady glare of the kerosene lamp. What think ye of this, students of other days, who were accustomed to flounder through the darkness and mud to see your sweethearts?"

The faculty continually struggled to uphold the academic and moral charge of the college. The faculty was still preoccupied by student transgressions and the handing out of punishments; the normal array of pranks and stunts—"rock rolling" in the Administration Building continued as prime entertainment—was mixed in with the more serious offenses of brawling and brandishing pistols. Faculty meted out sentences swiftly and without prejudice, including one to Professor Yonce's son Ivan who was "suspended for misconduct, after many previous warnings." Faculty admonished students about the dangers of "cramming," the unethical use of "ponies" (student translations of Latin and Greek texts carefully guarded and handed down from generation to generation), and the disgraceful practice of writing on the walls of the buildings.

The young women of Salem represented something of a challenge for the faculty too. The professors decried the common practice of these women approaching the campus seeking "interviews" with the students. The faculty pleaded, "Now ladies, don't take advantage of poor boys who are away from home and have no friends to care for them. As guardians of the institution, we do most emphatically remonstrate against any such proceedings."

Scholastic life progressed naturally into the 1880s. Students founded a Numismatic Society, a Teutonic Society (to promote the study of German life and culture), and a Mineralogical Society to safeguard Dr. Bittle's prized collection of rocks and fossils. Secret societies and the boarding clubs continued to thrive, and life in the "Buzzard's Roost" was never without a dull moment. The Roost, on the top floor in the Ad Building, offered a dozen rooms to a handful of students. The college provided only the space; the students had to acquire a bed, dresser, and all other furnishings. The faculty inspected their quarters routinely and encouraged the students to give their rooms "the cozy home-like" touch that would "enhance their academic performance."

Often, student events spilled over into the streets of town. The *Collegian* recorded this impromptu parade: "One pretty evening, about two weeks ago, several platoons of students, composed of dignified Seniors and sedate Juniors, boisterous Freshmen, and green Preparatorians, marched the streets of Salem with greased beavers [hats]. It was a sight, and the fair Misses of Salem looked on and smiled." Even the faculty could have a sense of humor. This published announcement offered some measure of relief: "The Review of the Senior class will begin immediately after Xmas vacation. This is preparatory to that time which decides whether it is necessary to order a tin case for a diploma, or to buy a railroad ticket home."

One of the first crises to confront Dreher's administration was a precipitous decline in enrollment. During the three previous years, the student body had numbered 171, 177, and 149. By 1878, the enrollment plummeted to 102; there was no marked improvement either in the next two years: 100 in 1879–1880 and 107 in 1880–1881. Much of the drop-off was attributed to a major epidemic of yellow fever that ravaged most of the Deep South through that time period. The *Collegian* recounted several fund drives and events that the students, with the assistance of the town residents, undertook for the benefit of the victims. College enrollment would not reach the 170 mark again until 1896. With tuition dollars cut by a third, the college clearly struggled for its continued survival. Faculty salaries were cut; college expenditures were reduced, and the college's future was severely compromised. Experimentation was demanded.

The Missionary Band played no instruments but served the students as a Bible class for a number of years.

MATRICULATION PLEDGE.

Roanoke College,

, 1888.

Duly recognizing the nature of the obligation assumed, I do hereby pledge myself as a gentleman to comply faithfully with the regulations of Roanoke College, and in all respects to conduct myself as a student and gentleman, so long as I remain a student at the Institution.

(Signature--
--Full name) _____

(Date of birth) _____

(Name of Parent or Guardian) _____

(Postoffice) _____

(State) _____

This "Matriculation Pledge" is not much different from the Academic Integrity pledge that students are expected to sign today.

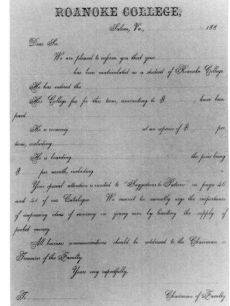

Professor F. V. N. Painter was affiliated with the college for over forty years as a language professor and published as much as perhaps any Roanoke faculty member in history.

Business Department of Roanoke College.

Prof. J. T. CRABTREE, A. M., Principal.
J. W. LAMM, Instructor in Penmanship.

During the present session (1887-'88) a large hall has been comfortably and handsomely fitted up for the Business Department of Roanoke College.

This Department is intended to meet the wants of that large class of young men who wish to carry forward their literary studies, and at the same time prepare themselves thoroughly for business pursuits. It is, also, suited to those who wish to prepare for business in a short time, and yet enjoy, during such preparation, the literary advantages of a College—such as a large library, a good readingroom, and excellent literary societies. All students in this Department are advised to enter regular College classes in English and Mathematics.

Students in the Business Course pay the usual fees (tuition $50 and incidental fee $10), and have the privilege of attending any of the College classes, without extra charge. Entire expenses for nine months from $149 to $204 (including College fees, board, fuel, &c.).

The Business Course is open, without extra charge, to students in any of the regular courses for degrees. As college graduates often need a knowledge of business methods, candidates for degrees are advised to take advantage of this opportunity of acquiring a business education.

In the Business Course, as well as in the other Departments of Instruction, a high standard of thoroughness will be maintained. Young men are advised to spend an entire session of nine months in the Business Course. When this is impracticable and the student enters well advanced, good work may be done in a half a session.

A certificate of proficiency in business methods will be given to any student who satisfactorily completes the course of study, provided he has also made respectable attainments in English.

COURSE OF STUDY.

ENGLISH GRAMMAR AND COMPOSITION—taught with reference to letter-writing and business correspondence. Special attention is paid to spelling.

Professor J. T. Crabtree was selected by the college to head up the Business program and served as its principal for three years.

By the early 1880s, Dreher and the faculty were not afraid of innovation or change as far as the academic program was concerned. Like Bittle before him, Dreher was always prepared to consider options and to weigh possibilities. The issue of a teacher-training program surfaced again in 1879; the college flirted with the concept and agreed to host a summer institute for teachers in 1882. The approach continued forward for a few more semesters but finally languished by 1885. Courses on the art of teaching were thereafter ably handled by Professor F. V. N. Painter, who became highly regarded as an authority on educational methods and history. His *History of Education* and his collection of articles entitled *Great Pedagogical Essays* were important publications for the period.

Further change occurred in 1880 when the college first offered its "scientific course." After his sophomore year, a student could elect to forgo additional Latin and Greek and instead adopt "the modern languages" (French and German) and undertake more rigorous instruction in mathematics and the natural sciences. The catalog described the course as including differential and integral calculus, "field work in Surveying and Leveling, Natural History, Botany and Mineralogy." The first two bachelor of science degrees were awarded to members of the class of 1881.

The college experimented with a business program during the decade of the 1880s as well. Indeed, as early as 1879, business courses were offered on campus, but no formal course of study was approved until 1887. Professor J. T. Crabtree was contracted as principal of the business department, which took up residence on the second floor of Trout Hall.

There were numerous other schemes that the trustees considered and, after careful reflection, laid aside. On several occasions, the college reviewed the possibilities of moving its prep school, either by renting the Lake Spring Hotel facility in town or by opening a distant campus in Wytheville, Virginia. In the end, the feasibility of all of those plans was rejected. Similarly, Dreher also pondered a school of "civil, mechanical, mining, and electrical engineering in connection with college," and somewhat later, a separate "school of commerce" was proposed. Ultimately, college finances dictated the more realistic course of action, and each of Dreher's dreams remained only dreams.

When the *Collegian* trumpeted in 1903 that "Roanoke College has had more foreign students than any other college in the South," it was no idle boast. Julius Dreher was a champion of international education as a means of fostering international and intercultural understanding. The president was dedicated to enabling his faculty to study and to travel abroad as a way of increasing perspective. Likewise, Roanoke students were encouraged to embark upon some European adventure. But for the majority of those who could or would not, Dreher was determined to bring at least a part of that experience to Salem.

As an initial reaction, greater college programming was a response. Through various events, lectures, and activities, the student body received increased exposure to international issues. Principal to that mission was the establishment of the department of history and political science, founded in 1882. Dreher himself was listed as professor of history, and to assist him in his labors, the college hired Luther A. Fox, whose teaching career would span the next forty-two years. Dreher was dedicated to combating this sense of American intellectual isolationism; introducing courses on the nature of Western civilization seemed an obvious course.

The graduates of the class of 1886 are in the outer circle with the faculty pictured around the center.

The "young" Luther Fox. The religion and history professor was already in his forties when he joined the faculty in 1882; he was still on the faculty when he died in 1925, at the age of 84.

"ANIMATED BY THE MODERN SPIRIT," 1880–1888   73

Another response to broadening the educational experience was the recruitment of students from other cultures to come to Salem and take up residence at the college. Through the balance of the nineteenth century, Roanoke was home to numerous international students. Several enrolled from Europe, several others from Canada, Mexico, and South America. The first oriental student, Hidei Fukuoka, entered Roanoke from Japan in 1888. The college's major international connection—its link with Korea—would occur shortly in the 1890s.

Above all, Dreher took greatest pride in his educational mission to American Indians. When he was a student himself, Dreher witnessed the first of thirty-five Choctaw Indians to arrive on the Salem campus. Jacob Battiece Jackson had arrived in 1870 and remained for four years. He returned to the reservation in Oklahoma and in time became influential in Choctaw affairs and served for a number of years in their tribal senate. His fond memories of his college days, coupled with Dreher's recruiting trips into the southwest during the 1870s, combined to channel a generation of future Choctaw leaders to Roanoke. Dreher took a personal interest in his "special guests." The last Choctaw to attend Roanoke departed in 1898.

There is little question that Julius Dreher spent most of his time while president away from Roanoke. His years as financial agent in the 1870s had impressed upon him the critical importance of raising and maintaining revenues. No other experience had better prepared him for assuming the reins of the institution. Indeed, as a man in his eighties back on campus to help the college celebrate its seventy-fifth anniversary in 1928, Dreher reflected on his tenure in office: "During that entire period of twenty-five years I played the role of a peripatetic college president in perennial search of a deficit extinguisher; but that deficit proved to be a sort of *ignis fatigues*, always a little ahead, and never quite overtaken."

Solomon Jones Homer, a Choctaw indian, was the valedictorian of the class of 1893. After graduation, he studied law at Harvard University and later represented his people as their special emissary in Washington.

James Alfred Dukes, '96, was the last Choctaw to graduate from Roanoke. He became the speaker of the Choctaw House of Delegates and later, the United States field clerk for his nation.

Dreher's schedule on the road was a demanding one. In a typical year, he would depart Salem by the end of September and not return until the close of term, often only a few days before Christmas. Then as the weather improved by early February, Dreher would take flight again, not to be seen until the end of May, just a week or two before graduation. In the college archives today are the trip accounts and financial journals of Dreher's thirty years of life on the road. They tell a story of sacrifice and unusual dedication, of long hours for often meager rewards.

As Dreher became president, the staggering financial crunch of lost revenues because of the sharp downturn in enrollments created instant financial adjustments for the school. But as soon as the initial crisis had been averted, Dreher and the board commenced a design for long-range planning. In 1880, the college adopted a program to establish formally a capital endowment. Dreher also dedicated his labors to augmenting faculty compensation as the board pledged to raise annual salaries to a dizzying height of $750.

Dreher also established a long-standing tradition of heading north for fund raising. The South, and much of Virginia in particular, was still in ruins after the war. Dreher could accept that fact but not the prevailing attitude that he could discern. "The Southern people are not rich. When they were, they did less than they are doing today. It is a sad confession but it is true, that there never has existed a benevolent spirit towards education in the South." With that complaint, Dreher headed north, cultivating fields that would provide the college bounty into the next century. Armed with letters of introduction and soliciting newspaper endorsements, Dreher entered the social worlds of Philadelphia, New York, Hartford, Newport, and Boston.

Life on campus through the decade of the 1880s continued much as before. Most of the fraternities and secret societies continued. Sigma Chi enjoyed life in "The Ark," their place of residence, and all the organizations took great pride in the annual spring planting of flowers in the shape of their badges in designated flower beds on campus. The debating societies—the Ciceronians and the Demostheneans—

each refurbished their respective parlors and sponsored their weekly meetings and monthly programs. The boarding clubs still dominated the extracurricular life of the students, offering room, board, and other amenities.

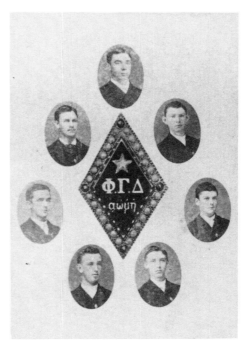

A carte-de-visite of the brothers of Phi Gamma Delta, a social fraternity of the period, which took great pride in their flower beds depicting their badge in the front of the campus.

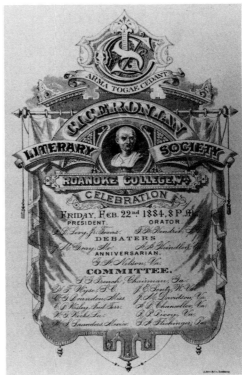

Not to be outdone by their rivals, the Ciceronians spared no expense on their invitations either. This one is from 1884.

C. Armand Miller was a member of the class of 1887.

The "campus committee," a group of interested students and faculty, supervised the general upkeep and well-being of the campus. Students frequently complained of wandering livestock on the property; some of the ubiquitous town cattle would frequently visit the inviting campus grounds, helping themselves to the lawn, trampling the gardens and shrubs, and generally making footing rather hazardous. Fences were constantly being repaired, and the college once even closed the front gates and moved the official entrance to High Street in an attempt to dissuade the cows. By 1883, the committee, in desperation, ordered the newly patented invention barbed wire to combat the problem; this was war!

A FAIR IN ROANOKE

"Silence held sway at Roanoke College. . . . The walks between the arching trees of the campus, which usually resound with the boisterous noises of Preps and Irregulars, now preserved a quiet broken, only now and then, by the birds chippering their astonishment at the unwonted stillness. At the village postoffice no pushing crowds clamored for mail, and the postmaster and his clerk wore pleasanter faces than they had been seen to have for many days. The dinner bells of the boarding houses rang less vehemently than usual. . . . It was evident that the students were out of town.

"Some time previous, hand-bills and posters had announced the second holding of the Roanoke stock fair. . . . On Thursday a number of boys . . . hastened . . . to board the vehicles designed to convey them to Roanoke. . . . After a ride of four or five miles, the boys . . . came to a long hill up which was toiling quite a line of vehicles bearing passengers going to the fair. From the top of the hill . . . could be seen a lovely view marred only by the town of Roanoke, which lay below in all its bran-new [sic] ugliness. . . . The fair proper was the least attractive feature on the grounds. Watching other people was more interesting, especially those who patronized the various gambling devices. . . . Some fine, and also some very poor stock was on exhibition. A good brass band at intervals enlivened the spectators, while all the time peanut and lemonade venders [sic], side show men, and such characters wearied them with their cries. Toward the end of the day some very poor races drew the people around the course.

"Our party of shabby vehicles reassembled at six o'clock and again took their seats in the wagons, now homeward bound. . . . Though all were tired, 'Won't go Home till Morning,' 'Going to Skip College To-morrow,' and many other songs, rose above the rattling of the wagon and made the distance seem short."

Excerpt from the *Roanoke Collegian,* December 1884.

The Ciceronians awarded the "Declamers Medal" to W. E. Main.

SMALLPOX!

"On Wednesday morning, January 3rd, we were startled by the announcement that the small-pox was in town. We were at first incredulous, but soon were satisfied that the thing was no joke. . . .

"Some three weeks ago Deputy-Sheriff Chas. Stevens and Judge Griffin went to Texas to bring back a fugitive from Virginia justice. They were in El Paso—where there was small-pox—on the trip. After returning to Salem, Mr. Stevens became sick, but not seriously so. . . . As he became better and assumed his duties his two little daughters, and a child of M. D. Strickler, became sick, having the same symptoms. [A] critical examination on Tuesday night revealed the fact of small-pox. Early on Wednesday morning all was confusion in the town. The Faculty quickly and closely investigated all the facts. At 2 o'clock a chapel meeting was called and the facts stated to the students, assuring them that all necessary and possible precaution would be taken for their safety. On Thursday evening, after close watching and mature deliberation, the Faculty, in the abundance of precaution, determined to suspend College exercises until the opening of the second term, February 1st. Most of the boys, residing near, have gone home. Some will remain and pursue their studies. . . . The town Council have established a hospital, and no new cases are developing—in fact the disease is now believed to be entirely under control. There is not, and has not been, a case in the College."

Excerpt from the *Roanoke Collegian,* January 1883.

Apart from the good times or the daily tribulations, life in the nineteenth century could rapidly turn brutish. To reveal that the college kept a plot at the ready in the East Hill Cemetery suggests how close death was to the people of the time. The campus long mourned the passing of a Choctaw Indian who died after a brief illness. Virtually every year, a student was lost to some affliction, and illness and disease were endemic. In 1881, an outbreak of the measles forced the postponement of several major campus events, and in 1883, the worst horror—small pox—invaded Salem. The college closed for five weeks, sending the students home in an attempt to avoid the pestilence. The outbreak proved less than feared, and the college survived unscathed.

"ANIMATED BY THE MODERN SPIRIT," 1880–1888   **77**

Through the 1880s, sporting events occupied much available free time. Baseball and football continued, and new avocations such as croquet, lawn bowling, and "jumping" debuted. Other "sports" still caught the faculty's watchful eye: for example, marble playing was discouraged, "whooping" at the Hollins Institute was not tolerated, and plastering keyholes in the Ad Building was absolutely denounced. Faculty had to chuckle when one student was called in to account for his actions the night before; he was spotted escorting his date through the streets of town holding her much too tightly. When the faculty inquired, his response was that "she was nearsighted and couldn't hear."

Dreher's labor in the North soon paid dividends in terms of donations for campus improvements. Several northern companies contributed the materials for much needed campus repairs. Three buildings were reroofed; screens were added to the Ad Building; the porch and basement were resupported; new locks were installed, and all was repainted: "The coloring, which had been applied in oil, has the appearance of bright brick. The penciling has been neatly done, especially in the front of the main building."

Chrisenbery Alexander Brown graduated in 1887 and became a Lutheran pastor.

WANTED: ONE JANITOR—APPLY WITHIN

"Messers Stebbins and Olinger having both applied for the janitorship of the college for the session of 81-82, it was after deliberation by the Faculty, agreed to divide the parties applying as follows for the term ending June 30, 1882.

"Mr. Stebbins is entrusted with the care of the main building, (its dormatories [sic] halls and lecture rooms), the ringing of the bell, the keeping of the chapel in order for service, and the post office. He is also to take general care of the College grounds, keep the walks in order, and see that general cleanliness is maintained about the buildings.

"Mr. Olinger is to carry the coal-house key and supervise the distribution of coal, to take charge of the two halls and the lecture rooms contained therein. He is also to sweep and dust the Library when needed, and do all the glazing about college which may be required. He is also to supervise the privy and jim if attention [is needed] by way of cleaning and disinfecting."

The Roanoke College faculty added several new faces in the decade of the 1880s and reorganized the college departments to begin the look of the college we know today. The stalwarts, Carson Wells and William Yonce, remained to lend a watchful eye and to insure the continued integrity of the system. To assist Wells in his labors, the college hired William A. Smith in 1885 as instructor to create a department of chemistry and physics. Wells continued in mathematics and astronomy until his death in 1900; Smith stayed until 1908. Yonce's department of languages saw greater academic defection: first, F. V. N. Painter appeared in 1878 to develop a program in modern languages and literature; then in 1885, the modern English department was born in the person of Wythe Morehead, who remained at his post for half a century, retiring in 1935. Yonce continued as professor of ancient languages until his death in 1895. And finally, as mentioned before, Luther Fox debuted in 1882 to teach religion, philosophy, and history; this beloved Tar Heel dedicated his life to Roanoke and remained until his death in 1925.

The faculty and trustees had experimented for several years with additional college administrative offices and positions. In the late 1870s, the board had in fact approved the creation of the position of vice president, but abandoned the title after only a few years. In 1888, the board also created the position of dean of the faculty, a person who would serve principally as the head of student discipline. The faculty elected, almost as a gag, Luther Fox to the post; Fox was so nonplussed by the assignment that he positively refused to have anything to do with the job. After two years of frustration, the board relented and let Fox out of that position, only to appoint him college vice president. Fox refused that post as well, and after a few more years, he was finally left alone by the trustees!

Professor William A. Smith taught mathematics and the sciences from 1885 to 1908.

Wythe Morehead joined the faculty with Smith in 1885 and stayed much longer—for fifty years, retiring in 1935. He was faculty emeritus the last four years.

Arthur Koiner, MD was a lecturer on physiology and hygiene from 1885 until 1891.

Relations between Dreher and the faculty were typically fine, but on occasion, the two sides could become rather prickly. When the president pledged to raise faculty salaries, things could not have been better. But in the late 1880s, when word reached the faculty that Dreher had negotiated a new deal with the trustees giving him a higher percentage of the funds he collected while he was away "at the North," the faculty balked. The professors felt that the "commission" policy ratified by the board was unbecoming a college president. Besides, if they had to work for a set wage, so should every member of the staff. The jealousy was resolved when the board agreed to review its decision. The principle of a percentage payment was retained, but that figure was reduced—from $7\frac{1}{2}$ percent to 5 percent. Dreher accepted the adjustment but still felt ambushed by his faculty.

A SOJOURN IN VIRGINIA

Noted clergyman Reverend Washington Gladden delivered the commencement address to the Roanoke College class of 1882. He later offered these observations about the college to the Springfield (Massachusetts) *Republican*.

"The next stage took me down the Richmond and Alleghany Road to Lynchburg, and thence to Salem, in Roanoke County, the seat of Roanoke College. . . . Salem is a handsome town of two thousand inhabitants, the neatest and most like New England of any I have seen in Virginia. The College buildings are well represented by the lithographs with which many of your citizens are familiar, and all that I saw and heard convinced me that the College itself is, as a prominent man in Richmond to-day remarked, 'the place where more education can be got for less money than in any other institution in Virginia.' The Faculty are men of good learning and high consecration; they stick to their work on small salaries, some of them refusing tempting offers to better their condition in other places; and they do not, like some other folks, seem to think it a thing to boast of, either. A large share of the students are from the middle class, and the spirit of the work and of self-reliance manifested by them is truly inspiring. In the baker's dozen of speeches by these young men in the contest for the prize medal in oratory, and on the Commencement stage, there was a revelation of the temper of the New South that bodes nothing but good to the section and to the whole nation. Without exception, the speeches were brave, manly, forward-looking. The fact that a new day had come to the South was the undertone of all this young thinking; and it was evident enough that these hopeful fellows were ready to spring to the front of the new movement, and make the most of its opportunities. National matters were referred to by most of them, and not one word of bitterness was spoken,—nothing that could have given pain to the most stalwart Northerner. In a literary way, the speeches were much more rhetorical than would be heard at Yale or Amherst, and some of them needed not a little chastening; but what they lacked in finish they made up in manliness. On the whole, I was greatly pleased with the indications given by the young men of this College, representing several different states of the public sentiment at the South."

In a special 1888 U.S. Bureau of Education report on the state of education in Virginia, Roanoke's programs are compared favorably to the other state schools. The report commended the college on its dedication and promise, and marveled at the school's sheer determination: "It is surprising that the college has lived; it is still more surprising that it has made so good a record for sound scholarship and for wide usefulness." With no endowment and no sponsoring patron, the college should have failed; that it did not do so is the principal theme of the nineteenth century. The report observed that "any one at all familiar with the difficulties of establishing good colleges, even in wealthy communities and under favoring conditions and influences," would know how truly taxing it was. For Roanoke to have survived proved the rule. The report found the valleys of western Virginia quite beautiful but not particularly wealthy. The lack of a sponsoring agency had limited the college's fortunes. "Although remaining under the auspices of the Evangelical Lutheran Church," the study noted, "the institution has always been conducted in a most catholic spirit, and has largely drawn both its students and its support from non-Lutheran sources. About two-thirds of its present constituency come from other denominations." The report concluded that Roanoke had done well. Only time would tell if Roanoke was to survive.

CHAPTER 7

"Hopeth all things,"
1888–1896

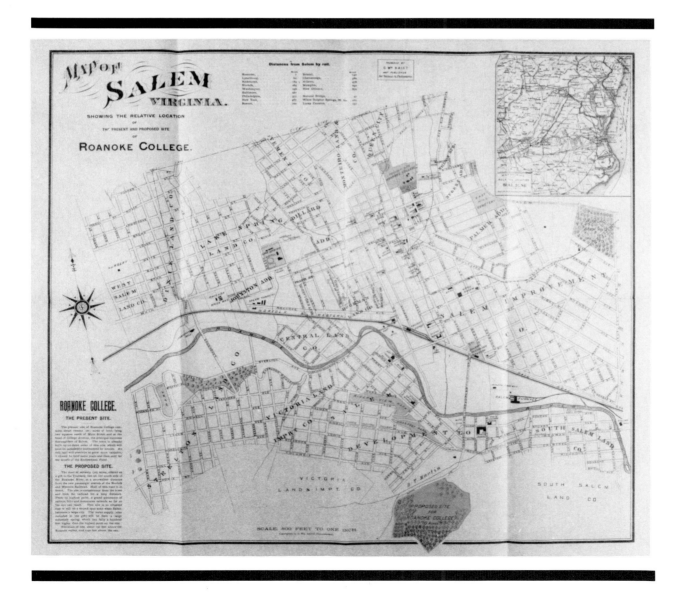

Headquarters of the Salem Improvement Company, in a photograph from the 1920s. (Courtesy Salem Times-Register)

The decade of the 1890s could not have loomed any more promising for the town of Salem. Ten years earlier, town fathers had misjudged the economic impact that additional rail links could make upon a community. With their rather lackadaisical attitude, Salem leaders scoffed when the Norfolk and Western Railroad chose the little town of Roanoke next door as the site of its major transhipment point and for the location for its shops. The growth of Roanoke shocked all observers, as the "Magic City" soon outstripped the older town and county seat of Salem before the decade was out.

SALEM'S RAPID AND SUBSTANTIAL GROWTH

"Since [April 1890] the growth of Salem has been more rapid and substantial than that of any other place of its size in Virginia. . . . [M]ore than 500 buildings, many of them handsome residences and costly business houses and factories, have been built. The population has increased from about 2,000 to nearly 5,000. The business of the post-office and telegraph office has increased 500 percent. The post-office has become an office of second-class this summer. The iron furnace about to go into blast and the factories in operation and actually secured will employ several thousand hands, including females, and insure the doubling of the present population in the near future.

"The improvements made in Salem are of a solid and substantial character. The new streets have been graded and macadamized on both sides of the river, brick pavements have been laid, the water-works have been extended, and an additional water supply secured to meet the needs of a large increase in popula-

tion. . . . [T]wo handsome iron bridges have been constructed to connect the two parts of the city. . . . College Avenue, seventy-five feet wide, extending from Main Street to the new passenger station of the Norfolk and Western Railroad, has been well macadamized. This is the principal business street of Salem, and as only brick or stone buildings may be erected on it, it is sure to become one of the finest thoroughfares in the State. . . . At the head of it stands the imposing group of brick buildings of Roanoke College, and at its foot the new stone passenger station of the Norfolk and Western, one of the finest on the line of its road.

"Visitors to Salem are impressed with the substantial and attractive character of the buildings that have been erected or are in course of construction."

Excerpts from *Salem, Virginia: Its Advantages and Attractions* (New York: The Giles Co., 1891).

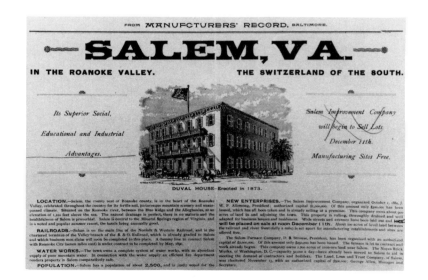

By 1889, Salem prepared for a counterattack. The town redoubled its efforts at economic promotion, and local entrepreneurs formed the Salem Improvement Company. This organization proved quite successful in attracting new industry to the town. The Salem Rolling Mills, the Corbett Machine Works, the Salem Steam Tannery, and the Salem Wagon Manufactory, to name a few, added their names to the business registry. Additionally, the Salem Improvement Company purchased huge tracts of land to be developed as housing sites. As a result of this activity, Salem burgeoned.

By the summer of 1890, nine other land companies climbed aboard the bandwagon. Building starts in Salem were astonishing: 211 new homes, 67 stores, and 39 manufacturing establishments. The town population had swelled from approximately 2,500 at the start of the boom to 4,350 by January 1891. Capping the new look for Salem was the majestic Hotel Salem, costing more than $100,000, on College Avenue, and the Academy Street School, just north of Main Street.

The college as well was caught up in the excitement. As land prices skyrocketed, the college property became more and more valuable. Members of the Improvement Company soon approached the college to begin discussions concerning the sale of the college grounds. Given the college's critical location in the town and its desired position, the developers were confident that they could offer the college a lucrative deal and still make a handsome profit in return. They offered the college a tract of land south of the Roanoke River and along the heights of Mt. Regis. The original offer stipulated sixty acres, but in the negotiations, the company raised the ante finally to 100 acres and "other considerations."

In September 1891, the college trustees conditionally, and somewhat surprisingly, approved the transfer. Today, it seems hard to imagine the college in any other location, without its front quad or its historic range of buildings. Still, the trustees felt that the prospects of 1891 were too good to pass up; they concluded "that it is highly desirable and important that the proposed site should be accepted and new buildings thereon as soon as practicable." Fortunately, the trustees added a qualifier when they suggested that "before taking final action on a question of so great importance, it is deemed wise and proper to ascertain the views of the friends of the college on whose hearty cooperation the success of the proposed movement depends." Luckily for future generations of Roanoke students, that cooperation was anything but "hearty." Students at the college found the proposal mystifying and closed ranks to protest. Even more outspoken, naturally enough, were the alumni. They found little merit in the entire plan and soundly criticized the college for even considering the option.

There was no place grander than the Hotel Salem. Its glory days were short lived; later it became home to the Lutheran Orphanage and was razed to make room for the new high school in the 1930s.

Visions of the future; the proposed new college campus is located at the bottom of the map. Soon the bubble burst and the town's offer was withdrawn.

If the eroding support were not bad enough, economic conditions in Salem soon were. By 1892, the glory days were over. As suddenly as it had begun, the excitement had dissipated. Along with the rest of the nation, Salem was hurled into the depression of 1893. The thought of a new campus with new buildings and an exquisite view of the valley passed with the other dreams of Salem's short-lived boom.

Life in Salem during the balance of the decade of the 1890s must have seemed positively tame in comparison to the pace recently experienced. The Duval House, the first town establishment to sport gas lights in the 1880s, now boasted electric lights while it continued as Salem's social centerpiece; special dinners, dances, and receptions were all hosted with "grace and charm" at the town landmark. Another fixture that remained was the Town Hall,

located near the school on College Avenue. For half a century, almost all major college functions were staged there— debates, worship services, parties, and commencements. Students often remarked about the taste and smell of hot roasted peanuts sold from a little stand in the rear of the hall.

Resigned to life in downtown Salem, the students and faculty were prepared to make the most of it. New requests were offered for a gymnasium, an expanded library, a science building, and a dormitory. Of those, only the library annex would be realized. By 1893, Bittle Memorial Hall was expanded in the rear with a transept addition to provide much needed stack space for the ever-increasing library and to serve as home to the Athenaeum, the library's reading room, which for years had been located on the first floor of the Administration Building.

An early view of the front quad in the 1890s. Notice the old Grub House to the right and rear of Trout Hall. The library's new annex is visible on the extreme right. With the exception of the tree in the left foreground, every other principal tree in the photo still offers its shade over the front quad today—a century later.

The "official" library card, good for a semester.

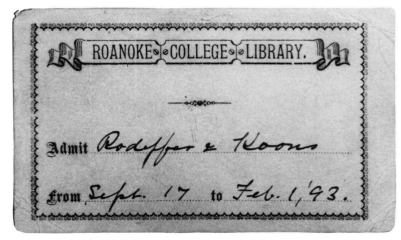

Throughout the 1890s, the campus physical plant was constantly being made over. Descriptions abound of the ongoing campaign to improve the buildings and their contents. The structures received countless coats of paint, wallpaper, varnish for the woodwork, mats and later carpets for most of the halls, a new steam-heating system, hot and cold running water, and in 1892 "the electrification of several buildings for lights." Students were often perplexed by the newfangled heating devices. One student recalled: "And the rooms in the College have got something like wasp-nests a-setting in the corner, which are made hot by the infernal heat of the earth." When the town of Salem introduced its new electric lights on Main Street, a freshman from the country wrote home, remarking, "You can see how to walk along the rock roads in town any time in the night. They've got mileposts every hundred yards with clothes lines stretched between them, and great big lanterns hanging down. You ought to be here."

Furnishings for the buildings were upgraded too. A steady stream of new "chairs and tables" made their way into the classrooms, as did new maps, other equipment, and the "latest scientific apparatus" to strengthen the instructional program. The chapel on the ground floor in Trout Hall was fitted out with a new organ in the early 1890s.

STEAM HEAT

"As it does not seem likely that the Trustees of Roanoke College will be in a condition in the very near future to accept the fine site of 100 acres offered as a gift, and to erect new buildings thereon, they have resolved to make many improvements on the present buildings so as to render them both more attractive and more comfortable. The buildings are to be repainted inside and out, and the brick work is to be restained and repenciled, thus giving them a new and fresh appearance. The students' rooms in the main building are to be wainscoted and ceiled with narrow pine strips, finished in hard oil; the other wood work is to be painted and the walls papered. Arrangements have been made for the students to buy carpet at a reduced price so that they may aid in making their rooms as neat as those in a nice private house. The chapel and recitation rooms will be greatly improved, and so will the hallways in the main building. Best of all, steam heat is to be introduced throughout the buildings—chapel, class-rooms, and dormitories; and hot and cold water will be put in the main building to supply the wants of the students. This building will be entered by self-closing doors, and sash will be put in the doors and windows on the second floor used for ventilating. Thus not only the rooms, but the hallways of the building, may be made comfortable in the coldest weather.

"Workmen are busily engaged in making these improvements, and when the boys return in September they will find the buildings so changed inside and out, as to seem like new edifices. All of which will be most gratifying to the students and friends of the College."

Salem Times-Register, 29 July 1892.

High atop Miller Hall was the formal parlor of the Ciceronians.

A view of the front walkway after a snowstorm in 1890. The rows of cedars were a campus fixture through the nineteenth century. Note the well-bundled students huddled on the steps of the Ad Building.

Henry Steere of New York City was a college benefactor who established an endowed chair in mathematics in 1890.

There was tremendous excitement on campus in 1893 when the board approved the drafting of plans for a gymnasium. The students were delighted. The administration promptly secured the services of a physical education instructor, and the architect presented his plans and construction estimates. And then all came to a screeching halt; the $12,000 price tag seemed far too expensive to the trustees, and they ordered the project suspended.

The campus also saw change through the decade. Various attempts at beautification highlighted the period. More shrubs and bushes were planted; more flower beds were introduced; and the thinning of campus trees was done in an effort to give the grounds a more kept look. A massive three-foot snowfall in December 1890 started the tree project, since it devastated nearly a third of all the trees on campus. The skating pond collapsed into disuse for a couple of years because of a continuing maintenance demand, but by the early 1890s the students resurrected the idea and reconditioned the old site. The "playground"—the new college athletic fields along Market Street—was fenced now too, and the students were delighted to hear the thwarted town cows offer "long deploring moos."

Julius Dreher's pace and duties continued unrelenting on through the 1890s. He still spent most of his time away from Salem, logging countless miles on the train in his endless search for college benefactors. His long trips into the North produced much revenue but never enough. Most of the entries in his ledgers are of a modest sort—$10, $25, and $50. But occasionally, Dreher would strike gold. In 1890, Henry J. Steere of New York City presented the college with a check for $25,000, the largest single gift the college had ever received. Whenever the president could not visit in person, his correspondence could. Dreher wrote thousands of letters, following leads and hoping for a willing ear to which he might present the college's case. He made his typical appeal to Cyrus McCormick, Jr., president of the machine works in Chicago. Dreher explained the state of the college, a brief history, and its attempts at improvement. Jokingly, Dreher suggested that the college motto could well be that Roanoke "hopeth all things" in its quest for greater prospects and for its future. He added, "After all these struggling years, Roanoke has not yet reached its first $100,000. But we are not discouraged."

The grueling pace of Dreher's job took its toll. Apparently his health was never particularly good, and on several occasions, Dreher suffered debilitating setbacks. In 1884, he was afflicted with a "severe attack of bilious remittent fever of the typhoid type. He was, apparently, very near to death's door." The *Collegian* reported that he was "wholly unconscious for a week and had the constant presence and attendance" of a team of town physicians. Again in the 1890s, he became quite ill while on business in New York City, but recovered after a lengthy recuperative period. Still, Dreher maintained a most active schedule throughout his tenure as president. By 1892, having made a cruise to Alaska, Dreher had visited every state and territory in the nation.

Throughout the balance of the nineteenth century, the relationship between the college and the Lutheran church remained at arm's length. Dreher continued

Bittle's practice of reporting to the synod each year as to the state of the college, but he made it clear that this was a matter of courtesy. Although the college charter had been amended in 1888 to require that two-thirds of the board of trustees be Lutheran, no formal connection existed. Dreher would routinely petition the synod for assistance in locating students and in the never-ending pleas for funds. The church would respond by endorsing the college's situation, pledging its support, and then occasionally sending some students but virtually no money.

As a result, Dreher was always prepared to consider proposals designed to support the college with students and funds. One such offer, in fact, came from the Episcopal Church and involved the establishment of a seminary on campus. Consequently, for a number of years the college hosted a seminary for the Episcopal diocese. The program faded by the mid-1890s as a result of changing plans for the diocese and also as a response to some resentment expressed by a Lutheran synod "Visitation Committee."

President Dreher poses with a student group in the late 1890s. (Courtesy George Kegley)

Suhr Beung Kiu, Class of 1898, was the first Korean student to graduate from an American college.

While on his travels in the spring of 1892, Dreher decided to pay a visit to the Korean legation in Washington, D.C., and in doing so, opened a fascinating chapter in the college's history. Dreher had a delightful visit with the secretary of the mission and invited him and his wife to visit the school in Salem that summer. The minister, Ye Cha Yun, and his wife arrived in July and thoroughly enjoyed their week-long stay. As a result, Korean students were soon directed to Roanoke, thus beginning a tradition that would last well into the twentieth century. In January 1894, Surh Beung Kiu became the first Korean student to enroll, and in 1898, Surh became the first Korean national to graduate from any college in the United States. Numerous others would follow, including his Imperial Highness Prince Eui Wha, the second son of the emperor of Korea.

Academically, the 1890s brought change and refinement to the college's curriculum. New descriptions were introduced for honor designations—"First Distinction" and "Second Distinction"—and written theses were required for all seniors by 1893. Graduation addresses were modified a few times. First in 1888, the graduates were allowed to deliver their individual addresses in English, no longer in Greek or Latin; and then by 1892, the students requested and the faculty finally approved having only a few members of the senior class deliver the commencement addresses. No doubt to the relief of many, only eight seniors had to give speeches that year!

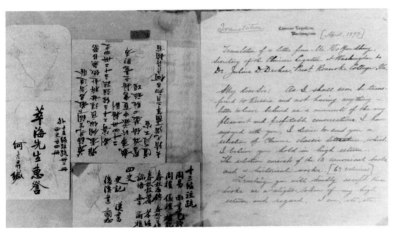

A letter of thanks Dreher received from the Chinese legation in Washington.

Prepared to make their way in the world, the graduates of 1897.

The college awarded this medal to Willie Eugene Main in 1885 for "Excellence in Greek."

The first elective courses were offered in 1893; before that time, all students took the same prescribed course of study. The college's Preparatory Division was transformed into Sub-Freshman Studies, and college tuition was kept low to be "attractive to students from all backgrounds and regions."

Instruction kept pace with the new decade; geology field trips continued up Bent Mountain and over the ridge into the Catawba Valley. The latest in laboratory apparatus allowed the biology classes to explore new frontiers, but only between December and March; the catalog reminded students that dissections could only be attempted during the winter months—the lack of refrigeration would prohibit much exploration at other times. In 1893, Professor Morehead and Dreher himself escorted twenty-six students to the Columbian Exposition in Chicago to view the marvels of the industrial age. And on the local level, there was always the "dummy line"—the trolley service into Roanoke—for a night on the town.

A view of the Demosthenean parlor on the third floor of Trout Hall.

On the road to Bennett's Springs and Mountain Day.

MOUNTAIN DAY

For the nineteenth-century Roanoke College student, hiking on Saturdays was a common diversion from the rigors of the school week. But in 1885, the faculty changed all that when they voted to hold classes on Saturday mornings. This limited hikes to nearby locations. Consequently, in 1887 the faculty granted a special holiday to allow students greater opportunity to visit places somewhat further away. Thus, on Wednesday, 2 November, "after an early breakfast several large parties were made up, having various objective points in view. 'McAfee's Knob' . . . seemed to be the favorite resort. Quite a large number of brave pedestrians made it their rendezvous and were amply repaid for their long walk by a sight of one of the grandest views in Virginia. 'Twelve O'clock Knob' had its pilgrims, too, and various other points were also visited. On the whole, our first 'mountain day' was thoroughly enjoyed, and all will look forward with pleasure to its future recurrence." Mountain Day continued as an annual event, with people calling it "a grand success," or "our most popular holiday." For the 1894 Mountain Day, one student wrote words to be sung to the tune of "Wander-staff." The song became Mountain Day's epitaph, because the faculty again revised the schedule; consequently Mountain Day was no more. Several attempts were made years later to resurrect Mountain Day but with little success.

Oh, our Mountain Day has come now,
In these bright October Days;
And with wander-staff and lunches,
We proceed our several ways.
For we climb the highest mountains
And we view the Valley o'er,
And by the scene enraptured,
We of text-books think no more.

Oh, we knew it was a-coming;
We petitioned long before;
And last night we made it lively,
Most of all on "second floor."
For we pitched our books and "ponies"
In a heap upon the bed,
And with rolling rocks and shouting—
Well, we almost woke the dead.

But today we climb the mountains,
Where we gaze the landscape o'er;
And enraptured by its beauty,
Think of class-room work no more.
And tonight we'll slumber sweetly,
From the climbing we have dared,
And will meet our "Profs" tomorrow,
With the same old "not prepared."

Harry Sturdivant was a local student who was enrolled in the "Partial Course" for several sessions.

James Burke's Garden in southwestern Virginia was begun as a German immigrant community in the late eighteenth century. The little valley formed a virtually self-sufficient society through most of the nineteenth century. Clinging to their German roots and Lutheran faith, the families of "the Garden" sent their sons to Roanoke for generations. College names like Peery, Gose, Scherer, Ritter, Grosclose, and Greever all hail originally from this little valley. (Albert S. Greever photo, ca. 1900)

The class schedule was always undergoing some revision. The week typically began by noon on Monday and ended by midday on Saturday. Sunday was to be regarded as a day of rest and relaxation and included a proscription against any studying. There is no recorded student protest ever against that particular ban! The *Collegian* reported that "a long contemplated change has been made to the satisfaction of faculty and students. Instead of prayers at the close of the day, we go to the Chapel now in the freshness of the morning, at a quarter past eight o'clock. The services over, classes go immediately to the various recitation rooms. The bell is then rung, on the half hours, until half-past twelve, which is dinner hour. There are no one o'clock recitations, and the work of the afternoon embraces from two to five o'clock."

The academic year stretched from September into June, with the first semester's exams taking place in January. The thought of a fall or spring break would have seemed positively frivolous—at least to the faculty. Even holidays were few and far between: Christmas netted the students only three days off from their labors, and Thanksgiving was unknown as any kind of national celebration. Still, the students would get excited about the approach of winter and its December holiday. The students celebrated the first snow and the opening of the skating pond. They eagerly awaited their "boxes from home" and enjoyed "the pine merchants and chestnut vendors."

The issue of coeducation returned as a major source of campus discussion by the late 1880s. Ever since the admission of women during the Civil War, the question of allowing women to attend Roanoke was never far from the surface. A favorite debate topic for the Ciceronians and the Demostheneans continued to be the question of the "merits of female education" in general or the presence of women at Roanoke in particular.

Students on the porch and balcony of Monterey. W.A.R. Goodwin, Class of 1889, and the restorer of Williamsburg, is on the porch.

The issue of admitting women was pressed and, interestingly, the student body supported the measure by a large majority. The faculty, save one, also voted to embrace the concept. Alumni support, as expected, was cool, but the board response was positively chilly. The issue languished for more than a year, but in 1889, a sort of compromise was effected. Women—or at least some women—would be admitted provisionally to the college as "Special Students." They could complete a course of study if they wished but never be awarded a diploma; after 1895, they could at least earn a certificate that signaled the successful completion of their studies. To be a "Special Student," the woman had to be a daughter of a member of the faculty or of the board, or be related in some other way. This rather unsavory compromise remained in force for more than thirty years.

Margaret Painter was the daughter of Professor F.V.N. Painter and a "Special Student" of the 1890s.

JULIUS DREHER ON "THE EDUCATION OF THE NEGRO IN THE SOUTH"

"The Education of the Negro in the South, taken in the broadest sense, is the most difficult problem before the American people to-day. . . . We are confronted with a great humanitarian problem, which is also economic and political, and which, while being national, is also in a peculiar sense, a Southern problem. . . . In the solution of our problem the fortunes of both races in the South are involved. . . . As the Republic could not exist half free and half slave, so no commonwealth can long prosper with one-half of its citizens educated and the other half illiterate. We must convince our people that no investment pays better dividends than that in brains. . . . In the South every effort should be made to lengthen the school term for the children of both races, and we ought to hear nothing more of that unwise and unpatriotic suggestion to divide the school funds between the races in the proportion of taxes paid by each. . . .

"The more education and property the colored people acquire the better for the State, for they will thus become more valuable citizens. If the Negroes of Virginia had as much property *per caput*, and as high an average in intelligence and education as the white people, does any one doubt that the State would be immensely benefited?

"Whatever may be the fate of the Negro in the future, we should not shrink from the responsibility of doing our duty manfully in the present; and, if we do the right as God gives us to see the right, we may with unfaltering faith leave the consequences to that gracious Providence which has blessed our nation through all the eventful years of its history."

Excerpts from Julius Dreher's address before the Southern Educational Association, Richmond VA, 29 December 1900, as recorded in its *Journal*.

The faculty mourned the passing of one of its twin pillars of the nineteenth century, William B. Yonce, in 1895. After a full day's work, Yonce was stricken in chapel that evening and never recovered; the students and his friends raised money for a commemorative marble tablet that was dedicated in his honor and placed on the wall in the chapel.

A final photograph of William Yonce, taken shortly before his death in 1895.

Along with preserving the academic code, the faculty still spent as much time upholding its moral one. The minutes of the faculty meetings were burdened with countless student charges and offenses—many serious but most harmless. "Top-spinning" and "leap-frogging" were the current rages, and the faculty cautioned students to be circumspect in their pursuits. The serious new threat confronting the faculty, thanks to local Roanoke manufacturing entrepreneur James Bonsack, was the advent of the cigarette. Bonsack, the inventor of the cigarette-rolling machine, had teamed up with Buck Duke of the American Tobacco Company to mass produce the new product. Like the rest of America, the students of Roanoke were hooked. The *Collegian* ran articles about the dangers of smoking, warning that if one was going to smoke, at least not to inhale. Another article related the story about the Yale student who, on a dare, chainsmoked forty cigarettes and died. The faculty set fifteen as an appropriate standard for the week.

Sports were bigger than ever by the 1890s. Baseball may have been king, as several Roanoke teams amassed impressive records, and two students—J. B. Brillheart and O. E. Burch—went on to play professionally in the major leagues. Football enjoyed ever-increasing crowds with its permanent position in the fall. As always, there were critics. One student wag reported for the *Collegian* about a recent showdown: "We came, we played, we lost!"

The earliest college sports photograph: the Football Club of 1894.

ROANOKE 2, VANDERBILT 1

Alexander Sanders, class of 1885, was the most heralded Roanoke College baseball player of the era. After graduation, Sanders pitched for the Philadelphia Athletics for a number of seasons before pursuing an engineering degree at Vanderbilt University. While there, he managed to pitch for his new school as well and talk soon grew of a rematch between Roanoke and Sanders' Vanderbilt club. In May 1892, the game took place in Salem; the Roanoke nine bested the visitors from Nashville in a great game, 2 to 1.

Seven years later, however, the truth was told. In a *Collegian* article entitled "Professionalism in College Athletics," the players fessed up. Here is their account:

"Knowing that the Vanderbilt team was one of the strongest in the South, we secured six men from the Roanoke League and to these we added the three best players we had, making a heterogeneous team which we called, for the sake of the occasion, the Roanoke College team. In the game that followed we won by the score of 2 to 1. The game was published in the newspapers as being a victory for Roanoke College; and during that summer and the following year, we told people about our victory over Vanderbilt, although when we did so our conscience was troubled with the remembrance of the six men from the Roanoke League. We acted unfairly towards Vanderbilt, and ever since then it has been our firm belief that it would have been far more honorable and far more manly to play our own men and be beaten than to win as we did by putting in professional men."

Excerpt from the *Roanoke Collegian,* May 1899.

The newest sports on campus were croquet and lawn tennis. The students got permission in 1892 to lay out the first tennis court on campus behind the Administration Building. Another competition debuted in November 1893. The *Collegian* reported: "This is a new and popular game, and ours is among the very first of the southern colleges to adopt it. It is played with a football, but this is manipulated with the hands only, and the point of the game is to get the ball into the baskets or goals at the two opposite extremities of the field. Any number can engage in the game, and as it is almost as active, though not so dangerous as football, it is likely to become one of the most popular of the college games." New organizations appeared (and disappeared) by the dozens. A glee club was first organized in 1884, a dramatics company in 1881, and a college orchestra—with students and faculty—by 1893.

Campus life included myriad activities. No annual event was more important to the students than "campus day," the day set aside originally to "clean" the campus by trimming trees and shrubs, raking leaves, and improving the walks. By the 1890s, that function remained, but after just a couple of hours of work, the fun commenced. The students delighted in the day's activities: "croquet parties, a moot court, a baseball match, and a botanical excursion." The college also adopted a "Mountain Day" for a number of years: the faculty would cancel classes for the day and head the students on an outing up to McAfee's Knob.

Campus attire kept pace with societal and academic dictates. Students commonly referred to their "stocks" (clothes) and especially to their "dike" (best suit). Knickerbockers had come of age by the beginning of the decade, which no doubt helped in the art of "drafting" (searching for a date). Class caps or beanies were in full use, and academic gowns for graduation and other formal functions also made their appearance.

An unidentified student of the nineties.

The brothers of Phi Gamma Delta enjoyed increased numbers in the 1890s. The decade before had witnessed faculty opposition and pressure from "the anti-frats", a group of fellows mostly made up of the ministerial students.

Boarding houses still catered to the vast majority of students. Room and board could be obtained at reasonable prices, and overall, the system served the students rather well. Nevertheless, such student comments as the following were not uncommon: "Sirloin is derived from the French; yet it would be hard to tell where some of our Boarding-House steak is derived from." Boarding houses also afforded other amenities. The *Collegian* noted that one "student has a telescope on top of his Boarding House to look at heavenly bodies but there is one in town that he especially likes to study." Fraternities continued as social centers for the students; each organization had its hall in town to hold its meetings and host its different functions. Turnover was fairly rapid, and membership rarely exceeded more than a dozen.

Probably the largest and most active organization on campus was the YMCA. These students organized numerous events, sponsored the chapel program, conducted bible study, formed prayer circles, and created a popular Missionary Band. Clearly, the faculty embraced the good works of these students and often assisted in their activities off campus as well.

Alpha Tau Omega fraternity was on campus from 1869 until its demise in 1893. The group's historian recorded that "it was itself a small fraternity; still essentially a southern fraternity; and it was happy."

The Alpha Tau Omega badge.

CHAPTER 8

"To build
up noble character,"
1896–1903

A turn of the century photograph of the Administration Building after a snow. Renovation plans would soon commence. (Courtesy Salem Times-Register)

The proposed grand new façade of 1900. Trout and Miller halls were to be connected, a third floor, new porches, and a towering dome were to be added to the Ad Building. After construction of the third story and the front portico, the money ran out.

As the new century approached, the Roanoke College campus was gaining refinement and sophistication in its appearance. With its gardens and groves, the front quad was increasingly well kept. A new path was constructed diagonally between the front gate on College Avenue and the High Street entrance. A tradition developed in the 1890s in which the senior class donated a tree for the front lawn as its gift to the school. The class of 1898 deviated from the custom slightly when it elected instead to plant ivy around the college buildings. For the next half century, Bittle, East and West Halls, and the main building were covered with the verdant growth.

The Administration Building received the most attention during the period. In 1895, the edifice first underwent significant structural renovation, both inside and out. The *Collegian* observed that "it will be divided by partitions into three sections. On the second floor there will be eight rooms in the middle and six in each end section, the latter rooms being reached by stairways at the ends of the building. The hallway on the lower floor of the west wing of the building will also be divided by a partition." The faculty had hoped to cut down the excessive traffic through the main staircase to the classrooms and to the Buzzard's Roost. With the project completed by the fall, faculty sighed that all was "peaceful and in order."

The summer's construction proved only preliminary to the truly massive facelifting envisioned by the board of trustees five years later. "A plan was adopted for the enlargement of the main building by erecting a third story for the scientific department, for connecting the east and west halls with the main building, and for remodeling these three old buildings. The interiors of the buildings are also to be remodeled and greatly improved." The building would be crowned by a massive dome measuring ninety-six feet from the base to tip, and the entire complex would span 243 feet in length. Despite the elaborate plans and a promising start to subscriptions, the campaign soon began to founder. By 1902, the fund-raising effort was obviously going to have a considerable shortfall; but so as not to scrap or jeopardize the entire project, the trustees authorized the start of construction with the hope that additional dollars could still be raised. Alas, the money was not forthcoming, and the present Administration Building is the result. The flanking pieces designed to connect the East and West halls were never attempted and, likewise, the dome astride the newly finished third story passed with the architect's vision.

New playing fields were introduced by the turn of the century; the faculty authorized the grading of new baseball and football fields located northeast of the library along High Street. Even temporary goalposts were erected near Bittle Memorial in 1896. The following year saw the "laying off" of the first campus tennis courts behind the Ad Building.

The town of Salem ushered in the new century with its typical "sober spirit." The community promoted its dedication to prohibition and temperance by boasting that there were "no bar-rooms in Salem." Even the college could echo those same sentiments in its selective advertisements about the school—those ads designed to appeal more to Mom and Dad than to the prospective student!

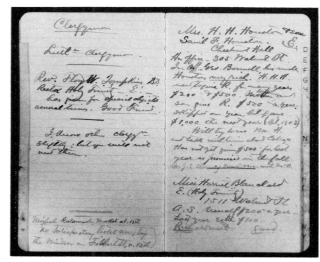

Pages from President Dreher's financial notebooks. Dreher kept trip journals for all twenty-five years he served as president; notice the last entry on the right page: "Rich old maid. Good."

Roanoke advertisement of the late 1890s. Notice the "No-Bar-Rooms" claim in the top flier. In 1897, the Collegian *recorded the following:*

An effort was made recently by one or two parties in Salem to secure a license to sell intoxicants in the town in connection with the drug business. We are glad to say that owing to the vigorous protest raised by many prominent citizens the license was refused. The prohibition sentiment is so strong in this section that there is not a barroom doing business legally in Roanoke county except in the city of Roanoke.

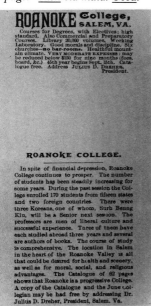

"MOTHER" BIGGS

"To say that 'Mother' Biggs is a factor in the social life at Roanoke College would be sad understatement; 'Mother' Biggs is the backbone of the social life at Roanoke; she is the pillar, the kind and guiding hand who has watched Roanoke College students at play for thirty-nine years, and always with a tolerance and understanding that only love can bring.

"It was in September, 1898, that Mrs. Biggs first chaperoned a Roanoke College dance. 'So many of my boys come to see me [still]. They bring me candy and flowers, and always want me to meet their wives and their children, and I love them every one.'

"Roanoke College on several occasions has publicly honored 'Mother' Biggs; to her 'sons,' however, she will be always 'The Sweetheart of Roanoke College.' . . . Like a mighty army, the 'Sons of Mother Biggs' are spread to the far corners of the earth. . . . [M]any were at one time 'Mother's special pets' for they roomed at her house on College Avenue while at Roanoke; but 'Mother's' beaux far outnumber her pets.

"At any dance, more active than the youngest debutante, 'Mother' Biggs is always found until the last strains of 'Home Sweet Home' have died away; she loves parties; her sprightly verve has not dimmed the least with the years.

"Eighteen ninety-eight is now far away and dim in memory. . . . And 'Mother' Biggs has watched all [the change over the years]; she has observed Roanoke College boys burst forth in bowlers and peg top trousers, discard these for baggy pantaloons and coonskin coats and finally lapse into 'beer jackets.'

" 'Mother' Biggs would laugh if one told her that she was a more precious part of Roanoke College tradition than the buildings or the legends that have come down; but, alive and keen and interested in her 'sons' she is far more precious than any songs or stories."

Excerpts from an article by John Thornton in the *Roanoke Collegian,* December 1937.

A view of the steps of the "kindergarten"—a favorite name of the students for the college. The amount of graffiti might be because of a scheduled "cleaning day" when the students would paint and otherwise improve the campus buildings and grounds; the faculty might have allowed the students a brief chance to express their creative talents.

Mother Biggs ran a rooming house for students from the 1890s until the Second World War. Her address on the boulevard was a true home away from home for generations of Roanoke boys.

Salem witnessed its first macadamized street in 1896 and a refurbished Town Hall soon thereafter. Still, the hall lacked real appeal for the students. A college critic described the "Town Barn" as "a conglomeration of brick and pine, a heterogeneous mass without order or proportion. Its architecture is the conception of a disordered brain and its workmanship, the expression of ignorance." Even the flying of a Cuban flag over the building in the spring of 1898 to express solidarity with the Cubans' plight against Spain failed to impress the students.

Back on campus, bicycles and pocket cameras were the rage. New shops opened on Main Street, eager to introduce these marvels to both student and citizen alike. The students were delighted when Limestone Alley, the little access road today that runs behind Bartlett and Lucas halls, was transformed into Virginia Avenue—nicely widened and blacktopped to provide a popular bicycle-exercise area.

Students continued their complaints about the campus food in the "Dining Hall," a first-floor room in the old "Grub" House. This two-story frame structure still stood in the back quad. It served as home to the college steward and also functioned as a boarding club for several students. The steward's duties included preparing the meals and also supervising the general upkeep of the college's buildings and grounds. The maintenance operation was, of course, quite nominal. The college owned no wagon or team, and for any major project, the tools and equipment were always borrowed from friends in town. The steward did manage to distribute the seven tons of coal annually to the respective building boilers, but the students commonly complained that the "radiators felt more like refrigerators."

Two principal college publications came into being during this period. In 1898, the first college yearbook, the *Röntgen Rays,* appeared and by 1900, the first *Student's Hand-Book*—known later to generations of Roanoke students as the *Cherobiblos*—came off the press. The yearbook staff clearly enjoyed its undertaking and took great pride in the finished product. Their tongue-in-cheek preface reflected their playful spirit; "the object of this work, as the name indicates, is to give in some measure an insight into our inner college life, to disclose, as it were, a few of our family secrets, or, in other words, to 'tell tales out of school.' " The staff suggested that the yearbook was intended first for the students, and second, for the faculty. The book would "show them what the college looks like on paper" and "tell them, when it is everlastingly and eternally too late for retribution, who greased the board, canned the cow, and rode the pony."

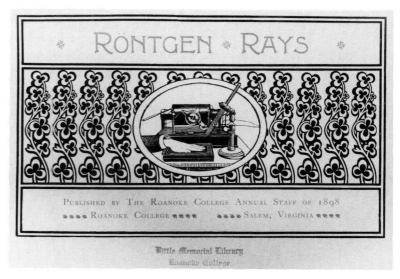

The title page of the first Roanoke yearbook, the Röntgen Rays *in 1898.* Röntgen *was the German scientist who had discovered X rays a few years before.*

A Hot Time in the Old Town Tonight

"But did you ever hear the story of the Roanoke College journalist who crossed the trigger-tempers of the Jeff Davis Rifles? . . . It was early in May, 1898. . . . On this particular Saturday, Salem was a bedlam . . . for the town was bursting at the seams with lusty young recruits of the Jeff Davis Rifles, who were to be off on May 10 to 'fit' the Spaniards in Cuba. . . . The Roanoke College journalist filed his story [on the recruits claiming that] 'they laid hold of all loose property and in every way maintained the reputation of the town company.'

"Quicker than you could say '23 Skidoo,' a squad of the Riflemen set out for the boarding house of [the reporter] with blood in their eyes . . . [but] when they reached the rooming house, nearly fifty College students were there to greet them. . . . [A] Jeff Davis haymaker and a Roanoke College left hook soon put to rout any thoughts of a peaceful evacuation.

"The brawl was on! Up Main street they went, College boys slugging it out with the volunteers.

"One student being hard-pressed by a group of burly soldiers ducked into a Salem tin shop, owned by one E. L. Maury. In desperation he grabbed a hot soldering iron out of the fire. Instantly, he struck, and his pursuers . . . went howling out into the open air, branded like young steers.

"Reports indicate that after some time the battle subsided. At any rate, one account says, 'The fighting was quelled without very serious consequences.' "

Excerpts from an account by John Thornton, Class of 1940, printed in the *Roanoke Collegian,* March 1940.

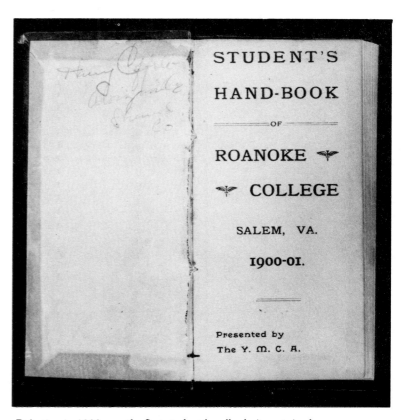

Debuting in 1900 was the first student handbook; it contained much useful information as well as helpful tips for freshmen.

The brothers of Sigma Phi Epsilon, circa 1901.

The handbook was printed by the YMCA to serve as a general guide and orientation device for new students. It contained pages of "helpful tips" too—of books "a student should read," a section on recommended field trips, and the always popular "Pointers for New Students." The page-long list addressed the topic of classroom decorum. Sample tips include "Be courteous to the Professors, and never fail to lift your hat to them"; "Don't be fresh. You are liable to be salted"; "Don't know it all. Leave a little for others"; "Treat every student with respect and he will respect you"; and finally "Don't ask too many questions. Professors sometimes get tired." By the following year, the students also formed a Reception Committee to assist further the incoming student.

America's "splendid little war," as Secretary of State John Hay called the Spanish-American War of 1898, apparently had little impact on the Salem campus. Apart from the debating societies' considering the merits of war over Cuba and a fictitious ad for "war pants" appearing in the yearbook, there is little other mention of America's venture into the Caribbean. No record survives of any student rushing off to join Teddy Roosevelt.

Frank Ford Cornelius was an Oneida indian from Wisconsin. He stayed at Roanoke for only one year (1898–99) and no doubt turned a few heads with his 6'3", 210 pound frame.

In the center is the Honorable Chin Pom Ye, the Korean Minister to the United States; flanking him on the left is Chong Ke Yi and Kiusic Kimm, on the right, as a freshman in this 1898 photo.

The war's impact, however, was felt in other ways. Always the humanitarian and believer in international understanding, President Dreher embraced the concept of the Cuban Educational Society by the fall of 1898. Within a short time, the college was home to two Cuban students who had come to this country to learn English and to pursue a college degree. Additionally, a half dozen Puerto Rican students soon made their way to Roanoke as well.

In the aftermath of the Spanish-American War, six Puerto Rican students made their way to Roanoke for the 1899–1900 session.

On the sports front, the college Athletic Association, founded in 1893, continued as the unofficial clearinghouse for all campus sporting events and teams. This group was a collection of dedicated volunteers—students, faculty, and friends—who organized and promoted different games and competitions. As the college sanctioned no teams directly, the association spent most of its time raising money to enable the students the opportunity to compete, both on campus and on trips to other colleges. As a result, the athletic record throughout the period was rather checkered. Some years, funding lagged, making it necessary to discontinue several sports. In the fall of 1901, the *Collegian* reported that the football team was having difficulty getting organized and that since funds for new uniforms were not forthcoming, the season had been canceled. Sometimes the association had better luck. Baseball, for example, enjoyed a more consistent record, and by 1897, the first track team was sponsored by the association.

This tough-looking bunch played football for Roanoke in 1897. The nickname "Maroons" was still ten years in the future.

These Roanokers sought fame and success on the diamond. Albert Hechel, seated in the middle, was elected captain for his senior season of 1903.

"TO BUILD UP NOBLE CHARACTER," 1896–1903   **103**

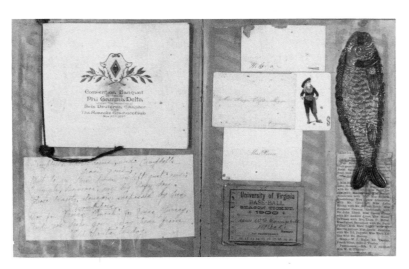

A page from a student scrapbook from the turn of the century.

The first formal photographic sitting of the Roanoke faculty. Taken in 1901, standing from left to right are William Smith, Charles Cannaday, Leonidas McReynolds, John Ambler, and John Peery. Seated are Wythe Morehead, Luther Fox, President Julius Dreher, F.V.N Painter, and Henry Hildreth.

A campus tradition began in 1895 known as "Field Day." Although at first associated with the events of commencement week, the annual college field day was shortly thereafter moved to early May and became the major date on the spring calendar. It was a day of fun and games, with the emphasis on the games. Students could take part in a host of athletic competitions, including "a hurdle race, running high jump, 100 yard dash, throwing the hammer, putting the shot, and pole-vaulting. A gold medal will be given to the man who does the best overall." And along with the major tests, the day included "scrub

TERM REPORT.

ROANOKE COLLEGE, SALEM, VIRGINIA.

A grade report from 1901.

features" between the events: "a potato race, shoe race, egg race, sack race, and a three-legged race" were offered to the delight of the spectators, often estimated at a thousand people. It should be noted too that the faculty once disciplined several enterprising students for attempting to sell lemonade to the multitude.

With the association's sponsorship, the college joined the state Inter-Collegiate Athletic Association in 1900. In the years before the Maroons were born, Roanoke competed in its customary "dark blue and steel gray" uniforms.

In Dreher's final years as president, the academic program of the college continued to be enhanced. Several faculty positions were added, giving both the professors and the students greater choice and flexibility in their schedules. New courses and electives were introduced, with Spanish and business offerings heading the list.

In faculty action, the professors raised standards both for admission to the college and for advancement between the classes. Another faculty committee studied the issue of coeducation in the late 1890s and concluded that beyond the environs of Salem, there was not much demand for "female education." Although sympathetic, they elected not to pursue the question at that time. In 1896, the faculty did support the establishment of a graduate program and the awarding of masters degrees. Upon application and completion of a written thesis, the candidate was eligible for the degree. The program proved successful and was continued for a number of years.

A final photograph of Simon Carson Wells. His sudden death in 1900 brought to an end over a half century's work and commitment to the college.

"SPECIAL" STUDENTS

When morning comes with rosy light,
With faces innocent and bright (?),
Why can't we to the chapel go,
And shout and stamp and clap also?
    We're "special."

When on the last night of the week,
The boys assemble, read, and speak,
Why are we banished from the hall,
And not allowed to speak at all?
    We're "special."

When Annual Celebrations come,
Why must we sit amid the hum
Of the old Town Hall, so bleak and bare,
And mutely at the speakers stare?
    We're "special."

And when Commencement comes at last
With all our studies duly passed.
Why can't we with our classmates be,
And get our richly earned degree?
    We're "special."

And when we meet in after life,
You'll wonder why, 'mid toil and strife,
Success has always crowned our brow,
This question may be answered now.
    We're "special."

Excerpt from a poem printed in the *Röntgen Rays,* 1898, following the photograph of six of the "special students." These "special" students are, of course, women.

---

code. The students pledged their support to a system predicated "on their honor as gentlemen"; no longer, theoretically, would the faculty need to scrutinize assignments or monitor examinations for dishonest behavior

On a less lofty plane, faculty busied themselves with the day-to-day matters of operating a college. They formed a committee in 1901 to consider the advantages and disadvantages of purchasing a lawn mower and, the following year, contracted the services of "a secret police" to investigate some on-going problems of vandalism.

The students managed somehow to get "Old man Hupp's" wagon onto the roof of the Ad Building for this early candid photo of 1898.

Faculty also considered the adoption of a summer school session in 1901, but elected to postpone its adoption for the time being. Not until 1917 did the college begin regular summer sessions. The faculty, doubtless, were delighted in 1903 when the students presented a petition and proposal for the first honor

Another student protest! Some college official hanged in effigy.

Discipline remained a major focus of faculty attention. Along with the regular list of charges and complaints, the faculty seemed preoccupied with the dangers of cigarette smoking, which was "no different," they reasoned, "than opium addiction." The *Collegian* cited numerous reports and articles that addressed the threat: "Cigarette smoking blunts the whole moral nature. It has an appalling effect upon the system. It first stimulates and then stupifies the nerves. It sends boys into consumption. It gives them enlargement of the heart, and it sends them to the insane asylum. I am a physician . . . and have seen bright boys turned into dunces and straightforward, honest boys made into miserable cowards by cigarette smoking."

CIGARETTES AND ALUMNI

Few people today realize the central role Roanoke College played in the cigarette revolution of the late nineteenth century. The inventors of the early cigarette-rolling machines, various cigarette company presidents, and the industry's early leaders were all Roanoke men. Here are some excerpts from a *Collegian* article written in 1939 detailing some highlights.

"In 1878, a student of Roanoke College sat dreaming in class one day. He was James Bonsack, a son of the owner of Bonsack Woolen Mills, about twenty miles east of Salem, where he had watched wool carded for blankets for Confederate soldiers. Out of the nebulous chaos that whirled in his mind revolved a shadowy shape that slowly took form and substance. So the cigarette making machine was born which was the forerunner of the present continuous rod machine. The first model was made of wood and unfortunately was burned in a railway station fire in Lynchburg, Va., while enroute to the Patent Office. A second was made and patented, and a company was organized by D. B. Strouse, '60, a lawyer of Salem, which operated for many years in Lynchburg.

"In 1889 the Comas Machine Company (later the Comas Cigarette Machine Company) was organized to exploit the Comas Standard Cigarette Making Machine. This entirely different machine was for the manufacture of the Spanish form cigarette with tucked ends. The first president of the company was D. B. Strouse, and among his associates was F. H. Chalmers, class of '73.

"As the years went by the interests of the Bonsack Company and the Comas Company diverged. D. B. Strouse continued as president of the Bonsack Company and J. W. F. Allemong became president of the Comas Company. In 1907 Dr. F. V. N. Painter, '74, teacher of romance languages at Roanoke College, writer of text books on English literature and associate of J. W. F. Allemong became president of the company, whose business by now had spread to many Spanish and Portuguese speaking countries. . . . In 1921 Dr. Painter retired and was succeeded by the vice-president, S. C. Markley, '09, who had joined the company two years before as an engineer and assistant to the president.

"Roanoke College can proudly say '[The industry] is the product of ideals and qualities which [it] instilled in its founder and its leaders.'"

Other issues were not quite so dramatic. During the winter of 1899, the *Collegian* playfully reported the "latest meteorological marvel: on the morning of February 1st, it was so cold that the college bell was frozen, and did not thaw out again until chapel time—the faculty has appointed a committee to investigate this strange phenomenon in the interests of science." "Science" was never apprehended!

By the turn of the century, Julius Daniel Dreher was approaching the end of his toils. He had talked of retirement before, and though he was still only in his early fifties by 1900, Dreher sensed that the time to move on was nearing. Dreher might not have been too old, but he might have admitted being too tired. As early as 1889, Dreher had threatened to resign over the flap created by the commission payment scheme of the board of trustees. And in 1901, forces almost came to blows in the dispute involving Professor Ambler's promotion to succeed Carson Wells. Some members of the board balked at Ambler's nomination and at the fact that the science professor was not a Lutheran. Dreher suggested that church membership should not be a prerequisite to college appointments and offered his resignation as reinforcement.

Dreher won the showdown, but it was clear that hard feelings resulted. The president took a two-month tour of Europe during the summer to help clear the air, and it did some good. Upon his return, Dreher used the approaching Semi-Centennial of 1903 as a means of refocusing his energies and excitement, and it proved successful. Soon he coupled in his own mind the fact that the college's fiftieth anniversary would also be his twenty-fifth as president and decided it would be a logical time to step aside as its leader. He announced his intentions privately in 1902, but had the responsibility of overseeing both the celebration and his retirement. The summer of 1903 was remembered as a bittersweet affair.

Julius Dreher at the Semi-Centennial in 1903 and the occasion of his resignation.

The President's House on High Street. The house was constructed by Professor Yonce and later purchased by Dreher. The college eventually bought the property from the president and made it the official residence. The house was razed in the 1910s and the present Roselawn was built in its place.

The town and gown joined hands for this significant celebration; this is the title page from the program.

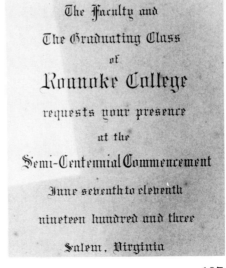

The Faculty and
The Graduating Class
of
Roanoke College
requests your presence
at the
Semi-Centennial Commencement
June seventh to eleventh
nineteen hundred and three
Salem, Virginia

CHAPTER 9

"A wholesome moral atmosphere," 1903–1910

The old Roanoke County Courthouse. Students often hopped the trolley for a ride into downtown Roanoke. (Courtesy Salem Times-Register)

"The Tabernacle" served as home to countless college events between 1901 and 1919. (Courtesy Salem Times-Register)

For the week of 7 June 1903, the college and the town of Salem joined hands for a joint celebration that would be long remembered. With news of President Dreher's resignation still secret, only the brightness and excitement of the times could be felt. The Norfolk and Western Railway ran special trains and offered discounted rates to those headed to Salem for the "grand celebration." The college published a commemorative volume to provide "an acceptable souvenir" of the festivities. It noted that

> the exercises throughout were of a high order; the audiences were large and appreciative, and the weather delightfully cool. The excellent music of the voluntary choir, the singing of the Semi-Centennial hymn and song, and the fine performances of the Salem Band were greatly enjoyed by all. The illumination of the campus for the promenade concerts was on a more brilliant scale than usual. Much interest was added to the celebration by the unusually large number of graduates, ex-students and visitors in attendance. Enthusiasm seemed to be in the air. It was an inspiring sight to see the long processions marching to stirring strains of music to

the auditorium, many old students and others carrying flags in college colors of blue and yellow, as well as many national flags, all bearing the figures 1853–1903."

The newly opened Tabernacle auditorium on the Boulevard in Salem served as home to the events. Dignitaries included the governor of Virginia, the Honorable A. J. Montague, and a host of other well-wishers from numerous colleges across the state and region. The five-day celebration included an almost endless number of speeches, receptions, and commencement itself with the "awarding of Prizes and Distinctions." All in all, the festival was an unparalleled success save for the announcement, on the second day, of Julius Dreher's departure. That news tended to dampen spirits slightly as the time of recollection and celebration turned into a moment of reflection and farewell. As the board of trustees announced the passing of the presidential torch, they also made public their offer of the presidency to Dreher's would-be successor.

Inside the Town Hall for a Demosthenean Literary Society meeting in 1909. A student numbered the dignitaries on stage: number one (extreme left) is President Morehead; number eight is Luther Fox.

"J. D. DREHER
    PAPEETE, TAHITI"

With his new bride and new post, former president Julius Dreher steamed out of San Francisco bay, leaving behind a city still smoldering from the previous year's devastating earthquake. Dreher must have embarked upon his second career as a United States diplomat with a measure of disbelief. Here he was, a smalltown boy from South Carolina, a veteran of the Civil War, for twenty-five years a president of a struggling college in Salem, Virginia, now aboard a freighter bound for that almost mythical place—Tahiti.

The journey took the Drehers almost two weeks, but in a real sense the trip back in time was even more dramatic. The Tahiti they discovered in 1907 had changed little in hundreds of years. Although Europeans had been present for more than a century, change and development had come slowly to the islands. And Dreher elected to record and calendar all that he saw and heard for the next three years—before the onslaught of civilization would alter or destroy it for all time.

With the fervor of a true academician, Dreher wrote report after report of all that he could observe about traditional island life. His voluminous studies ranged from family structure to dietary habits, from agricultural techniques to tropical diseases. To supplement his studies, Dreher and his staff took hundreds of photographs.

Dreher's days in Tahiti came to a close in 1910. Although his time there had been fascinating, the former president had definite professional aspirations as far as the U.S. Foreign Service was concerned. Being posted as consul in the distant South Pacific to a French colony could hardly be considered the fast track.

The Drehers moved on to assignments in Jamaica, Canada, and finally to Panama, where they witnessed the opening of the Grand Ismithian Canal in 1914. The former president finally retired from the service in 1924 at the age of seventy-seven.

Thirty-six-year-old John Alfred Morehead was no stranger to Roanoke College. Indeed, since his birth in Pulaski County, Virginia, in 1867, Morehead was never far from the school—either geographically or psychologically. His mother, Katherine Barbara Morehead, was Professor William Yonce's sister, and his older brother Wythe served on the English faculty at Roanoke for fifty years commencing in 1885. It was the very next year that John Morehead enrolled at Roanoke as a sophomore and was graduated in the class of 1889. Upon graduation, Morehead was extended an offer to stay on as an instructor of

The youthful new president: John Alfred Morehead served as college leader from 1903–1920.

Former president Dreher (without hat) aboard ship in the South Pacific on his way to Tahiti as United States Consul.

Dreher took hundreds of photos while he was on station in Tahiti. Here is one he took of the main street of the capital, Papeete.

mathematics and natural sciences, and he willingly accepted. Soon, though, Morehead felt his calling, and after just one year at Roanoke, he set off for the Lutheran Seminary in Philadelphia. By 1892, he was ordained and received a call from a congregation in western Virginia. Two years later, he headed off to Richmond to take over another church, and by 1898, Morehead's rise to prominence within the church was enhanced by his election as president and professor of systematic theology at the Lutheran Theological Southern Seminary in Charleston, South Carolina. Roanoke honored him in 1902 with an honorary degree of doctor of divinity.

In July 1903, Morehead formally accepted the board's offer of the presidency. For the sum of "$1,500 cash, or its equivalent, per annum, guaranteed," John Morehead, his wife, and their small daughter packed up and returned home to Roanoke. Morehead's election represented, in some ways, a changing attitude among the board of trustees. By the 1890s, several board members complained about the "liberal atmosphere of the college and Dreher's apparent indifference to Lutheran church connections. Several "visitation committee" inspections from the two synods in Virginia reported that the extent of religious instruction and the moral climate on campus left much to be desired. The board mandated that a Bible course be incorporated into the curriculum and also directed the faculty to be more diligent in monitoring chapel attendance, with an additional reminder that faculty should avail themselves of the opportunity to worship as well. The faculty might have grumbled about board interference but, on the whole, went along with the changes.

The issue came to a head over the affair involving Professor John Ambler and his promotion to Steere Professor of Mathematics in 1901 after the death of Professor Carson Wells. The board opposed the appointment because Ambler was not a Lutheran; Dreher was irate. In his reply to the trustees, Dreher stressed the principles of academic freedom, the professional nature of modern colleges, and to underscore these points, he offered his resignation as evidence. As mentioned earlier, the board backed down, but the battle had cost Dreher valuable capital. Two years later, when Dreher offered his resignation again, there were several board members who were doubtless perfectly content to accept it.

A principal actor on the board was Demetrius Bittle Strouse, a prominent Salem business and civic leader, member of the College Lutheran Church, and organizer of the Salem Holiness Association. It was Strouse, in fact, who in 1901 constructed the Tabernacle to house various gatherings and revivals that were anticipated. When the opportunity arose to find a suitable replacement for Julius Dreher, D. B. Strouse was prepared. The qualifications of such a man were obvious: academic credentials were necessary, of course, but Strouse also hoped for a minister with strong church connections and an undying dedication to the ideals of Christian education. Who better than a president of a seminary to lead the crusade? John Alfred Morehead possessed all of those qualities.

Morehead's inauguration occurred along with the 1904 commencement. In his address, he outlined the course of the college for years to come. He pledged a new and improved curriculum; more faculty receiving better salaries; an expanded physical plant; prompt repayment of the debt incurred by the recent renovations to the Administration Building; a particular emphasis upon a new endowment campaign, and finally, and no doubt to Strouse's satisfaction, a rededication to the principles of Christian education. In his "The Mission of the Christian College," Morehead identified the principal themes of the new order:

> In contrast with the present day secularizing tendencies in education, the Christian college is pervaded with the Christian spirit. While such an institution is devoted to the cause of truth in the broadest sense, its atmosphere is harmonious with the Bible and favorable to Christian faith. . . . An institution which comprehends within its system of educational means, forces for the development of character . . . , is justly entitled to the name of Christian college. Accomplishing the work of Christian education, such a college is fulfiling a distinctive mission among the educational forces of the country.

A commencement program from 1904

Reflecting the newfound spirit of the school, the *Collegian* began to echo a similar sentiment. Through the years 1903–1907, the publication became more a proselytizer of approved college values and practices than a responsible monitor of student and college behavior. Gone were the silly tales of campus revelry, of pranks and stunts, of off-color humor, and of the sordid encounters of the night! The newly approved and antiseptic editions focused upon life at Roanoke almost as some would have imagined it, rather than the way it was.

SONGS AND FANTASIES

In the days prior to the literary magazine, Roanoke students frequently had their works included in the *Roanoke Collegian.* Another method was to have one's work privately printed. Such was the case with John Heiskell Booton and Edwin Latham Quarles when they published *Songs and Fantasies* in 1900. The little book contained twenty poems and was dedicated "to those friends who have not frowned when we dallied to pluck a flower."

I Dreamed of Thee

Last night I dreamed of thee—oh, joy replete!
Did earthly eyes e'er such a vision meet?
No seraph's song on moonlight summer seas;
No wingéd sylphs; no fairy-haunted leas;
No serenade was heard from angel choirs;
No magic chord was struck from golden lyres.
The night, with beauteous canopy above,
And thou were all I saw and felt but love.

As through the casement in the silent night
There floated streams of purest silver light,
Thy sleeping form reclined in my embrace;
Thy golden tresses played about my face;
And balmy breezes fraught with fragrance rare
Caressed thy cheek and marbled shoulder fair.
In ecstacy my heart was throbbing fast.
I thought not of the future, knew no past.

And then, ah then, thy sweet awakening came,
And pressing thy soft hand, I breathed thy name.
The moonbeams with their gentle beauty fell
Upon thy cheek soft tinted as some shell
Oft washed by foaming seas. In silent bliss
I pressed upon thy placid brow a kiss.
The countless eyes of Nature looked in thine
Which rose and cast their love-light into mine.
Ah yes, I dreamed thou wast mine own, mine own—
Can all my joy be in the dream that's flown?

E.L.Q.

The Dramatics Club in a 1906 photograph; the women could be special students or those recruited in town. The club offered two or three presentations each year. Standing third from the left is future biology professor, George Peery.

The main focus of attention for student reporters was naturally the YMCA. Although arguably the largest student group on campus, the coverage the Y received made one wonder whether it was the only group in operation. Its meetings and services, special events and dinners, and the functions of its Missionary Band were all carefully recorded and neatly described. The paper proudly trumpeted that "eighty-five percent of the student body was a member of the Y and that eighty percent attended the Christian churches in town regularly."

Student enrollment moved steadily forward and, for the first time in college history, exceeded the two-hundred mark in 1905–1906. For a couple of years thereafter, enrollment held firm, but by 1907, the numbers began to slide again. The unpredictable nature of student recruitment further served to convince the administration of the need to redouble its energies where the endowment was concerned.

The *Collegian* duly noted the establishment of the Vigilance Committee, a group of dedicated students and faculty who pledged to uphold the honor and well-being of the college. This group reported acts of deviant behavior and generally served as a kind of campus watchdog with regard to acts of violence and vandalism. With administrative approval, the Vigilance Committee even managed to thwart the long-standing campus tradition of depositing a "furniture and vehicle collection" on the front porch of the Administration Building on Halloween.

Also hailed was the establishment of the board of regents, a type of student government that monitored the classes and championed the fight against hazing. The regents also regulated the college honor code, judging cases and several times asking that the faculty expel convicted offenders. Students were likewise encouraged to maintain a stricter social and moral code. Condemned were the usual offenses of drinking, smoking, profanity, spitting, and "other unseemly behavior."

REQUIREMENTS AND PROHIBITIONS (1908)

"It is the constant aim of the Faculty to encourage in every possible manner a spirit of earnest work and true manliness. To build up a noble character is regarded as the highest function of education.

"3. Students are required to be punctual and regular in attending recitations and chapel exercises. When absences are unavoidable they must be accounted for at the end of the College week in which they occur; otherwise one or more marks will be retained as a penalty for neglect. Excuses must be written and must be presented in person to the chairman of the Faculty at the regular excuse period of Thursday afternoon from 3:30 to 4 o'clock. . . .

"6. Class attendance in all cases affects class standing, and as many as ten absences from recitation, excused or unexcused, will subject the student to investigation by the chairman of the Faculty. . . .

"9. Discipline is administered both for misconduct and for neglect of work. It may take the form of admonition, demerits, correspondence with parents or guardian, summoning before the Faculty, probation, enforced withdrawal, or formal expulsion, according to the degree of the offense.

"10. Hazing and other forms of unkind treatment of students is forbidden.

"11. Visiting pool or billiard rooms or saloons at any time during the session is forbidden.

"12. Drinking intoxicating liquors at any time during the session or bringing them into the rooms of students is prohibited. Any student who shall become intoxicated will thereby sever his connection with the College. . . .

"17. All places of rooming and boarding must be approved by the Faculty.

"18. Students will not be permitted to board or room at hotels or public boarding houses. . . .

"22. Discretionary power is vested in the Faculty to meet all cases not provided for in these regulations.

Excerpts from the *Roanoke College Catalogue*, 1908–1909.

The sophomore class banquet featured turkey with all the trimmings. A local hotel hosted the event.

The members of the
Demosthenean
Literary Society pose
for a yearbook picture
outside of Bittle Hall.

For the students, no night
was more fun than
Halloween. This early
morning shot from
November the first records
a part of the evening's
plunder.

By 1908, it was evident that much of the earnestness of the previous years had dissipated. In any event, whether campus life had changed all that much or whether it was just the reporting of the *Collegian,* campus lifestyles seemed to be as before. No new club was more popular than the Minstrel Club, which entertained audiences on campus, in town, and because of popular demand, performed on several trips through southwestern Virginia. These performers, often in blackface, provided a range of entertaining acts in the best vaudevillian style. The Mandolin Club debuted in 1907 and reflected that popular rage for a number of years. And the college orchestra, reorganized in 1909, provided countless hours of "dancing pleasure" for a multitude in the course of several decades.

Class Day, a pastime from the 1890s, was reintroduced in 1908. This event featured an evening of skits and acts offered up by a troup of players formed from each of the four student classes. The players "entertained the audience with a continuous flow of wit, humor, and burlesque." Halloween also came back to haunt the administration by the end of the decade! The *Collegian* reported the highjinks of 1909: "Hallowe'en was celebrated both on Saturday night, October 30, and early Monday morning, November 1st. All sorts of things were heaped artistically on the front porch of the college. Unfortunately, each time the janitor spoiled the marauders' handiwork before it could be admired by the light of day. Everything was in attendance from broken-down wagons to aged and enfeebled grindstones. The great 'rat' parade was also held with great success. Happily no one was arrested."

The poor freshman rat was an easy target for decades. The following letter home would come as no surprise to upperclassmen: "A Rat's first letter home: 'Dear Dad, they've got box cars here that run so fast down hill that they run all the way to Roanoke without stopping, and they've got lightning bugs tied up in bottles for lamps. They have wells and springs made out of pipe in their houses. They've got a lot of doctors in College, but I never do see them carrying medicine bags.'"

COLLEGE FRIENDSHIPS

[A]fter a new student has been initiated into the mysteries of students' life, if he has manifested the proper spirit, his friends begin to multiply fast. Soon he is in danger of having too many friends, but he does not understand everything yet. He begins to feel very much at home with the boys, and thinks perhaps they are very good fellows after all.

"One night he hears a knock at the door, and, upon opening, is proud to find some five or six visitors who have come 'to see how he is getting along.' He secretly congratulates himself upon finding that he has friends that he knew not of. He puts on his very best manners and seats his visitors as comfortable as possible, or rather helps them to seat themselves, for they have a way peculiarly their own of making themselves at home on all occasions.

"When he has answered the usual questions, one of the callers settles himself to tell one of those classic college yarns with which everybody is familiar. After the fun is all laughed away the man who has been hanging on the trunk near the door draws forth a bag of the very vilest smoking tobacco he could buy, fills his pipe, and passes the bag to his comrades. Soon clouds of smoke are rising to the ceiling and spreading throughout the room.

"Their uneasy host sitting on the foot of the bed begins to realize that he is the victim of a 'smoke out.' But when he attempts to raise the window, his *friends* will not hear of it, but declare that the ventilation is good enough for them.

"[A]s time passes on the new student, as by degrees his native verdancy wears thin and he gradually becomes accustomed to the ways of the college world, soon learns to distinguish the bogus article, and at the same time realizes that after all there is such a thing as true friendship among his mates. . . .

Excerpts from the *Roanoke Collegian*, January 1907.

The *Collegian* also returned to printing stories that would have been considered playful or even risqué a few years before. In its January 1909 issue, the magazine offered this view: "It is related that some one asked a member of the faculty if his wife was entertaining this winter. And, not understanding that giving parties, etc., was referred to, he replied 'Not

Very.'" The first mention of that newfangled invention, the automobile, came in the fall of 1908. "A school-girl was asked to write an essay of 250 words on automobiles. She submitted the following: 'My uncle bought a motor car. He rode way out in the country and it busted up and broke down. I guess this is about twenty words. The other 230 are what my uncle said while walking back to the city. They are not for publication.'"

On the sports front, the college's Athletic Association continued as the unofficial clearinghouse for teams and competitions. The group did a creditable job of fielding teams throughout the period and continually exhorted more students to join and lend their support. Technically any student who competed for Roanoke had to be a member of the association, but typically there were always many who were not. These students were a constant source of frustration for the leadership, who often sacrificed dues for victories as the big game approached. The faculty even had to step in on one occasion to discourage the practice of picking up players from town who were not students at all. Such indiscretions prompted the faculty to form its own Athletic Committee to provide additional oversight.

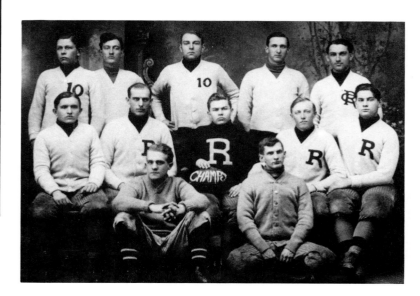

The "Champs" of 1909; these "Maroon and Grays" were ready to take on all comers.

SEASON TICKET

FOR

Base Ball, 1910, Roanoke College

NOT TRANSFERABLE   VOID IF DEFACED

This Admits *Miss Mary Keister*

SIGNED *N.H. Copenhaver*
Treasurer

Mary Keister's season ticket for 1910; N.H. Copenhaver was the student treasurer of the athletic association and a member of the team.

Sporting their maroon uniforms, these are the originators of today's college nickname: the baseball team of 1907.

The association perpetually exhorted the student body to improve its spirit. Article after article implored the students to be faithful supporters of the various activities. Class competition was encouraged to promote greater unity and to instill in the students a pride in themselves and in the college. An increasingly popular spring event was the class baseball tournament, which was always staged at the conclusion of the regular baseball season. Field Day also continued as a day of epic contests and performances. Recreational sports came and went; the students attempted to reconstruct the ice rink in 1904 to "accommodate ice hockey competition," and the first mention of horseshoe pitching appeared a year later.

It was not until November 1908 that the first reference was made to the college athletic colors as **maroon and gray**. The *Collegian* reported this story: " 'Just look at that little fellow coming up the field,' cried the girl as she kept a large maroon and gray pennant waving over her head. 'Oh! That big man has knocked the breath out of him.' " Two years later, the football team donned its new "maroon and gray suits," replacing its old red ones. Lacking any official nickname, let alone mascot, the paper began referring to the team as the "Maroon and Grays." Soon, the name would be shortened to just the "Maroons."

Athletics took a major step forward in 1910 with the completion of the long-awaited gymnasium. Although tiny by today's standards, the gym must have appeared awesome to these students of the early twentieth century. After decades of using spare campus rooms or cramped little storefronts in town, the students had a legitimate place to play and to exercise. It even afforded space for spectators—a single row of seats on one side of the gym floor plus a balcony that offered standing room for fifty more. Students and faculty alike were suitably impressed. The faculty encouraged the students to take full advantage of the new resource: "Too many students sacrifice their health for want of exercise. By spending one half-hour daily in the gymnasium, these evils can be avoided, and not only that, but the students may also secure proper physical development."

The decision to have an official basketball team was not as automatic as one might think, given the above statement. Considerable lobbying went into the team's creation. In January 1909, the *Collegian* suggested that "basketball, which is for the most part played in gymnasiums, is daily gaining in popularity, and many are of the opinion that the game is destined to take a rank equal even to that of baseball. . . . Many students, unacquainted as they are with the game, are laboring under the erroneous impression that basketball is a feminine amusement."

With the construction of the gymnasium, the College was now ready to sponsor a basketball team. Here is the very first Maroon team in the winter of 1911.

Berta Mae Reynolds, a special student of the class of 1906, was allowed to wear a cap and gown but not graduate with her fellow classmates.

From an academic standpoint, the college moved forward dramatically under Morehead's leadership. No statistic is more telling than that of faculty size, which mushroomed from eleven in 1904 to twenty just five years later. The turnover in the old guard was even more striking, since professors Painter, Smith, and Ambler all elected either to retire or to resign. In fact, by 1910, only three faculty members survived from the nineteenth century: Luther Fox, Wythe Morehead, and Leonidas McReynolds. It was a new order, to be sure.

Certainly, the college was not left in the lurch; in the new cast of members were George Peery, professor of biology; Wilbur "Happy" Mann, business instructor and bursar; and D. R. Carpenter, Steere professor of mathematics and registrar. All of these men faithfully served the college through the next half century.

Morehead even hoped to establish a new chaired position in intellectual and moral philosophy and to have it named in honor of the college's founder, David Bittle. After a couple of years of trying, the effort was aborted to concentrate on more comprehensive campaigns. During the decade, the faculty again studied the issue of coeducation, established a department of education to teach pedagogy, and several times raised academic and admission standards to "achieve national norms" by 1910.

Jerry Price had been born a slave on a plantation in 1849; he worked for the college from the 1890s until the 1910s.

Another key objective of Morehead's strategy was the redoubling of college efforts at fund raising. The new president was prepared to take a multifaceted approach. True to his election promises, Morehead turned a part of his attention to the Lutheran synods of Virginia. He challenged each to help in specific campaigns, and the churches responded with record contributions. Second, Morehead studied the record of Dreher's trips and contacts in the North, and armed with a letter of introduction from the former president himself, he set off to reap the harvest of many years of careful cultivation.

The staff of the Grub House poses on the steps of the building in the Back Quad.

A view of the campus looking from High Street into the Back Quad. The library in Bittle Hall is on the left and the Grub House stands to the right.

Finally, along with ongoing support from alumni and friends, the school successfully attracted the interest of the Carnegie Foundation in 1906. The foundation pledged $25,000 to the endowment campaign if the college could raise an equal amount. For the next twelve months, the school raised money as never before. Faculty and students subscribed; friends and associates all contributed. When the dust settled on the appointed date, the trustees met to tally the funds. They were still $2,000 short. Creating high suspense, one of the trustees presented his checkbook and covered the difference. The college had made it—if barely. Carnegie's canceled check was framed and later hung in the college archives, signifying the importance it played in establishing the college endowment.

With all the energies devoted to the careful raising of money, one would think that Morehead and the board were reticent about spending it. Nothing could be further from the truth. Once the president had paid off the debt incurred by the renovation of the Administration Building, he was more than eager to press for new studies and projects. Morehead formed a committee in 1904 to examine the need for a dormitory, and a year later, the group was refocused to consider all campus needs and resources. The renovation of West Hall, which occurred in 1907, resulted in a newly equipped physics lab replete with plumbing and modern facilities.

A.M. Bowman, Sr. served as college benefactor, trustee and Chairman of the Board. Bowman Hall today stands where his house and orchards stood a century ago.

By 1908, major change was afoot when the trustees appointed a property committee to consider the whole question of planning. The *Collegian* reported that the board "felt that the next step in the development of the institution is the erection of additional buildings, and that a wise policy demands that all projected building should be in accordance with a general harmonious and permanent plan that will provide for the larger Roanoke of the future." That "plan" was assigned to the architectural firm of Rommel and Company, based in Philadelphia. Their report and drawings envisioned a Roanoke College that was radically different from any the board might have considered previously. Rommel and Company proposed to turn the college on its side to reorient the campus and grounds to the west and Market Street. Incredibly, the plan called for the razing of all existing buildings and the construction of a series of new structures in the "collegiate gothic" style.

Just as surprisingly, the board approved the plan and in 1909 authorized construction to begin on the first three pieces—the Commons, the gymnasium, and a dormitory. As the new decade dawned, the college celebrated its new look with confidence and optimism.

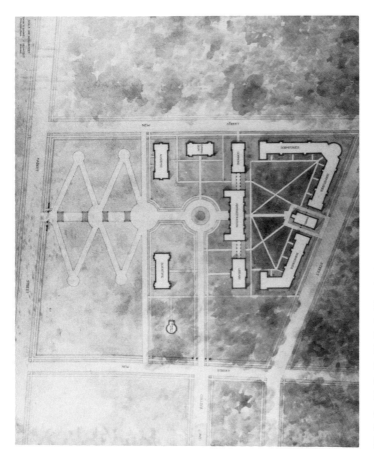

The image of "the Greater Roanoke." The College adopted this campus planning model from the Philadelphia architectural firm of Rommel and Company in 1909. Market Street is located at the left and High Street to the right. The plan called for the razing of all of the nineteenth century buildings and the construction of a new campus in the rear. The gym, the Commons, and the Sections were soon built in accordance with this model.

CHAPTER 10

"The greater Roanoke," 1910–1919

The snow-capped mountains north of campus frame the newly finished gymnasium in this photograph from the teens.

Although spartan by today's standards, the dining room of the Commons when it opened was "elegant."

The decision to begin construction on the back quad of the Commons, the dorm, and the gymnasium was hailed by all as a major step forward into the twentieth century. Ever since the renovation of the Administration Building in 1903, the college had been unable to offer any dormitory space to interested students. As a result, the college became completely dependent upon boarding houses in town. Such a situation also meant lost revenue. The *Collegian* reproted that

> owing to the increased cost of living and to changes in the habits of our people, the problem of obtaining for our students satisfactory board at reasonable rates has become more and more difficult. The old 'club' system, which has long served an excellent purpose, is no longer entirely satisfactory. The authorities of the college are convinced, therefore, the problem can be properly solved only along the lines of the best scientific knowledge and the most approved methods in the selection, preparation, and serving of food in attractive surroundings, and on such a scale as to secure both economy and efficiency.

The campus additions did not come without some cost. By April 1910, a reporter from the newspaper waxed nostalgic in observing that "the removal of old landmarks, no matter how necessary or advantageous, is often a matter of regret from the standpoint of association and sentiment. Such, doubtless, will be the

feeling of many former students when they miss from the college grounds the old group of buildings known as the steward's quarters in the rear of the main building. These, being no longer needed, have just been removed. They were the only frame buildings belonging to the college, and their removal has made a great change in the general appearance of the campus." Alas, the old Grub House would be seen no more.

Once the Commons building was constructed, it was "attractively furnished" with chairs and tables. There was a silver setting and monogrammed china emblazoned with an RC. The steward's quarters were located above the kitchen in the rear, and a special faculty dining room rested above the foyer in the front. Overall, it was a commodious addition. Running a major food-service operation proved taxing for the newly appointed college steward. After the first year's operation, the commons posted a serious deficit and the steward was dismissed. The following year, the trustees contracted another manager whose salary was tied to the "efficient and profitable" running of the hall. Sure enough, the commons finished in the black the next year, having made a whole $60 profit. New, more stringent measures had had to be implemented, however, including charging for seconds at the meals. With that, the Commons demonstrated continued strength and financial return for the college, even withstanding the first-ever recorded food fight on 23 April 1915.

The Sections under construction. There were as many "overseers" as workers in this photo from the summer of 1910.

The completed Sections and a tree-less Back Quad. The first three sections were opened in 1910 (Wells Hall) and by 1913, the next two were finished (Yonce Hall). The final wall of fifth was finished without windows or doors because the College expected to add another piece soon. When Sixth Section was completed, forty-five years had passed! Fox Hall opened in 1958.

Students and faculty alike celebrated the opening of the first three sections in the fall of 1910, but when the students continued their celebrations on into the semester, the faculty became less enchanted. Having so many students under one roof proved a new and challenging experience for the professors, who had forgotten whatever lessons they had learned a few years before when students lived in the Ad Building. The faculty meetings of that fall are rife with faculty complaints and responses to student transgressions. The faculty passed numerous measures trying to codify student behavior. Students were forbidden to throw objects from the roof, and when that edict failed to have the desired effects, the faculty simply banned the students from the roof. Students were requested not to hang their wash from their windows and thereby offend campus sensibilities. Noise persisted as a problem, and when the faculty measure to install numbers on student doors failed to achieve greater accountability, the administration was prepared to play tough. By the end of September, the three most junior members of the faculty moved into the student quarters. Doubtless, the students were less than pleased, not to mention the reactions of those three lucky members of the faculty.

A typical student dorm room from the teens; here the Gose brothers no doubt get in a little last minute studying.

Clarence P. Caldwell, Sr. was the first student to occupy this corner room in First Sections in September 1910.

Students captured this stunt on film in 1912; the cow was successfully removed from this class room on the second floor of the Administration Building.

There was no dignity in being a rat! Here a couple of freshmen (Class of 1921) are asked to hold on to a wandering bovine in the fall of 1917.

The maroons of 1915. Manager Everet Burnette Bonham is standing on the left and Coach Pinky Spruhan is standing to the right.

In the early years of the decade, campus highjinks appeared at an all-time high. President Morehead noted in his report to the board the host of "troublesome spirits" that were plaguing the campus, and the board responded by suggesting that the college purchase especially "heavy furniture" to withstand the wear and tear. Hazing was always a problem, at times worse than at other times, but the faculty continued to do battle. The Reception Committee still served to help orient the new students with sessions and meals designed to assimilate them into the college routine.

A CHILLY STREAK FOR JUST 50¢

College students are known for their crazy fads, like swallowing goldfish or seeing how many students can pack into a Volkswagen. The craze in the mid-1970s was "streaking," stripping off one's clothes and running naked across campus. Masks or head gear were optional, depending upon whether the streaker wanted to be recognized or retain anonymity. But there was a streaker on the Roanoke campus long before the students of the 1970s were even born. The story came from an alumnus, Cecil W. Gray, who revealed the tale in a letter written during the streaking phase in 1974.

"Among the students of my time was one named Keys [Carson Keys, Class of 1917?], whose nickname was 'Two Gun.' He lived in the 5th section dormitory and he was a whimsical fellow.

"One night at a bull session, Two Gun said that for fifty cents he would strip naked and run around the street light pole at the corner of Main and College Streets, where the Dillard drug store used to be.

"His offer was accepted and at the stroke of midnight old Two Gun shed his bathrobe near the Administration Building and stark naked he circled the light pole and returned to the campus for his fifty cents.

"Hardley Erb . . . and Julius Prufer probably were witnesses to the famous run of old 'Two Gun' Keys."

Much to the dismay of the faculty, the college also witnessed a new spectacle entitled the Feasts of the Frats, a rather loosely defined series of parties and receptions designed to introduce the students to the Greek system. The *Collegian* gleefully reported a day-long battle in 1912 between the sophomores and the "rats," with the control of the Administration Building as the spoils. The class flags took turns waving from the front portico roof and then being hauled down in disgrace. The faculty, the tireless peacemakers, finally interceded to arrange an armistice. The practice of housing visiting sports teams in the dorm was also curtailed in 1914 when a rival baseball team apparently started batting practice a little before they took the field.

Halloween continued as the biggest night of the year on campus, and typically took place in town. The students complained that the Salem police force deputized half the town in an effort to deflect the students' "rowdyism." Still, the students could have fun, and by 1912, there was no better target for their fun than the Roanoke Women's College located just a mile across town. The college men, in any given year, presented their "plunder" as if in the form of some sacrifice and dutifully serenaded the recipients of this "treasure." Most of their booty was harmless enough, but on occasion Morehead did complain—as, for example, in the instance when the students acquired "excessive poultry" on a scavenging expedition.

Morehead complained about more serious problems too, and nothing gave him greater concern than the "increase in licentiousness" evident at the college. Several students each year were charged, convicted, and expelled on that count. The editors of the *Collegian* complained too about different aspects of student behavior. Nothing proved more frustrating to student leaders than the perceived lack of spirit. The *Collegian* suggested that student "deadbeats" and "sluggards" would be the ruin of any institution, Roanoke included. The editors decried the paltry interest in subscribing to the yearbook and, to make matters worse, were forced to start paying students for their articles to the magazine.

As mysteriously as the previous few years had been boisterous and unsupportive, the student body of 1914–1915 proved positively delightful. The newfound spirit and outlook were transformed into a host of new organizations. A series of "home clubs" appeared and united students from the same geographical region: the Southwestern Virginia Club, the Tar Heel Club, and several others. The Glee Club continued strong, as did the college orchestra, and a pep band was organized to assist at athletic events. Numerous academically related societies also became active: a Spanish Club, the Classical Club, a Literary Club, the International Polity Club, and the German Club, which had social overtones as well. The German Club made fashionable a new drink on

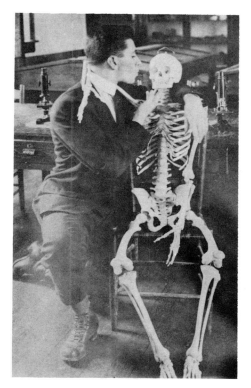

There was nothing like that special friend in biology class.

This photo from a student scrapbook was entitled: "The Sophs pay a visit to Lizzie." Elizabeth College had come to town in the teens.

The graduates of the class of 1915, replete with their "class canes."

The Salem Club poses on the steps of the Commons in 1914.

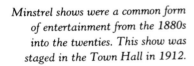

Minstrel shows were a common form of entertainment from the 1880s into the twenties. This show was staged in the Town Hall in 1912.

campus, beer, and introduced its "hops, which are held most every week."

The YMCA continued to provide outreach to many students. Some others joined the Intercollegiate Prohibition Association and accepted the challenge on confronting "demon rum" on campus. The debating societies, the Ciceronians and the Demostheneans, offered continuing outlets for those students so inclined and commonly hosted intercollegiate competitions while sponsoring a combined team.

For sheer entertainment, nothing could beat College Night during the teens. Staged in the commons and held following dinner, the evening featured selected faculty and students in a series of skits, songs, and readings—with the emphasis on fun. The show of 1916 found more than 200 students, faculty, alumni, and friends all craning their necks for a better view. The decade also brought "moving-picture shows" to both Salem and Roanoke, and even Buffalo Bill and his Wild West Show stopped off in Roanoke.

Roanoke's only undefeated basketball team; the state champions of 1916. That's Pinky holding the ball.

The first issue of the school paper went untitled but offered a year's subscription to the student with the best name; the following issue, the Brackety-Ack *was born.*

One Year's Subscription
FOR THE BEST NAME FOR THIS PAPER

Volume 1   SALEM, VIRGINIA, TUESDAY EVENING, OCTOBER 19, 1915   Number 1

ROANOKE COLLEGE 0; A. & M. 0

V. P. I. 26; R. C. 0   **Coach Hegarty's Men Are**   **R. C. 62; R. M. A. 0**

Roanoke College Fails to Show Her Full Strength   **Given a Big Surprise**   **Bedford Boys Fight Hard Though Vastly Outclassed**

ROANOKE'S BACKFIELD STARS

Renewed spirit and interest must have been related in part to greater success on the athletic front. To monitor better the accomplishments on the field and court and to rally the support of the student body, several students organized a little paper in the fall of 1915. The first issue was unnamed but contained an offer of a year's free subscription to the student submitting the best name for the newspaper. The next week the *Brackety-Ack* was born, and the fledgling publication had much to celebrate. Within two years, Roanoke's athletic prowess had become redoubtable. The football team of 1916 became the state champions, and the basketball team showed marked improvement. After some humbling defeats in the initial couple of seasons, the basketball team gained championship form by 1916.

No one was more responsible for that success than Coach Guy "Pinky" Spruhan. With his arrival in 1913, he revolutionized Roanoke athletics. He provided a permanence and coordination that the program had never enjoyed. After twenty years of guidance under the Athletic Association—the student-run volunteer governing body—the college embraced athletics officially in the 1910s. The General Athletic Association was organized, consisting of faculty, students, and of course Coach Spruhan. To support the program and to offset the expenses of maintaining the gym, the association introduced "a compulsory athletic fee," which was levied on each student. The three-dollar surcharge soon became five dollars, then six, but there seemed to be no major student protest. The tax was a small price for victories!

A home game on the Market Street Field. The Pi Lam house today stands where the house on the left was; the other two are still standing.

The student body of 1916. Notice the guy standing in the back row, extreme left and far right. He is the same person! Cecil Gray pulled off this fairly common stunt of the teens. Given the exposure setting of the camera, a person could remain motionless for 10-

Spruhan oversaw the construction of new grandstands on the Market Street field and popularized the notion of playing a couple of big games in Roanoke's old Victory Stadium to maximize press attention, crowd size, and revenue. He also introduced the idea of an athletic award and appreciation banquet each winter, a popular event that continued for years. Additionally, Coach Spruhan was influential in the formation of the *Brackety-Ack* and the establishment of the Monogram Club, an organization for those athletes who had won "the R."

Academically, the college had never enjoyed a better reputation. The increased admission standards, changes in the curriculum, and physical transformation of the campus all combined to give the school a much-enhanced profile. To confirm what many on campus suspected, the United States government Bureau of Education published in 1912 a review of all colleges in the state and listed Roanoke as second only to the University of Virginia in terms of reputation and quality of instruction. Morehead reveled in that news and also complimented the board of trustees on its foresight in constructing the new range of campus buildings. The president noted the explosion in Virginia high school education, from a handful of schools at the turn of the

century to several hundred high schools by 1915. Roanoke's expansion could not have come at a more fortuitous time.

12 seconds, then duck down and race behind his fellows and show up at the other end of the line, then stand still for another 10-12 seconds. If everything worked, you show up twice!

A little book dusting in Bittle library.

Faculty responsibilities continued as before. Teaching occupied the lion's share of their time and professional development—their research, writing, reading, and continued graduate training for some—was promoted as never before. Morehead exhorted the faculty to remain current in their designated fields and recommended to the board that promotion to full professor should be contingent upon an earned doctorate. The faculty responded well to the board's suggestion that the faculty should visit the "backward communities" of western Virginia, to represent the college and to be of service to the localities.

The professors began the fall of 1914 by compiling a list of the college's three biggest needs. First, to no great surprise, the faculty suggested that more—and better-paid— professors should be the college's highest priority. Second, the library needed attention, especially to eliminate the overcrowding of the stacks as more and more volumes took their places on the shelves. And finally, the faculty suggested that the "Visitors Gallery" in the gym should be made "more inviting for the viewing of the athletic contests."

The faculty introduced several new features into the academic program during the decade. The buzzword of the 1910s was clearly "system"; reference was always being made to the "Athletic System" or to the "Dormitory System."

The "Group System" debuted in 1910 and gave students greater flexibility in massing their electives around various areas of study. Assigning students to faculty as "advisees" in the "Advising System" also began as did the "Coaching System," a faculty-supervised, student-based tutoring program linking stronger students with those in need of additional assistance.

Other faculty duties ran the gamut from selecting the topics for the senior thesis to helping with the new cataloging of the library's collection. Discipline was never far from faculty attention. The normal list of charges and offenses persisted, with the dormitory heading the concerns. The faculty grappled with strange cases—as, for example, the time a town family used the college grounds to bury their recently departed child. The faculty insisted that the family remove the body or else the college would be forced to take matters into its own hands. Less weighty issues surfaced too, including a faculty debate in 1913 concerning replacing the old college bell with a gong. Somehow Henry Hill, the school's longtime custodian and timekeeper who started work in 1911, just would not look quite right hitting his gong to sound the change of classes. And finally, the faculty members enjoyed their evening in Roanoke listening to an address by former president William Howard Taft in the special box provided by a college donor.

Under Lutheran auspices, a college for women opened in Salem in 1911. First called Oakmont, the school soon changed its name to the Roanoke Women's College and, symbolically at least, attached itself to the men's college. Although there was never any institutional relationship, the two schools cooperated in a number of ways. By 1912, Roanoke deferred to the women's college and refused to accept any new female students. When the administration of the women's college questioned Roanoke about a joint commencement exercise, however, Roanoke balked. Roanoke's faculty suggested instead that the respective college literary societies hold a combined celebration. Roanoke never considered the women's college (by 1915 renamed Elizabeth College) a rival; on the other hand, Roanoke did not consider it a true sister school either.

In the aftermath of the Elson controversy, Morehead and the trustees had their work cut out for them, at least as far as local fund raising was concerned. The poisoned relations between the college and the towns would take several years and Morehead's eventual departure to register any real improvement. Despite the president's best efforts, church sources reverted to a trickle as congregational support amounted to just a few hundred dollars annually. Morehead's letter to "Cousin George" Brown, synod treasurer, is typical: "Have you any funds for Roanoke College in your treasury now? If so, I shall appreciate your remitting [them as] we shall have a struggle to 'make ends meet' for the balance of the year." Morehead continued his journeys to the North, and although his harvest was far from bountiful, he did at least manage to collect enough each year to keep the college afloat.

Given the college's meager prospects and its building debts of 1910 and 1913, it is little wonder that the trustees spent the vast majority of their time "planning" and "studying" proposals and projects rather than attempting to implement them. Seemingly undaunted by the balance sheet, the board developed a veritable wish-list of proposed buildings and schemes. A new chapel headed the agenda, followed by a science building, more sections to be added onto the dormitory, and a new home for the president. Of all those items, only the president's home would reach fruition during the decade. A review committee appointed in 1914 concluded that the president's house was in such a sorry

The fine stone building of Elizabeth College. The sister school was about a mile from the Roanoke campus and the site of the Elizabeth campus today.

Judge W. W. Moffett, a longtime trustee, became embroiled with the college over the Elson history controversy and resigned from the Board.

In 1910, the college became embroiled in a remarkable controversy. It started as a local squabble between a concerned parent and his daughter's professor but soon evolved into a story of national scope and attention. For newspapers from New York to Chicago, the college was a champion of academic freedom, a stalwart defender of instructional liberty and integrity; however, to the local papers and people, the college had become a villain, a traitor to its heritage and past traditions.

Sally Moffett was a "special" student in Professor Henry Thorstenberg's American History class. One evening at home, Sally apparently left her history textbook out on a table and her father happened to pick it up and began to thumb through it. Her father, a Roanoke County judge, was not pleased; the book, Henry Elson's *History of the United States,* was published by Macmillan and was considered to be a most respectable professional history. Yet the judge was appalled by the book's alleged northern bias and its less than flattering references to the South. As a result, the judge demanded satisfaction.

Judge Moffett was not only a parent of a student, he was also an influential member of the college's Board of Trustees. Accordingly, he took his case directly to President Morehead. The judge proposed that the text be withdrawn and that Professor Thorstenberg's lectures be monitored. And in the future, he said, the trustees should play a more active role in supervising the academic content of classes and readings. For Morehead, the issue was squarely one of academic freedom. No college president wants to confront his own board. For this cause, however, Morehead was prepared to do battle. Predictably, the faculty closed ranks around their colleague, and the lines were drawn.

The controversy raged for several months. In the end, the president proved stronger than the judge and his allies on the board. In frustration, Moffett led several board members in resigning in 1911. The local press had a field day with the affair and charged that the school had turned its back on its Southern heritage and had forever dishonored its once-proud Confederate record. The local frenzy also spawned a number of ugly incidents involving the college and featured numerous pieces of hate mail, including death threats to Morehead.

By 1912, tempers had calmed and Morehead tried to mend fences. Thorstenberg tendered his resignation and was happy to leave Salem for good. The college might have won the principle of the debate, but it clearly lost its standing in local eyes. Morehead's ability to raise money in southwestern Virginia was effectively at an end.

A final touch of irony can be added to the story. Only later was it revealed that Professor Thorstenberg was actually Morehead's second choice for the history position. Who had the president tried to recruit for the chair? None other than Henry Elson.

state and so badly in need of repairs that it would be far cheaper to tear down the old nineteenth-century house of Professor Yonce and Dreher than to attempt to fix it. By the summer of 1916, the president and his family moved into the present structure known as Roselawn.

The trustees also entertained numerous plans and programs that, while never being fully realized, were nonetheless seriously considered. Several scholarship campaigns were embraced, including one proposed by an alumnus from his missionary school in Japan for the training of some of his most promising charges. Yet while all of these ideas proved promising, the capital to implement any of them was simply lacking.

The college's precarious financial state was threatened even more drastically by the onset of the first World War. With American entry proclaimed in April 1917, the college and its student body faced an uncertain future. The trustees considered emergency measures almost at once. Predicting a marked decline in enrollment for the fall and expecting college donations to be dramatically curtailed as well given wartime government fund-raising measures, the board prepared to tighten the college's belt. Three junior faculty members were let go by the summer of 1917, and the college's first summer session was held for reasons that were probably less educational than they were financial. The faculty, expecting further inroads into their number possibly as a result of required government service, supported the notion of trying to attract "lady teachers" as a stopgap measure. Those anticipated draft calls never materialized, and the faculty was not forced to effect such "extreme measures."

Life on campus in the fall of 1917 brought some changes but nothing like the transformation the school would experience in the following year. At first, students were encouraged to be diligent, to contribute to the war effort, and to help raise their own food in the college's "Victory Garden." Still, students were students, and without the regular degree of dorm surveillance—the three dismissed faculty members were the ones who lived in the Sections—dorm living resembled life in the Jurassic Period. By the middle of the semester, the faculty had regained the upper hand, though.

Fun and games soon gave way to the more serious business of war. Many college students had been organized into the Student Army Training Corp (SATC), which effectively turned Roanoke into a camp. Fifty-four students initially signed up for military training, and by 1918 the vast majority of the students were involved. The college *Bulletin* offered its version: "The college was organized upon the principles of a camp. The curriculum was torn asunder, and drill, military science, War Aims course, mathematics, physics, and chemistry took precedence over everything. The campus was truly a camp. Literary societies, intercollegiate athletics, the regular YMCA, and the student publications were suspended until the demobilization of the SATC." Even Coach Spruhan was called away, if only to Lexington to get the cadets of VMI in better fighting trim.

The college erected a special flagpole to honor the 175 Roanoke students and alumni who were already in the service, and the college flew a Battle Flag from the balcony of the Administration Building to commemorate the students in action in Europe. Tragedy struck the campus corp in the fall of 1918 as the scourge of influenza assumed pandemic proportions. Of the tens of millions who died worldwide, a million and half Americans can be counted in that toll; and in Salem, the corp of students was infected and quarantined from the rest of the town. The Ciceronian Society hall became a hospital, and local physicians and the Red Cross did battle. Of the dozens who were ill, only two students succumbed.

A final effect of the war was ultimately the loss of Roanoke's president. The Lutheran Church had tapped Dr. Morehead to lead its relief effort in Europe following the end of hostilities in 1918. Morehead obliged and threw himself into the effort with all the energy and dedication he could muster. After a year and a half, Morehead realized that his greater calling would keep him in Europe. Regretfully, he tendered his resignation to the college trustees in the spring of 1920. His new life's work had just begun.

David Bittle's pride and joy—the remnants of his mineral cabinet as it appeared in this lab room in the Ad Building.

President Morehead as he departed for Europe in the spring of 1919; his letter of resignation would reach the college the following year.

CHAPTER 11

"A child of Roanoke,"
1919–1926

With President Morehead's departure to Europe in 1918, the Board of Trustees appointed Professor George Peery as acting president and dean of the college. The assignment to step in and direct a school in the throes of the "revolution of the SATC" must have been a daunting experience. Peery vowed to make the best of it. Even after the war had come to a conclusion and peace had returned to Salem, life on campus proved more than taxing. In his report to the board, Peery decried the state of affairs. He felt a certain "restlessness" in the air because of the uncertainty of Morehead's return and the general confusion caused by the dismantling of the corp. Peery was alarmed by the disaffection of the faculty, the slumping of student enrollment and morale, and the virtual disintegration of the campus physical plant. The financial coffers of the college were about empty, and prospects seemed no brighter. Postwar inflation played havoc on faculty salaries, and in general the college came as close to the brink of collapse as at any time since the death of David Bittle.

Such conditions demanded action, and Peery, although without a lasting charge or endorsement, was prepared to wade into the surf. With board approval of course, the interim president proclaimed a half-million-dollar endowment drive that would begin at once. That effort proved to be more an "announcement" than an actual "campaign"; nevertheless, it did serve psychologically to rejuvenate college spirits.

Always the good professor, Peery turned his attention next to faculty concerns. He urged that salaries be raised and introduced the notion of the nine-month contract. In an age of increasing specialization, faculty were to be more specialized too. Peery suggested that faculty should not be expected to perform added duties—such as summer school— without added compensation. Further, the nineteenth-century notion of the faculty's providing administrative services was curtailed. No longer would faculty be required to "canvass for students" or be expected to help raise money or to facilitate the handling of college correspondence.

The earliest glimpse of the campus from the air is captured in this 1921 "aerograph."

One of Dr. Charlie's first assignments was to try to soothe relations still strained by the Elson controversy ten years before. Here the president (standing in the rear) hosts a reception in Roselawn for a group of local Civil War veterans in 1921. (Courtesy Salem Times-Register)

George Peery's other principal contribution came in the way of curricular reform. Given the shambles of the old order when the SATC was demobilized, Peery and the faculty reasoned that the opportunity for overhauling and updating the academic program was at hand. Remarkably little sentiment existed for attempting to resurrect the old system, and the faculty hoped to make the best of a bad situation. First, the college reintroduced the bachelor of science degree, dormant since the early 1890s, and rededicated itself to the teaching and promotion of science. Peery, the biologist, was doubtless pleased. A renovation of all of the science rooms and laboratories was anticipated. There were other modifications too: Latin and Greek were slowly losing out to the modern languages; and an "expanded system of election," the electives of today, would give students greater choice and flexibility in their schedules.

When Morehead's letter of resignation arrived in May 1920, it did not take long for the board to consider his replacement. Ever since his graduation in 1901, Charles J. Smith had kept an eye on Roanoke and the college an eye on him. He was invited back in 1915 to receive an honorary doctorate, and in 1919 Smith was on campus to deliver a series of lectures to the college

YMCA. Smith's connections were even more far-reaching than that, though. In the first paragraph of his inaugural address, "Dr. Charlie" introduced himself.

Dr. Bittle, the first president of Roanoke College, rescued my father from the commonplaces of a country printshop, befriended him through all his courses at Roanoke College, and became the inspiration for his rich life of earthly service and eternal victory. Dr. Dosh, the second president, imported to Salem his own sister-in-law, saw to it that my father made her acquaintance, and, though not usually given to humor, watched, with a merry twinkle in his eye, while acquaintance ripened into love, upon which in due time was founded the home of sweetness and of light from which I sprang. The third president, Dr. Dreher, a gentleman of great culture and exact purpose, presided over my own education and, by his personal confidence in me, made possible my post-graduate training at a great university. The fourth president, Dr. Morehead, directed my thought to the Christian ministry and became my trusted colleague, counsellor, and friend. Surely I am a child of Roanoke College and enter today into the richness of that heritage which has been built for me by the noble company of my illustrious predecessors.

Looking up Main Street in the mid-twenties. (Courtesy Salem Times-Register)

This "child of Roanoke" set upon his presidential duties with a vengeance. Upon his arrival in Salem in the summer of 1920, "Dr. Charlie" was horrified to discover what he found. He minced no words in his report to the board:

> The buildings and grounds were in an evident state of disrepair. . . . The wood-work and plumbing in the buildings were rotting and rapidly becoming worthless. Every available corner was filled with refuse and junk. . . . The equipment for work was poor. Laboratories were in cramped quarters and without the necessary apparatus for scientific work. Classrooms were dirty and the campus was growing up in filth. The college was in a grievous financial condition. . . . The student morale was bad. A comparatively small number of men remained at the College for any considerable length of time. . . . The Church, the community, and the alumni were apathetic. Past controversies, the tension of war situations, and the general breakdown in the institution, together with the lack of morale among the students, had spread into our whole college constituency. I am quite willing to confess that the problem seemed almost insurmountable.

The "Child of Roanoke," Charles J. Smith.

One can only imagine if any college president ever assumed a more challenging project. It is little wonder that Smith later admitted that he accepted the presidency for "sentimental reasons."

A panoramic shot of the front of campus taken in the early twenties.

The president and his faculty. Flanking Dr. Charlie on the left is D.R. Carpenter, longtime registrar, and to the right, Charles Brown, the first dean of the college.

Key to Smith's approach was the term administration. For all intents and purposes, the modern governance of the college dates from 1920 and Smith's arrival. To get the college back on its feet, the new president believed in delegating responsibility. Chief among his officers was the newly redefined and expanded position of dean of the college. Smith appointed history professor Charles Brown to the post, a position he would hold for the next nineteen years. To assist Dean Brown and to handle all matters of admission and correspondence, a post for the secretary of the college was established. Former faculty member D. B. Welsh returned to assume those duties. And finally, a superintendent of buildings and grounds was appointed to oversee the physical plant operation. "Happy" Mann continued as bursar or business manager, and D. R. Carpenter remained as registrar. Those men became the nucleus of college management and planning for the next three decades.

Along with Smith's responsibilities as general college overseer, he recognized that his first priority was that of fund raiser. If his alma mater was to be saved, it would be because of his powers of persuasion. He at once began to use his greatest gift—his ability as an orator—to attract audiences to Roanoke. Dr. Charlie took to the road tirelessly in his quest for interested

PRESIDENT'S RECEPTION

"On Monday evening from 8:30 to 10:30 P.M. at the president's home, 'Rose Lawn,' President and Mrs. Smith tendered a reception to the alumni, inauguration and commencement guests, and friends of the College in the community. The evening was clear and cool, with a bright moon, and the guests, after having greeted the hosts, congregated in the porch and lawn, where refreshments were served. The grounds were illuminated by Japanese lanterns and rows of electric lights. In the receiving line were President and Mrs. Smith, and Dean and Mrs. Brown. About five hundred guests attended the reception."

From the *Roanoke College Bulletin,* July 1921.

friends, benefactors, and prospective students to the college. Through his efforts, the Alumni Association was revitalized, and chapters began springing up across the East and the South. Moreover, local relations with Salem and Roanoke still needed mending after the scars left by Elson ten years before. In typical fashion, Smith won over the hearts of the school's most important constituency.

Even though the college was in desperate financial straits, Smith and the board realized that immediate improvements must be made to the campus's physical plant or the college's ability to recruit and retain students would be seriously impaired. Although it meant going deeper into debt, the college felt obligated to adopt its course of action.

The first target of renovation efforts was the third floor of the Administration Building. The science classrooms and labs for both biology and chemistry were completely overhauled and refurbished. The board had also authorized $10,000 for new equipment in its bid to reclaim some of the program's lost luster. The floor was fitted with new electric lights that made it "possible to conduct the laboratory work without interruption by darkness during the winter months." Additionally, the physics rooms in West Hall on the main floor were similarly reappointed and a "baloptican" was installed. The ground floor of the building, previously used for storage, was partitioned into three new rooms for added departmental space. Peery's dream of a new and improved science program had been realized.

The west wing of the first floor of the Ad Building was similarly transformed into new executive offices for Dr. Charlie and his staff. Campus beautification was on the agenda as well, no doubt enhanced by the purchase of a "new power-mower" in 1921. The college purchased its first new property in years in the early 1920s. Moving beyond the traditional front gates of the campus, the college began its slow expansion into the northern limits of town. It purchased a frame structure adjacent to the front gates on the west side of College Avenue, and lacking any other expressed need for the house, the college promptly rented it to the Pi Kappa Phi fraternity. By 1923, the college had decided on a better purpose for the site and so picked up and moved the fraternity house back to the rear of the property and rotated the structure so that it faced the college's front quad. In the vacated lot, the school constructed a handsome brick building that contained four five-room apartments for faculty. It remained a faculty residence until 1964 when "College Hall" was made home to the Business Office.

"MANY IMPROVEMENTS WILL BE MADE"

"During the summer, many improvements will be made in the college plant. The entire west end of the first floor of the Administration Building will be remodeled. Partitions will be removed and the present classrooms converted into executive offices. A steam heating plant will be placed in this building, which will supply heat also to East and West Halls. An electric master clock will be installed which will operate gongs in all of the college buildings. The heating plant in the Gymnasium will be enlarged. The exterior of the Administration Building and the interior of the Dormitories will be painted. Rooms in the Commons Building will be prepared for the College Store which will be operated under the direction of Coach Spruhan.

"The wireless apparatus, which was installed during the past winter, has been in operation for several months. Besides catching messages going to France, Germany, and Italy, the college station has been in regular communication with numerous stations in our country, including those at Arlington and Annapolis, from which time has been received. The apparatus has a sending radius of six hundred miles; but, because of the delay in receiving a license, so far no messages have been sent."

From the *Roanoke College Bulletin*, July 1921

The newly-illuminated Sections is featured in this snow covered scene. (Courtesy *Salem Times-Register*)

The Pi Kapps were delighted with their new quarters outside the college gates on College Avenue. The college would soon move the house to the rear of the property and evict the brothers.

The student yearbook catches the three college custodians at ease; that's Henry Hill on the right.

There is no question that the major Board of Trustees' action of the decade concerned the all-out campaign for endowment. The dream of a meaningful endowment had been a hope of the college's since the days of David Bittle. Dreher had invested much time in the project but with little real return. The official account had been opened in 1882, but when the president retired more than twenty years later, the balance sheet was anything but impressive. Morehead had carried the project forward, but by 1921 the endowment amounted only to $130,000—and the college was in debt for more than half that amount.

If the financial reasons were not compelling enough, sobering academic news was received as well. The recent national trend to standardization and accreditation of America's colleges had led in 1921 to a preliminary review of Roanoke. The findings were anything but satisfying to college officials. The review found the school deficient on a number of counts, and given the association's requirement of a minimum half-million-dollar endowment, Roanoke recognized

the inevitable decision. The unofficial "substandard" rating alarmed the faculty and trustees alike. The college had plummeted in just ten short years from one of the state's best schools to a condition of quasi-probation in which its program and diplomas might have their legitimacy called into question. Given those prospects, Smith and the board prepared to do battle.

Key to campaign prospects was the hope of attracting some sponsoring group that would be willing to match a college amount or at least challenge the school with a given donation. After several years of pursuing other contacts, the college succeeded in interesting John D. Rockefeller and his General Board of Education. To assist the college in its drive, Rockefeller's board agreed to commit $165,000 if the college could raise $335,000. The terms were signed in the spring of 1922, with the college required to have pledges and subscriptions completed in a year. If it was successful, the college was then to be given three more years— until 1926—to collect those pledges in cash or in securities.

With the agreement signed and the clock ticking, Smith, the board, and a New York fund-raising firm went out to collect money as the college had never done before. The faculty subscribed, students paid, and the alumni contributed in record numbers. Major support came from the newly united Lutheran Synod of Virginia, to the tune of $100,000. Illustrious alumni John Thomas Lupton, a founder of Coca Cola, and James Ellwood Jones, a coal baron of West Virginia, each contributed $50,000. The passing of "the old man," Luther Fox, after more than forty years on the faculty galvanized student and alumni support to raise an additional $50,000 to help fund a chaired professorship in philosophy and religion in his name.

John Thomas Lupton '82, offered Americans a taste of "the real thing." He was one of the three founders of Coca-Cola.

The "Old Tar Heel," Luther Fox, confers with some students. Fox was stricken while lecturing in Trout Hall in late 1924. He recovered from his stroke well enough to return to the classroom for the fall semester but his health soon began to fail. He died in November, 1925.

THE COKE MAN

People expected great things from John Thomas Lupton. And graduating as the valedictorian of Roanoke's class of 1882 was only the beginning. He moved on to Charlottesville and obtained a law degree from the University of Virginia and then to Chattanooga, Tennessee, to pursue some business opportunities.

He never lost touch with his alma mater. He served in the Alumni Association, helped plan the college's semicentennial in 1903, and certainly aided the school as a benefactor. Lupton had made many fortunes in his lifetime and gave the college one of them; when he died in 1933, he had donated more money to Roanoke than anyone else in its history—more than a quarter of a million dollars.

Lupton was generous with his money, but then, he could afford to be. He had entered into a little business proposition with two partners in 1899. You may have heard of the result: the Coca-Cola Company.

THE FORTNIGHTLY CLUB OF ROANOKE COLLEGE

The Fortnightly Club of Roanoke College was founded on 21 January 1921 with ten charter members. Composed of faculty wives (there were no female faculty then), its purpose was the literary and cultural enrichment of its members. The group met— of course—fortnightly! Members discussed topics of current interest or presented papers. Occasionally a professor gave an address or book review. Each woman brought a book that was exchanged with other members until it made its way back to the owner.

In the days of a much smaller Roanoke College, the members of the Fortnightly Club had many social responsibilities. In the 1920s they gave formal tureen suppers either in the commons or in private homes, and included the faculty bachelors on the guest list. During the 1930s, they hosted the yearly alumni dinner, both greeting guests and serving the dinner. Fortnightly Club members often assisted the president's wife in formal entertaining, arranging flowers, serving at receptions, and sometimes even housing guests. They also helped chaperone at dances. In a time when there were few activities for students on Sunday afternoons, they held monthly teas. In the 1950s, the women expanded their offerings to the students in the form of sandwiches or baked goodies during exam study breaks. That practice ceased the time their efforts were greeted with "less than appreciative" remarks by some of the boys, who had opened the sandwiches and returned them to the serving trays!

The Fortnightly Club members donated more than their time to the college. The cherry trees along High Street were purchased in the 1930s, and over the years the dogwoods in front of Roselawn and other landscaping projects were funded by Fortnightly. Members purchased china and silver for the dormitories, and in the 1940s and 1950s, when meetings were held in Smith Dorm, the women contributed some gift, such as curtains, to help make the dorm more attractive. The group has also purchased works of art by local artists. In 1991 they donated the media and reference desks in the Fintel Library in memory of the two presidents responsible for the building of the 1962 library, H. Sherman Oberly and Perry F. Kendig.

As Roanoke College grew in size, so too did the Fortnightly Club, increasing its membership to include female faculty and staff, and wives of the male employees. Additionally, the focus of the club changed, with less emphasis on social duties and entertaining and more emphasis on service to the college in other ways. The annual children's Christmas party—a tradition begun in the 1940s—continues, with fun and games and a visit from Santa. The formal dinners gave way to potluck suppers and an "after-the-Washington-and-Lee-basketball-game" chili supper. Two fund-raising projects begun in the 1980s—the Midnight Buffet (an exam study break in December) and "Survival Kits" (boxes of goodies given in the spring)—have enabled Fortnightly to sponsor not only the Cardinal Key cash award to a senior, but also a $1,000 scholarship to an upperclassman.

When the dust had settled, the college had made it with little to spare. Having completed phase 1, the college's arduous task of converting pledges into dollars began. By the June 1926 deadline, the college was still short; the foundation's board kindly granted a three-month extension upon the college's assurance that the final money was forthcoming. The principal culprit in the delay had been the Virginia Synod; it had promised $100,000, but the church was still short by $38,000. To prevent a crisis, Smith and several trustees traveled to Richmond to meet with church officials and to effect a compromise. The college got its money, but several critics alleged that it was more a "ransom than a payment." The church agreed to borrow the balance if the college would pay the interest and agree to a change in its charter requiring **that three-fifths of its board of trustees henceforth be Lutherans from congregations in Virginia.** For the synod, which a few years before had requested Smith and the board to turn the college over to the church, the compromise gave them the role and leverage they desired in monitoring college affairs. Smith had obtained the money, but he must have wondered at what cost.

As Dr. Charlie attempted to rebuild the college's fortune, the students of the 1920s set about the business of recasting campus life on a stronger footing as well. More and better students— whom the college labeled "the clean, manly, type"—appeared soon and quickly reassembled the clubs and routines of college life. The literary societies, dormant since the war, emerged with an enthusiasm unseen in years. Dedicated students formed the Farm Battalion to assist local farmers in the harvesting of crops as a gesture of student "goodwill." The college commons, back to using student waiters after an experiment with a buffet line, established a tradition of serving Thanksgiving dinners to the community as well. The faculty even decided to close its separate dining room and sit among the students at the head of the tables. Special seating arrangements were made for "foreign language tables" and other similar interests.

New clubs and organizations grew up as well. The Cotillion Club became the premiere social group on campus in sponsoring dances and receptions; the German Club soon succeeded the Cotillions as the best party-givers on campus. Fraternities returned in fine fashion with the reorganization of Sigma Chi in 1923 and a new chapter of Kappa Alpha the next year. To better coordinate the affairs of the various houses, the students first formed a campus Interfraternity Council and then a Pan Hellenic Board. Students in general reorganized their student government and campus publications: the *Röntgen Rays,* the *Brackety-Ack,* and the *Collegian*—now strictly a literary magazine—never looked better.

The YMCA continued its campus and community service and even introduced a couple of billiards tables into its Trout Hall home—at "2 ½ cents per man per game." The Glee Club was reformed by 1924 and offered its first radio concert on WDBJ in 1926. The college orchestra boasted nineteen pieces and even spawned interest in the "Maroon and Gray Jazz Band" by mid-decade. The "Harlequins" presented numerous dramatic offerings, and when all else failed, the college radio could pull in "a concert almost every night."

Long-standing traditions were restructured too. Class Day and Mountain Day, begun in the 1890s, were combined into a full day's outing of fun, food, and freedom at Bennett's Springs. And of course no day was complete without a hike up to "the Knob." Lakeside Park opened to thousands of swimmers and picnickers, and visitors to town included Roald Amundsen with "actual pictures of the South Pole" and John Phillip Sousa entertaining audiences in Roanoke in 1925. On a more somber note, students mourned the passing of "Lizzie," or Elizabeth College; it burned to the ground in December 1921.

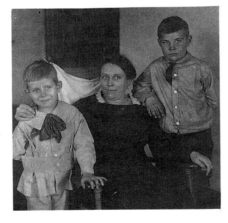

The cooking in the Commons just would not have been the same without the efforts of Mrs. Price. Here she is posing with her two sons.

Lakeside was quite the place for plain old fun. (Courtesy Salem Times-Register)

The old gym (now the Ballroom) decorated for a big dance in the early twenties. (Courtesy Salem Times-Register)

There was not much left standing of Elizabeth College after the fire of December 1921. The women were allowed to finish their studies at Roanoke for the spring term but no more.

The "Lizzie Girls" pose for this photograph in happier times.

The freshmen are caught doing the "Snake Dance" during the Rat rush of 1921. (Courtesy Salem Times-Register)

The most familiar corner in Salem. Dillard's Drug Store was an important meeting place for decades. (Courtesy Salem Times-Register)

The Rats in their party clothes in 1922. This shot from a student scrapbook reported that there was "not much Sophomore spirit."

The automobile appeared in such increasing numbers that the imperiled faculty was forced to ban them by 1925; a campus wag asked, "How is a classroom like a Ford?" The answer was, "Each has a crank in front and is full of nuts." If the faculty introduced "freshman week" to be kind to the new student and to help get him settled, the rest of the student body took up from there. "Ratting" became the major student avocation of the decade. Through the fall months, the freshman "rat" was subjected to all kinds of treatment, most of it bad. The rats could be found "cleaning" the intersection of College and Main streets by Dillard's Drugstore with their bricks at about any hour; they could be easily spotted, too, carrying around their pillows on campus in anticipation of a paddling that was inevitable at the hands of the sophomores. Nothing gave the upperclassmen more glee than watching the bewildered rats sort through the huge heap of shoes on the back quad—"the Shoe Scrimmage"—hoping to reclaim a pair that looked vaguely familiar.

The campus newspaper kept the students fairly up to date on current affairs. Warren Harding and his troubles with Teapot Dome apparently cost the Republicans the campus election of 1924, as the students soundly defeated Calvin Coolidge. The starry-eyed faculty, true to form, "firmly supported the Progressive Robert LaFollette however." The paper also reported the latest national polls on "necking," and did its best to encourage school spirit and to support the athletic program. Even the editors, though, could admit that school spirit could be carried too far. After a particularly rewarding football victory, the paper pleaded with its readership to "refrain from painting the score in the future on the houses in town; the sidewalks would do just as well."

Coach "Pinky" Spruhan was welcomed back as a campus hero in 1921 and took up where he left off, as exemplified by a 186-0 shellacking of Randolph-Macon in 1922. The football teams enjoyed continued success through the period. Having people with Hollywood-sounding names on the teams—the captain of the 1924 squad was Hunk Hurt—how could they lose? The Monogram Club opened a student store to sell supplies and snacks in an effort to underwrite athletic program costs. The campus witnessed its first volleyball tourney in 1924, and long before Adolph Hitler, the college sponsored its "Swastika" Tennis Club in 1921.

The Monogram Club was organized to help sporting events and raise money for the teams. They ran a snack bar for years to supplement the athletic budget. (Courtesy Salem Times-Register)

Another Roanoke victory from the early twenties. An anonymous letterman remembers: "Coach Pinky Spruhan was a demanding—and to some of the players—a heartless and cruel martinet. On a particularly hot afternoon, Spruhan required one-half of the players to face the other players in crouched positions. Spruhan, at one end of the double line of players, would tip a football and yell, 'Charge!' As the players in the two lines charged repeatedly against each other, sweat appeared on all players and blood appeared on some. After one of the vicious charges, a player looked at his hand that had wiped blood from his partially-ripped ear. Spruhan yelled, 'Yes, G— d—! That's blood. Now get down all of you and CHARGE!!' "

The Maroon starting five of 1923 take photography to new heights in this yearbook shot.

The clothing has changed but the site of graduation has not. A commencement on the front quad in the early twenties. (Courtesy *Salem Times-Register*)

Academic affairs would also rebound nicely by the mid-1920s. Admission standards were raised to new heights, and for the first time, an imposed "system of scholarship" was implemented. It introduced minimum academic averages necessary to remain enrolled. In its first year in place, thirteen percent of the student body flunked out; the new standards had a sobering effect on those who remained behind. Smith called for the termination of the Prep School, calling it "an evil situation" that had no place any longer in a college setting. After a couple of years, the student body had certainly become leaner but undeniably stronger too.

The faculty introduced a number of new courses and programs. A department of commerce and business administration appeared in 1921, and a host of new offerings in journalism, physical education, the languages, and especially the sciences were added to the catalog. Letter grades appeared for the first time in 1923, replacing numerical averages, and that hated icon of the student, the blue book, was first introduced three years later. The senior thesis was finally abolished in 1925. In order not to appear lax, however, the faculty had passed a "Bad English" resolution the year before requiring that any student who produced written work that was judged to be substandard would have to repeat a basic English composition course. The "Bad English" resolution appeared in the college catalog until 1939, when it was called the "Poor English" resolution, thereby correcting the faculty's "bad English."

The college reestablished its summer school in 1923, opened an extension office in Roanoke City, and offered special summer institutes for community educators, including separate workshops for the area's black teachers. To right a past wrong, the faculty voted in 1922 to grant degree diplomas to all the women who had successfully completed a course of study at Roanoke; thus the "special students" had finally been rescued from limbo.

With the successful completion of the endowment drive and the regirding of the academic program, the faculty rejoiced when the Southern Association elected in 1927 to accredit the college.

"HARD-DRINKING, CIGARETTE-PUFFING, LICENTIOUS AMAZONS"

What could be more harmless than an address by Dr. Charlie entitled "The Social Life of Our College Students" given before the National Lutheran Educational Association? Or so he thought! But the day after his 9 January 1924 speech, the account in the *New York Times* was far different from what Dr. Charlie thought he said.

According to Smith, in a letter addressed to the *Times* on 18 January, his main argument was that American society was suffering a general moral breakdown, not only in "the homes of the humble" but in "the homes of many so-called best families." The cure came not in legislation, not in the expectation that schools and colleges would correct bad habits developed in the home, but "in the building of proper homes and in sympathetic Christian education."

The *Times* reporter heard a far different speech.

The girl of today, and in particular the college girl, was the subject of bitter denunciation yesterday by a Lutheran educator, who characterized them as voluptuous, decried their thirst for strong liquor, and condemned their petting parties. The attack was delivered by Dr. Charles J. Smith, President of Roanoke College, Roanoke, Va. . . . 'Some women in every age drank liquor,' said Smith, 'a few even enjoyed a smoke, many of them threw away their honor, but the world has never known the turning loose of such an army of hard-drinking, cigarette-puffing, licentious Amazons as walk our streets and invade our campuses today.

Dr. Charlie received hundreds of letters, some of support, some of protest, especially from women's colleges across the United States. The furor was incredible. Smith called the report "most unjust to the great body of American college women, as well as to me. I trust I am too chivalrous to make such a generalization as your paper suggests." Julius Dreher consoled Smith from his post in Panama: "I sympathize with you in the annoyance of having your remarks misunderstood and misrepresented. . . . You have a wonderful facility in the use of language, and I suppose that you have to be on your guard often not to let it become a 'fatal facility,' as I once heard it described."

CHAPTER 12

"A temporary expediency" 1927–1934

The view to town. Looking down the path from the front porch of the Administration Building.

Dr. Charlie resisted coeducation for as long as he could; with the Stock Market crash of 1929, the admission of women in the following year was "a temporary expediency."

The timing could not have been any better. With the endowment finally won in the summer of 1927 and full accreditation to follow in the fall, everyone was primed for a party. The spring of 1928 provided the perfect opportunity—not only to celebrate the college's recent good fortune but also to commemorate the college's Diamond Jubilee, seventy-five years since its charter of 1853.

For three days in June, the college revelled in its past and eagerly anticipated its future. The festivities were carefully planned, and all went off without a hitch, save the weather, which proved singularly uncooperative. Two days of rain washed out several events and forced folks attending a couple of other activities to go scurrying for cover. A special dedication service in honor of S. Carson Wells at the East Hill Cemetery had to be moved back to campus and into the gym. The weather could dampen the setting but clearly not the spirits.

Hundreds of sons of Roanoke had made it back to alma mater. Of those, none were more senior than Dr. James Henry Turner, Class of 1867, the oldest living graduate of the college. His remarks captivated the overflow audience in the gym: "I entered Roanoke in September, 1859—the same year and month in which the first oil well was discovered in this country. Take note of what has happened since and you will get some idea of the distance your speaker has traveled. In 1859, it was little Roanoke; little in plant, little in number of faculty, little in student attendance, little in finance, little in public appraisal. One exception, however, must be noted to this diminutive stature. I speak of the three men who conceived the idea of founding a college, viz.: Bittle, Yonce and Wells. They were men of sterling worth, men of vision, of courage, of faith."

None of the dignitaries in attendance was any more illustrious than former president, Julius Dreher. Now in his eighties, Dreher had taken command of the college at the young age of thirty-two and had invested the next twenty-five years of his life at the helm. Another quarter century had passed since then as Dreher reminisced in his address. He joked with his audience by suggesting that "if you could understand the agonizing struggle of the garrulity of age with the problem of compressing one thousand and one memories into a ten-minute address, you would feel the deepest sympathy for me in the present circumstances."

Buoyed by the excitement and optimism of the celebration, President Smith and the board got back to the routine business of operating a college with a new-found sense of dedication. A 1927 independent survey had prioritized campus needs and had concluded that the number-one concern must be a new gymnasium. Although the much anticipated and heralded present gym was fewer than twenty years old, it had become wholly inadequate. The study concluded that Roanoke's athletic facilities might indeed be the poorest of any college in the state. Armed with that kind of evidence, Dr. Charlie convinced the board to move ahead and begin construction. By the spring of 1929, contracts were approved, and excavation was underway. By January, 1930, the first basketball game of the season was played in the Maroon's new home.

Prospects loomed bright when the board met on campus in mid-October 1929. With the endowment safely in the bank and after a year to catch his breath, President Smith was prepared to strap on the armor again and move out to do battle. If the recently completed $500,000 dollar campaign had seemed fabulous at the time, Smith's announcement of a new one million dollar fund-raising effort must have sounded incredible. Believable or not, the board ratified the campaign and the college was prepared to redouble its endowment effort. Needless to say, before the ink was dry on the board's report and before Smith had purchased his first train ticket out of town, Wall Street laid its famous egg.

Now an old man, Julius Dreher returned to Salem in 1928 for the Diamond Jubilee celebration. The occasion marked the fiftieth anniversary of his election as president in 1878 when he was only 32.

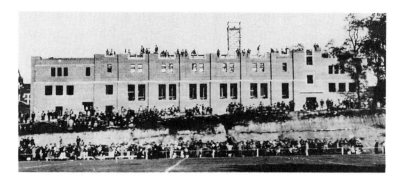

Alumni gym going up in the summer of 1929. It was home to Maroon basketball for over half a century.

The finished product; the gym sparkled for its dedication in 1930.

At first, no one sensed the enormous repercussions of the Crash; however, by the winter and spring of 1930, the nation and the college became painfully aware of the enormity of the collapse. With the spring board meeting, the college's cards were on the table, and every conceivable option was considered—from changing nothing to ending the college's very operations. Compromises and contingency plans were the order of the day. One option considered a potential merger of Roanoke with a suitable partner, thereby achieving a greater financial base to endure the crisis. Another plan explored the possibilities of curtailing a part of the college's program and becoming a junior or community college. Further discussion once again introduced the notion of coeducation.

Of all the combinations and possibilities, the board felt that coeducation could promise the greatest reward with the least amount of institutional dislocation. Coeducation could be achieved quickly,

and if the results were less than those required to succeed, more serious steps could then be added. Above all, the board made it clear that this business of coeducation was entirely a matter of "temporary expediency." No charter amendment was anticipated; the women might attend for a session or two—perhaps a year or two, before things would return to normal. After all, David Bittle had done the same thing during the Civil War. For the next several years as the Depression continued, the board routinely passed a statement announcing that women would again be permitted to attend the next year. In time, by 1934, such an announcement seemed so obvious and unnecessary that all concluded that women could continue for the time being. In a couple of years, the issue had become sufficiently blurred so as to confuse the whole question. Women simply stayed. Even today, over fifty years later, the status of women at Roanoke College has never been finally settled by the board of trustees!

One of the last student body shots; this one is in front of Bittle Library in the spring of 1927.

Through the next several treacherous years of worsening depression, the trustees steered a careful course between Scylla and Charybdis. The college was never forced to adopt the most drastic measures it had earlier considered, but always remained ready. The trustees labored tirelessly, in a time of failing banks and crumbling economy, in monitoring the endowment fund and in manipulating the college's holdings from one account to another. The college was forced to impose a ten-percent pay cut on all employees at one point, but conditions never deteriorated beyond that extent. The college had to borrow against its endowment when the Virginia Synod, having borrowed money from state banks to make good its subscription to the endowment drive originally, came back on the college with a request: that the school borrow the money against its endowment to give the financially strapped synod the ability to repay the loan. The church agreed to pay the college a four percent interest charge.

And if the Depression were not bad enough, death would claim the two leading benefactors of the college: James Elwood Jones in 1932, and in the following year, John Thomas Lupton. When all seemed dark, the horizon grew even darker without those two generous patrons.

Campus developments throughout the period obviously reflected the heavy hand of the Crash. The hundred-thousand-dollar price tag of the new gym hung around the school's neck like a noose. No new building projects would be started for a decade. Instead, the college had to make do with existing facilities, and "renovation" and "adaptation" became the buzzwords of the thirties.

Now a senior churchman and much heralded world figure, former President J. A. Morehead posed for this photograph in 1930. Even a partial list of Morehead's awards is impressive: Honorary degrees from Gettysburg College, the University of Leipzig, University of Paris, and Elizabeth University in Hungary; the German Order of the Red Cross from President Hindenburg; Knighthood from Denmark and Finland; nominated as a candidate for the Nobel Peace Prize by Sweden, Finland, Germany, and Denmark.

The subject of much campus competition, the old gym (on the left) became the "Lab-Theatre" in the thirties. The commons stands to the right.

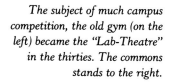

Once the new gym was opened, the old gym became quite the target of a campus bidding war. Discussions considered the space alternatively as the new library, a new chapel, a new science building with ample laboratory space, and an auditorium. Although Bittle Hall was hopelessly overcrowded with books and stacks, the cost involved in accommodating the collection in the old gym proved prohibitive. With that move stalled, the renovation of Bittle Hall into a chapel was postponed indefinitely; Bittle remains today that building on campus which looks most like an old chapel and never was but might have been! For competing interests, the battle for the old gym became a showdown between the science proponents and those who favored the establishment of a theatre on campus. The "laboratory-theatre" controversy was settled when President Smith decided in favor of "theatricals." The unofficial nickname "Lab Theatre" survived as the only name the room would ever know. When the building was renovated in 1978, the room was stripped of its rows of theatre chairs and became today's Ballroom. In the basement under the theatre, at least some of the library's overcrowding was eased by the locating of government documents and other voluminous special collections.

To assist the needs of the newly-arrived women students after 1930, the college acquired the use of a house on High Street located just north of Roselawn where Antrim Chapel sits today. The Ferguson home, the long-time residence of the college's librarian Janet Ferguson, offered the women a safe haven to study or to relax. There were several sitting rooms upstairs and a couple of parlors on the first floor to accommodate the women. Given the temporary nature of their admission, the college had not accepted any female boarding students. For the first eighteen women who arrived in the fall of 1930, and over the next several years, the Ferguson house was the best they could expect.

If the school could not generate the funds to construct a new building, it could at least hope to recondition some of its older structures. One such project took place in 1932 when the college acquisitioned the hallowed hall of the Ciceronians atop West Hall. The literary societies had been struggling anyway, and the Demostheneans had ceased operations for a couple of years after 1928. The space was simply too precious for the college to maintain in the interests of a few students. The Ciceronians were invited to double up with their long-standing nemesis on the other side of the Administration Building. Needless to say, the students were less than pleased. The vacated third floor was turned into additional space for the Physics Department and as home to its Engineering Lab.

The interior of the library was cramped and dingy. The students still managed to get their work done, though not without complaints!

The college undertook another renovation project in 1930, but this one was unintended. Fire had swept through a part of Yonce Hall and had caused eighteen thousand dollars damage. The school had adequate insurance to cover the rebuilding expenses; otherwise the college would have slipped ever farther into debt.

A final campus note was beautification. In many ways, the "Back Quadrangle" was born in the early thirties. A new system of roads and paths was laid out as a class project by the engineering students, and trees and shrubs were introduced to transform the **barren rear campus into a new Eden. The class of 1933 donated the funds to build an attractive brick** entrance off High Street, and a few finishing touches served to produce the Back Quad much as it still appears today.

Life in the Commons continued as always—a place of conversation, nourishment, and inevitably as a source of student complaints. Friday fish, in deference to the Catholics in the student body, served most typically to offend. Students routinely worried about "excessive beans," "poor bread," and "cold ham." Students often wondered why dead horses disappeared so quickly in Salem until the *Brackety-Ack* reminded them of "their sausage at breakfast and their hash at dinner." Stealing cream at the evening meal was an art, and back in the dorm, when the students added ice and fruit, the taste treat was something to write home about. Conduct in the dining hall was usually respectable enough as the students sat according to some club membership. Rival groups gleefully recorded Dean Brown's admonition to the Shenandoah Club one evening as he scolded them to "sling hash in a more manly way."

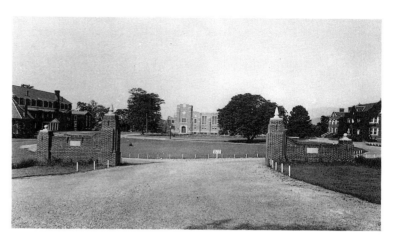

The new and improved Back Quad. The class of 1933 donated the entrance gates and the student engineering class helped lay out the road pattern.

BEANS TAKEN OFF OF COMMONS MENU!

A wave of protest and dissatisfaction prevailed about the Campus yesterday when it was officially announced that beans were to be taken from the Commons' Menu. Strudwick's office was the scene of a near riot and practically the whole student body was present and voiced its protest against the unprecedented action. Strudwick refused to comment, other than to say: "Boys, I've always bean good to you, but the bean must go."

A demonstration parade was held on Main Street and College Avenue and banners containing the following were carried: "We want beans, and more beans;" "They can't take them from us;" "John Paul Jones fought for the navy, we'll fight for the Navy Bean."

A petition has bean drawn up and signed by 241 students, 117 townspeople, and representatives of the following companies: Van Camp, Heinz, and Campbell, and it is expected that this petition will serve its intended purpose in restoring the bean to its esteemed place on the Commons' Menu.

Rawenoch, 1927

Student life through the late twenties and early thirties continued almost as if the Jazz Age had never ended. When Dean Charles Brown was asked what students needed most, he replied to the faculty "that the two essentials were that they be kept busy and clean." This is probably not what the students had in mind. In fact, in response to a *Brackety-Ack* survey in the fall of 1928 in regard to student "needs," one respondent offered this list: "smoking in classrooms, more liquor, co-education, cars for resident students, better food, erection of a stadium, hot orchestras for dances, and stickers that are really maroon and not red."

The nation's latest fads lost no time in reaching Salem. The advent of the yo-yo, checkers, ping pong, criecino, and numerous card games were all registered before the decade was out. When "that man Hoyle was on campus," there was action to be found; bridge was big, but poker was the rage. Stunts continued to occupy an inordinate amount of the students' creative potential. Blackboards suddenly turned white, and when the door knob to the third sections was hooked up to the wire door mat and all of that to the light socket, it gave a new meaning to the term "Welcome Mat." There were virtual battles over the rights to the Town's water tank and the privilege to inscribe the class's year in numbers on the side.

Fraternity life picked up in scale and excitement. "Rushing" and "pledging" were terms of the twenties and by 1930, all four fraternities had their own houses. Academics often suffered as evidenced by the semester's report of 1929: the four fraternities amassed grade point averages of 1.20, 0.92, 0.89, and 0.89 respectively. It should be noted, however, that that was based on a 2.50 scale.

Ratting continued in unfettered form, and the Rat Council wielded almost omnipotent power. The Rats could be accused, tried, convicted, and punished without any other college review. Only when the sentence was "expulsion" would the faculty step in to consider the case. The Rats were subjected to the normal abuse; the year was organized into three "periods"—the first ending at Thanksgiving, the next in February and the beginning of the spring semester and finally with Easter. At each stage, additional liberties were restored but hardly enough to make the year "fun." A Rat could not date until after Thanksgiving, and always had to be seen outside his room with his cap on, be available for chores or errands at any hour, and be able to sing or recite the appropriate song or ditty on command. Not to be outdone, the Rat Council still made the Rats cheer a certain football yell every time they passed an old tree inside the gate where the road forked in the Back Quad. The only problem was that the tree had died one summer and the college had had the tree cut down. The upperclassmen were even more amused that next fall in watching the Rats cheer for the stump. With the arrival of "the local maidens," the Rat system was taxed but not defeated. After some confusion and heated discussion, the Rat women would have to wear caps and participate in most of the demands of the season.

Clubs and organizations by the dozens came and went through the period. Of those more seriously minded, the Aegis Club and Blue Key, established in 1930, attracted some of the brightest students. Departmental organizations flourished with the likes of an English Club, a Biology Club, the Chemical Society, a Classics Club, and a college debate team which won the state title in 1934. Who better than Henry Fowler to help found the "Credit Investment Committee" in 1928, a group dedicated to helping students invest their savings. The Harlequins continued to entertain audiences, and in the days before women students, the men had to play all the roles. Seeing future executive and Chairman of the Pennsylvania Railroad Stuart Saunders "in drag" in the production of "Tom, Dick, and Harry" would have been enough to startle even the most seasoned railroad investor. The first college choir offered its selections in 1934.

STOP! LOOK! THINK!
The Brackety-Ack
BOOSTING ROANOKE COLLEGE

VOLUME 13 — ROANOKE COLLEGE, SALEM, VIRGINIA, WEDNESDAY, MARCH 20, 1929. — NUMBER 17

What Is Wrong With Roanoke College?

Editor-in-chief Henry Fowler's parting shot at the Administration. Despite all that was wrong, the paper felt that the college could be salvaged.

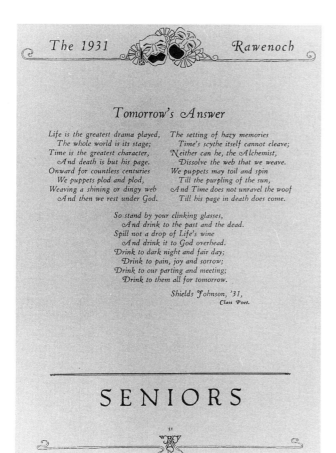

Class poet Shields Johnson went on to a career in journalism.

Maroon And Gray Loyalty Song

Words by
E. PENDLETON HOGAN '29

Music by
I. M. ELLIS '28

Marcia

Let ev-'ry stu-dent take his place,———— The bat-tle
Old Roa-noke's men will win this game,———— By fight-ing

cry rings loud;———— The stands are
hard to-day;———— Our men are

full, our men will face A foe that's strong and
strong and have the same Old loy-al spir-it

Copyrighted,1928, by Roanoke College
Published by Thornton W. Allen,113 W. 57th St.,New York City

*That song writing team of Hogan and Ellis offered this
rendition to the students in 1928.*

"THE GOLDFISH CLUB"

One day someone told three old students by the names of
Rochelle, Carr, and Repass that he wouldn't swallow a live goldfish for a dollar. Those three guys thought the idea over and
decided to see whether or not it was worth a dollar. So each of
them swallowed a live goldfish! And with that experimental act,
one of the most unique organizations of all time came into being
on the Roanoke Campus. They called their brainchild The
Goldfish Club.

It was some society! They had a Grand Goldfish for president,
and a Grand Porpoise (I think) for secretary, and all sorts of
incredible names for the other members. People clamored for
membership—they literally itched to be among the select few.
But, boy, the select few were choosy! When you got a bid you
were really honored. And what was more, you had to pay a dollar
initiation fee and the initiation consisted of swallowing a live
goldfish! I suspect that the three perpetrators of the scheme made
a lot of money.

The news spread around and the Associated Press took
pictures of the group. Even College Life heard about it and
devoted a long paragraph in eulogy. I had an uncle in Chicago
who read it and sent me the clipping. The Goldfish Club did
more for Roanoke College in the way of advertising that year
than Shields Johnson did with the whole news bureau.

It's a pity it died out. In fact, no one seems to know just what
did happen to it. Mike Reiley was the last surviving member,
bless his soul, and he is with us no more, alas.

"Vanishing Roanoke" by Walter Knobeloch. In *The Brackety-Ack,*
4 October 1933.

"WHAT IS WRONG WITH ROANOKE COLLEGE?"

By any measure, it would have to be considered one of the
most notable editions in the history of the *Brackety-Ack*. The
issue was no farce, no attempt at parody, no April Fool's edition.
Rather it was a scathing attack upon the Roanoke College
establishment. The banner headline asked "What Is Wrong With
Roanoke College?" and with that, the editor and staff launched
their offensive. They suggested that this paper should be
interpreted not as an attempt at "journalistic vilification," but an
honest, if painful, review of present college conditions and
policies. In short, the newspaper found the students *uninterested,*
the faculty *uncaring,* and the administration *unresponsive.* Roanoke
College had lost its mission, its purpose—"stagnation," the paper
said, had won out over "progress." The *Brackety-Ack* cartoon
pictured the college as a mongrel with the caption "A whipped
dog wondering what's the matter."

The list of grievances seemed endless; the general student
apathy headed the list. "Why," the editor asked, "are
administration edicts accepted without a murmur by a too pacific
spiritless student body?" The paper recounted the numerous
student organizations that had, over the previous few years, fallen
by the wayside. The athletic program was in disrepair,
intramurals—a shambles, and traditions by the score had become
lost and forgotten. Faculty morale was decaying, and so too was
the physical plant. The paper's assessment of that year's freshman
class was contained in an article entitled "Can You Squeeze Blood
Out Of A Turnip?" Day students took more from the college
than they gave; petty fraternity squabbling only factionalized
things more, and overzealous campus police made it all even
worse.

The issue closed with the comment: Our "intentions were
of the best, and results are longed for in action, rather than in
anger."

But the editorial staff was prepared for anger. The students
expected some response, they recall today, to be disciplined or
perhaps, even dismissed. Sure enough, the next morning they
were summarily ordered to the President's office where they were
sternly lectured and reprimanded but nothing more. That issue
of the *Brackety-Ack* had been intended to have been their last—
their parting shot, so to speak. The next year's staff was already
in place, eager to begin their assignment.

Ok—enough with the suspense. When did all of this take
place and in regard to the editor—who was that masked man?
The date was 20 March 1929—and the editor-in-chief? None
other than our own, beloved Henry H. Fowler!

On the lighter side, the list of social groups is just as
long, if not as impressive. A secret society, "The
Mystic Knights of the Sea," left its name if not its
purpose to posterity, but the "Bi-Weekly Bath
Association" made its avowed purpose pungently
obvious. The Owl Club specialized in late night
entertainment while the Goldfish Club was one of the
earliest student groups in the nation to popularize the
"art" of swallowing goldfish. The Associated Press
even sent a reporter to interview the students and to
witness the initiation of several new members.

May 4, 1927

Dear Roanoke College Mother:

We are planning to have all the mothers of Roanoke College students in Salem on Saturday and Sunday, May 14 and 15, and we want you to be sure and come.

We assure you that at no other time will you be able to see college life in cross-section as well. Luncheon, athletic contests, dinner, Glee Club and Dramatic Club performances will feature our program. Every minute, from 11:30 A.M., Saturday thru 6:00 P.M. Sunday will be taken.

This is the first affair of its kind that we have attempted. We are all proud of our mothers and we want them to see college life as it really is and to entertain them with our various activities.

If your son hasn't already written you please write him about this matter. Advance reports show that there will be a goodly number present.

This is not an invitation from a single organization. Faculty, student body and civic organizations of Salem join in with us.

Next week we will send you a duplex card on which you will be requested to signify your intention, and please be sure to say "yes."

You will find enclosed a tentative program for the occasion. Mother, you know you can't miss it.

Effort is being made to secure homes to house visiting mothers and it is expected that all will be cared for.

A. D. SMITH, General Chairman
Roanoke College Mother's Day

The tentative program mailed to mothers included a morning chapel service, luncheon for out-of-town mothers at the Roanoke Country Club sponsored by the Fortnightly Club, an inspection of dormitories and buildings *(Clean up those rooms, boys!),* a track meet, a tea hosted by the Junior Woman's Club of Salem, dinner in the Commons and a play "Tom, Dick and Harry" presented by the Harlequins. Sunday's activities called for a Mother's Day Service with Dr. Charlie giving the sermon, and an "Automobile Tour of Surrounding Country." Sixty mothers attended the event. "From the arrival of the first mother on the campus until the last entrained for home not a minute was spared them in dullness. Faculty, students and townspeople entered wholeheartedly into making it a red letter day for the college."

It did not take women long to form their own groups. The Sphinx became their first sorority, and others followed close behind. A YWCA was soon organized, and women enjoyed general invitations to join most other groups on campus as well. All things considered, the integration of women into the college routine was accomplished with remarkably little protest or confusion.

Campus activities and events always provided ready outlets for student involvement. Halloween continued as a "special" time, made even more memorable the year the students managed to get "Dad" Strudwick's truck up on the porch of the Administration Building. During the maneuvers, the vehicle got loose and almost careened down the front steps and was saved only by one of the pillars which it nicely gouged. The scars on the pediment were a source of student pride for years. The college sponsored its first May festival by 1930 and also offered Mother's Day in the spring and Father's Day in the fall so that Dad "could watch a football game." After a few years of juggling both events, Parents Day became the solution.

The first Mother's Day was held in 1927, boasting luncheon, teas and tours. Here are some moms assembled outside of the Commons for the Annual Mother's Day in May 1931.

There were always dances and none in the early thirties more popular than "mid-winters." And with dance bands like "Al Katz and His Kittens," these affairs had to provide unforgettable memories. Talkies debuted in 1927, and soon thereafter, Salem and Roanoke offered a number of brand-spanking-new "movie palaces." Roanoke's Grand Theatre opened in 1928 with "Ben Hur," long before the Charlton Heston version. Students found plenty to laugh at when the Salem Theatre opened with the Marx Brothers in "Coconuts."

Life in the "Sex-tions" could be challenging. The normal highjinks could always be counted upon, and when Mr. Bowman's apples were in season, the roof atop Yonce Hall doubled as "the fort." To the unsuspecting visitor down below, a simple stroll through the Back Quad could become a harrowing adventure. Sections' rivalries took on an added dimension in 1931 when each hall, except third, published its own newspaper. The students joked

about Dr. Charlie and his never-ending references to "our depression" and loved reporting that Dr. Longaker "studebakered" into Roanoke one evening to deliver a speech on "Memory," but had to return quickly to Salem to retrieve his notes, which he had forgotten.

Jetts on Main Street and the College Inn, between the bank and Town Hall on College Avenue, served as the most popular college hangouts, and the "Bulletin Board" in the Ad Building kept students apprised of the action on campus. Al Smith beat Herbert Hoover in the 1928 campus election, and Franklin Roosevelt's supporters stuffed the ballot box four years later. Students decried the kidnapping of the Lindburgh baby in 1932, the most sensational crime "since the Crucifixtion" according to H. L. Menchen. They marvelled at the announcements of the building of the Blue Ridge Parkway and the Appalachian Trail in the following year.

The Jazz Age had nothing on these guys; the Maroon and Gray Orchestra was in existence for several years.

Parking was at a premium in this busy Main Street shot circa 1930. (Courtesy Salem Times-Register)

The students celebrate a football victory over Virginia Tech with a bonfire. Salem residents lived in dread of too many Maroon victories; bonfires often claimed porch furniture, wood piles, and even fences.

Football continued as the sport of choice, and in 1927, the college hosted the familiar "Homecoming" pageant for the first time. Most seasons were begun with a pep rally and a bonfire and the blaze of 1928 was particularly impressive. The Rats did an outstanding job in collecting sticks, branches, and available lumber throughout north Salem. Unfortunately, some of the material was not actually "available," and when the residents complained about losing porch furniture, parts of fences, and piles of firewood, the college was forced to keep an eye out in the future. To travel in style, Pinky Spruhan acquired the "Parlor Car," a team bus to enable the Maroons to arrive at the site in comfort and also to allow them to attend other games that "they ought to see." Cheerleaders were popularly elected and the Monogram Club continued its store for supplies and snacks.

A Darn Doggish Dog

"He's not much to look at, that's easy to see"—but he's every inch a dog. And that speaks a volume. Harry, Jr., the new college mascot, was officially accepted as part of Roanoke College during the summer months, and returning students have greeted the cross-bred canine as if he were a welcomed character in the annals of college life.

It has been said the best friend a man has in the world may turn against him and become his enemy, and the one absolutely unselfish friend that man can have in this egoistical world, the one that never deserts him, the one that never proves ungrateful or treacherous, is his dog. Such a statement exemplifies the true, intelligent and faithful trust that can be placed in a mere brute.

Harry, Jr., as doggish as he appears to be, has already won his place in the affections of the majority of this student-body. His presence lends an atmosphere to the campus that can be appreciated only by true lovers of dogs.

The Brackety-Ack, 5 November 1931

The pride and joy of Roanoke athletics: the "parlor car" ready for a trip in the late twenties.

For a big game against Richmond one year, the administration announced that it would pay the way for any student who wanted to attend. Many did. Back in Salem, a new field and concrete and steel bleachers opened in 1928; lights were installed two years later; and in 1932, the addition of a loudspeaker made the game a real experience. Under the lights, the "Maroons" first appeared wearing gold and blue uniforms, close to the actual school colors, since it was reasoned that those colors would be "more flashy and visible at night." Whether it was the uniforms or not, Roanoke slipped by Bridgewater, 53-0.

When Coach Spruhan resigned in 1930, Gordon "Pop" White took the helm as head football coach and Director of Athletics. With the completion of the new gym in that year as well, Pop White had his hands full directing the new activities that the gym afforded. The new 20 foot by 60 foot pool in the basement allowed the college to offer a water polo team in 1931 and its first swim team by 1932. Volleyball, tether ball, and medicine ball were all introduced to the gym's facilities as was an intramural handball tournament in 1931.

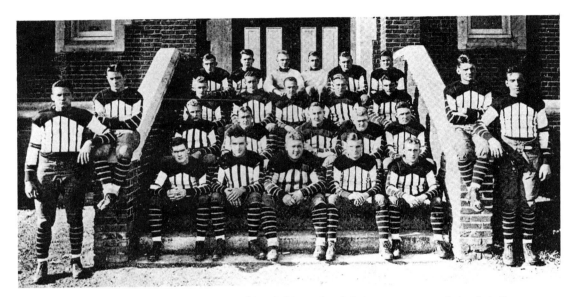

Sporting their new uniforms, these Maroons could probably confound their opponents merely by their "test-pattern" design.

Ready for the kick-off at a Roanoke home game; looking north up Market Street.

Baseball was halted in 1929 but returned by 1932 because of student "demonstrations." Basketball continued in popularity, and the program introduced wrestling in 1927, boxing in 1928, and the first golf team in 1934. Women cheerleaders debuted in 1931 and so did the school's first official mascot: "Harry, Junior," a dog. The football team also saw other service when Franklin Roosevelt came to town in 1934 to dedicate the Veterans Hospital. After the dedication, there was a brief motorcade through the streets of Salem, and there, marching beside the Presidential convertible, was the Maroon football squad, offering a little extra "secret service."

The Academic program suffered the same kind of institutional retrenchment that affected the campus as a whole. There was little thought of expansion, but rather greater effort was applied to bettering the existing course of studies. The college officially awarded its last Masters degree in 1927 but enhanced its undergraduate program by instituting special honors courses into the curriculum. The program was made more flexible in 1933 with additional electives and a pre-Engineering department represented an actual net increase to the college's course offerings. The first "Dean's List" was published in 1931 to recognize outstanding student achievement. Faculty attached a special code of "moral integrity" to final degree requirements, which no doubt embarrassed a few would-be graduates.

Bachelors of Science outnumbered Bachelors of Arts by three to one. All students were invited to hear the likes of philosopher-historian Will Durant and journalist Lincoln Steffens as they addressed campus audiences. The faculty first donned academic regalia for the opening convocation of 1928 and struggled with official bookstore order forms for their courses booklist. The "bookstore," such as it was, was located under the stairs on the first floor of the Ad Building and was open for the first few days of each semester—long enough for students to make their purchases. For the rest of the time, the little room served as the campus post office.

A new chapel schedule was introduced in the late twenties which officially ended the religious requirement of chapel attendance. Chapel was still held three days a week, and students were of course invited to attend. On the other two days, attendance was required, but the program was of "a secular nature" with a campus topic under consideration.

The chapel doors of Trout Hall; services were held in Trout into the1950s. The second and third floors could be reached only by an outside porch and second-story entrance.

The old campus looking west from High Street.

The library had been successfully reclassified into the "new" Dewey system by 1930. A couple of years later, it celebrated another Carnegie foundation gift of eight thousand dollars for books.

Several new faculty members appeared on campus during the period, including long-time classics and fine arts professor Miles Masters, and to head the physics and engineering programs, Charles Raynor. All full professors were housed in the Ad Building where they might keep one eye on the students and another trained on the administration. Professional development for the faculty became an increasing commitment. By the late 1920s, there was a specific budget amount to enable faculty to travel to professional conventions and meetings. On campus, faculty sponsored their "Round Table" for discussions and also threw "paper parties" where faculty members offered a paper or a presentation to the others assembled.

Roanoke had weathered the crash and had been made more lean by the resultant depression. By mid decade, the college was prepared to move ahead.

CHAPTER 13

"The ivy still grows," 1934–1941

With an article entitled "The Ivy Still Grows," Dr. Charles Smith inaugurated the return of the Roanoke College *Collegian* in 1935. This publication, started by Bittle himself in 1875, had been dormant for over a decade. Its return as an alumni magazine was hailed not only by graduates but by current students and faculty as well. Dr. Charlie's comforting message reassured the alums that all was well back home at alma mater. In several ways, the little article set the tone for the period before the cataclysm of a second World War.

If the early twenties had been a time of crisis and stern reflection, the middle years of the decade offered a frenetic pace in the pursuit of endowment. If a moment of peace and prosperity existed by 1928 and 1929, that tranquility had been dashed by the dislocation of the depression. By the mid-thirties, Roanoke had become a leaner institution. Women were present but not permanently; programs entailed few frills, and the student character had become overwhelmingly local. By 1935, after several years of self-denial, perhaps both the student body and the institution were prepared to move forward and moreover, to have some fun.

President Smith's annual report to the board of trustees seemed to reflect a growing confidence and spirit. "It should be noted," Dr. Charlie said, "that up until the present moment our College has weathered successfully the storms incident to a disturbed financial situation the world over. Since the onslaught

of the so-called depression, we have steadily increased our enrollment until it is now at full capacity and we have also enhanced the effectiveness of our strictly educational program. All of this has been done on a pay-as-you-go basis. In these lean years we have borrowed no money either for capital expenditures or operating accounts. This record has won for us in the educational and business world the reputation of being a stable and soundly managed institution."

The college's enrollment had indeed taken off. From a paltry one hundred and thirty-six students in 1920, the college had almost tripled in size to attain in 1940 a record enrollment of 396 students. Indeed for the first time, Smith had asked the board to limit enrollment by "25-50" in 1935. The demand for tuition dollars was too great, however; and the college could not heed the president's request. The strain on the campus physical plant was real enough too. During the two decades, the college was able to add only a gym to the register of facilities. There were no new dorm rooms to handle the influx of new faces and no accommodations whatsoever for women. When the fall enrollment of 1937 swept onto the campus, hard-pressed administrators were busy stashing students all over campus in any available space, including the commons, storage areas, and the YMCA rooms.

In attempting to keep pace with the bounty of students, Smith resolved to increase both the faculty and the administrative staff. Although the number of

Dr. Charlie wasn't kidding about "the ivy still grows." In this shot, the ivy is about to engulf Trout and Bittle Halls.

professors and professionals moved steadily upwards, from twenty-six in 1920 to forty in 1940, the improvement in no way matched the marked growth in the student body. A key element involved in the president's strategy was the restructuring of the administrative network of the college. Between 1936 and 1940, the prototype of the modern college cabinet system made its appearance. The institution combined the positions of treasurer and bursar into the newly-created Vice-President for Finance and nominated Happy Mann for the post. The first director of alumni affairs was Miller Ritchie in 1936, and by 1940, he was appointed the college's first admissions director. In that year, the trustees also named their first development officer, Stewart Hanks, as Director of the Living Endowment. As college promotion became a larger concern, the first full-time public relations officer appeared, and by 1941, with the ever-increasing and more permanent looking women's enrollment, Helen Hobart was hired as the college's first Dean of Women.

Reform as well came to the membership of the Board of Trustees. Since the last charter amendment in 1927, three-fifths of the board were to be Lutherans maintaining membership in a congregation in the Synod of Virginia. While the change made the college more mindful of church interests, the decision had rendered the board more ecclesiastical than financial. More simply put, there were just not enough wealthy Lutherans in Virginia. The board had served the college well in rendering advice and in steering a difficult course through the treacherous waters of depression. But what the college needed most was more money and less advice. By 1941, the college was more than one hundred thousand dollars in debt. President Smith and the trustees recognized that some new accommodation with the church was in order. Accordingly, in 1937, discussions began which resulted in a new relationship between the board and the Lutheran synod. In exchange for deleting the three-fifths requirement for the board, the college and church agreed that as long as the president was a

The faculty in the mid-thirties. In the front row (from left to right) are Dad Strudwick, Frank C. Longaker, President Smith, Dean Charles Brown, and D.R. Carpenter.

Lutheran of good standing, the college would be protected. Moreover, the church was given the right to approve all future trustee selections. Finally, the number of trustees was increased to thirty to provide further opportunity to broaden the college's financial base. The changes were ratified by the respective bodies of both institutions and certified by the state as a chartered amendment in 1939.

To get matters off on the right foot, the newly reconstituted board asked to meet with the entire faculty so that the two groups might get better acquainted. Plus, there was another celebration to get ready for. During the late 1930s, the college began rechecking some dates and asking a few questions. It was still true that the college had been chartered in 1853, but its institutional history had not begun then. Eleven years earlier, in 1842, Reverends Bittle and Baughman had opened their little school at Mt. Tabor. Why not, several key officials queried, list that date as the official beginning of the school? The phrase "founded in 1842" soon replaced "chartered in 1853" on all college publications and stationery. And of course, that eleven-year slight-of-hand meant that 1942 instead of 1953 would mark the college's centennial. If that was the case, there was much to be done. Doubtless a few students must have wondered in examining the *Cherobiblos,* their Student Handbook, how the academic session of 1938–39 was the college's eighty-sixth year and in returning the next fall, found 1939–40 labeled as "our 98th year."

The pressures of a decade and a half had begun to take their toll on "Doctor Charlie." By 1936, the president had begun to tire, and in the spring of 1937, he asked the board for some time away. The board willingly acknowledged and wished the president a speedy recuperation. The new administrative structure proved immediately successful in helping to pick up the slack caused by Smith's departure. An assistant to the president was hired to handle many of the routine duties of the office. Although the president did not officially return until the fall of 1938, Dr. Charlie, in many ways, had never fully stepped out. He was still around for official functions and major decisions, and he never once missed his column for *The Collegian.*

With respect to the campus during the period 1935–1941, the first five years found the college making do with existing facilities under a policy of on-going renovations. In the last years of the pre-war period, the school dedicated two new structures within a couple of months. In 1935, the college spent fourteen thousand dollars in an attempt to spruce up the aging library, and to improve the heating system and to add new baths to the Sections.

TRIBUTE TO A CONSTRUCTIVE DREAMER

Most of us dream dreams. Some of us only dream—we do not have the energy and resourcefulness to transform our vision into reality. Many of us made the effort but fail. A few succeed.

Those of us who mourn the recent passing of Dr. W.A.R. Goodwin, '89, have the satisfaction of knowing that he was one of those few . . . that he saw the great dream of his life come true.

That dream was a restored Williamsburg, a recreated colonial city that might stand as a symbol of the proud history of the Virginia colony and that might bring Americans to a more enlightened appreciation of the lives and deeds of Washington, Jefferson, Henry, and other colonial patriots.

Williamsburg, on the day the dreamer died of heart disease after two years of illness (September 7, 1939), approximated or exceeded his original dream. The principal buildings had been restored, with an expenditure of more than $17,000,000, the streets once more followed the colonial plan, the colonial capital greeted the visitors who drove eastward on Duke of Gloucester, Bruton Parish Church the oldest Episcopal edifice in America in continuous use, was undergoing final restoration touches and over the entire community historical homes of individuals had returned to their original guise.

It was the happy combination of Goodwin's dream and Rockefeller's money that brought about the present status of Williamsburg as perhaps the nation's number one historic shrine.

Now Williamsburg is indeed a dream town. Along the quiet, broad streets, paved with material that resembles the gravel on a country road, a coach-and-four may be seen, mixed in among the modern automobiles of the latest make. Young ladies bedecked in colonial costumes welcome visitors to the famous old homes that have been restored and are open for public inspection.

No son of Roanoke has ever been more loyal. No one has ever reflected more wholesome credit upon the name of his Alma Mater. The dreamer has passed on . . . but his living dream and the inspiration of his achievement remain to challenge us who pay tribute to his memory.

From an article by Miller Ritchie in *The Roanoke Collegian,* October 1939.

By 1938, the college had added new walkways to the front and rear campus, and had also made improvements to the rear porch of the Ad Building: Henry Hill's tolling station had never looked better. And speaking of Henry Hill, the students and faculty toasted the campus guardian with a special celebration in 1936, marking his twenty-fifth anniversary of service to the school. The natural beauty of the campus was enhanced too with the planting of new oak trees on the front lawn and new hedges between the Ad Building and the Lab-Theatre in the Back Quad. Dad Strudwick's legendary squirrels had a new home in which to nest.

After the ill-fated attempt at banishing automobiles from campus had failed, college officials finally acknowledged the obvious and in 1939 paved the first parking lot right behind the Ad Building. It served as a central point on campus. A service road continued up Colorado Street, behind present day Bartlett and Lucas halls, and then turned behind Miller Hall to connect with the Back Quad and onto High Street.

Old Miller Hall. The entrance door was moved from the side porch to the front in the early thirties. The door was moved again in 1947 when the building was expanded.

Surveying his domain. President Smith is caught on the Ad Building steps in this 1939 photo. (Peter Boisseau photo)

"THE YEAR CHRISTMAS CAME LATE

Henry Lucas was a tool manufacturer from Cleveland, Ohio, who happened to be in Salem on business one bright December day in 1939. Lucas's attorney, R. M. Calfee, was a Roanoke College graduate and a member of the college's board of trustees. In the course of their association, Lucas surely must have known of Calfee's alma mater but he had never been on campus before and had never met with the president, Dr. Charlie. From all accounts, Lucas had never been solicited for financial help either.

Unbeknownst to his friend Calfee, Henry Lucas paid a little visit to campus on December 28. He found President Smith in his office and the two men struck up a conversation. When it finished, Lucas had embraced the president's project of a new chemistry building to the tune of fifteen thousand dollars. The president was delighted over his good fortune.

Immediately, plans went forward for the design and construction of the science facility. Dr. Charlie, apparently never afraid to look a gift horse in the mouth, decided to press his luck. In September 1940, the president took the building's architect and Dr. Harry Johnson, the head of the chemistry department, to Cleveland to meet with Mr. Lucas again. Once more, Lucas was impressed and agreed to Dr. Charlie's request for an additional $25,000. Additionally, Lucas offered a final $20,000 for furnishings and equipment several months later so that if the building could not be the biggest, it might be the best.

Henry Lucas returned to Salem only once—a year later for the dedication of his hall. Death would claim him suddenly only a few months later. Henry Lucas's hall still stands on campus today, a testament to one man's good will and a symbol of the college's good fortune.

At his tolling station, Henry Hill waits to signal the end of a class period. Today the bell hangs in his bell tower, still marking the class schedule, but is driven by a computer. Somehow, Henry did it better.

Two residences opened during the period as the first two dormitories for women. The old Pi Kap house, located behind the faculty apartments at the front gates of campus, was renovated into one home for women. Professor Henry Hildreth's former house, located along the campus loop road where the Life Science Building now stands, was transformed into "Hildreth Hall" and served as a women's residence for a time.

A major step forward for women finally came in 1941 with the completion of Smith Hall, named in honor of the college's president, and promptly nicknamed "The Coop" by the male students. Tucked away in the extreme southwestern corner of the campus, the hall was geographically at the point farthest from the Sections . . . and the males. The hall faced the front campus, and its back door bordered the town alley. Once across the porch and inside the door, any visitor would have found the formal parlor on the left and Dean Hobart on the right—an effective buffer to the women beyond!

The Ad Building saw additional improvements by the end of the decade. The academic offices of the dean, registrar, and guidance officer were all moved into the newly renovated east side of the first floor. The engineering students were put to good work again by designing and establishing the campus phone/intercom system which operated well into the 1950s.

The final act of the period was easily the largest. The dream of a science building had dated back to the days of Julius Dreher and a "wish list" of the Semi-Centennial of 1903. Now, on the eve of the Centennial, a science building materialized. Henry Lucas, a stranger to town and campus, offered his help to enable the school to realize its dream. When the building was dedicated in October, 1941, the college had one of the finest chemistry facilities in the nation.

This 1939 aerial photo shows Roanoke before the addition of Lucas and Smith Halls in 1941. (Peter Boisseau photo)

In the world of academic affairs, 1939 became a watershed year in terms of policy and progress. The culmination of two years of study and review, the faculty report outlined a series of new academic procedures designed to make Roanoke and its graduates more academically sound. The policy included higher admission standards, a new freshman advising and guidance system, the separation of the student body into junior and senior divisions, and the formulation of a new honor code to reassert the ethical underpinnings of the entire structure. The impact of the new system was immediately felt. Of the 268 applications for the freshman class in 1939, only 136 were accepted. By the end of the fall semester, the president, reflecting the tougher college standards now in place, summarily dismissed thirty-two students for "bringing no credit to themselves, their families, or their college."

Frank Longaker, Luther A. Fox Professor of Philosophy and Psychology, headed up the new guidance center. To assist Longaker, ten faculty members acted as special freshman advisors to help these new students initially in getting settled and to continue to guide them until they declared "a major course of study." With that declaration supported by sound academic performance, the student would be permitted into the senior division. The class of 1941 was the first from Roanoke to graduate with specific "majors."

Grade distribution reflected the renewed sense of dedication to academic quality. And academic integrity went hand in hand. Students were told that the only thing they needed during an exam was "a pen—there was no need of paper, conversation, or leaving the room."

There were other academic changes as well, and none more significant than the resignation of the college's first true Dean, Charles Brown. After nineteen years, Brown had decided that it was time to return to the History Department and to full-time teaching. Moreover, he had just been elected Mayor of Salem and felt that he just did not have the additional time to do justice to both jobs. In any event, Associate Professor of Psychology Earl Broadwater assumed the duties of the office.

Smith Hall debuted in 1941 as the first dormitory specifically designed for women; the college boys soon knew it as "the Hen House" or simply the "Coop."

The college offered an engineering program for years; the old Ciceronian Hall atop Miller Hall was renovated as a drafting laboratory for the students.

Audio-visual education made its appearance in the thirties. The students demonstrate the latest in film projectors for this public relations photo.

Dad Strudwick poses in front of his Commons. The much-beloved student confidant died suddenly in the fall of 1935. The students erected a bench in his honor which stands today in the quad.

The faculty recommitted itself to coeducation in 1940 and hoped that the board would do likewise; alas, the trustees felt unpressured by the measure. The faculty also reaffirmed the "integral nature" of summer school in 1940 and took steps to develop its potential even further. The faculty watched intently during a workshop presentation entitled "Visual Education" as the wonders of audio-visual instruction appeared on campus in 1937. New courses continued to be offered, like Business Law taught by Judge Frederick L. Hoback; and by 1940 nothing caused a greater stir than the introduction of an "aeronautical course" sponsored by the Civilian Aeronautics Authority.

The age also marked the passing of an era. Since the 1860s, the college had not been without Julius Dreher. As student administrator, president, and faithful advisor, Dreher marked the summer of 1938 as the sixtieth anniversary of his election as president. Two months later, Dreher was gone at the age of

ninety-one. The college had lost its other former president just two years before, when John Alfred Morehead, in declining health after a decade and a half of tireless European labors, returned to Salem to make his peace. Death had claimed his brother, Wythe, the previous year bringing to a close a half-century of dedicated service to the English Department. The students were stunned by the sudden death of "Dad" Strudwick in 1936 and constructed a bench to his memory. It still stands in the front lawn today, watching visitors admire the campus that he worked so hard to beautify.

The period also marked the true final demise of the two ancient debating societies: the Ciceronians and the Demostheneans. After more than a decade of sporadic activity, the death knell was sounded finally in 1939. The trustees mourned their passing, and the English Department offered its first course in public speaking in an attempt to fill the vacuum.

"Join the Literary Society," are words of ironic wisdom doled to freshmen in the "Rat Bibles." For many past years the Literary Society has been the Freshman forte. More than one future Maroon leader received his training in the late Ciceronian room.

But now the Ciceronian has admittedly given up the ghost. After a brief struggle against overwhelming odds and non-student interest, the Literary club died this fall as quickly as a chick embryo placed in sulphuric acid.

Students, who have been here longer than others, may scan their memory books to recall that many years ago Roanoke boasted two literary groups, the Demosthenians and the Ciceronians. Many were the happy hours spent by the two forces in patting each other on the back with knives. It was a friendly rivalry. But one morning the College awoke and discovered it was minus one literary society. The Demosthenians had gone to join that ancient Greek from whom they had taken their name.

Rapidly the ranks of Ciceronians swelled and contentment reigned in Ciceronian hall; but with the advent of the radio, the campus literati found little time to spare from their loud speak-ers. Graver and graver grew the plight of the Ciceronians and late this fall it unwillingly decided to join the passing parade by a bygone era. . . .

One thing no one denies: The need for a campus self-expression outlet through the medium of a literary organization is essential. What appears most singular to the Brackety-Ack is that the large number of students who are, ostensibly, preparing themselves for the ministry or law are not grasping the advantages offered by such an organization as a literary club or debating society where forensic opportunities are afforded. It is these groups who should lead the way. . . .

The Brackety-Ack has long sensed the day when a literary society would be spoken of in the past tense. It has forecast the apathetic decline in debating. But now rather than grind the mill writing obituaries, it would suggest than an organized student forum be established. A forum with definite, faculty sponsors, definite, elected leaders, and specific programs. Student interest is ripe for such an endeavor.

An editorial from the Brackety-Ack, *Feb. 2, 1940.*

Students and faculty alike enjoyed the "Bull Sessions" made popular in the late thirties where both teacher and pupil could informally share thoughts and ideas. The library struggled to find adequate stack space, not to mention study room for the students; by 1935, the library first offered Sunday hours in an attempt to avoid overcrowding. Student assistants also appeared for the first time, with several assigned to duties in the gym, a few others in the library, and thirteen selected as assistants to professors.

The student world of the late thirties echoed the sentiments of the nation as it first emerged from the depths of depression in 1935 and 1936, and then watched with quiet despair as Europe plunged back into the chasm of war by 1939. The enthusiasm and "collegiate" spirit of mid-decade were soon tempered by the sobering realities of world war. Student life at Roanoke found time for fun and games, but, increasingly, the figures across both oceans cast longer shadows.

Socially, life on campus had many dimensions. Students knew that short collars were in and with them, the bow tie or "bat tie" was the rage. Black suits were passé; blue suits, everyone knew, were the thing. Students scrambled for tickets to hear Nelson Eddy and Artie Shaw and their orchestras when they were in town and long complained that the college never managed to book "name bands" for them.

A much improved Bittle Library reopened in the late thirties. A new balcony and improved lighting made the old structure a much brighter place for study.

The pageantry of the May Court. May Queen Thelma L. Garst reviews members of her court in this 1937 photo.

Along with Homecoming in the fall, the May Festival each spring, replete with Queen, court, and dance, was a centerpiece of campus life each year. First staged in 1933, the May celebration contributed good times and lasting memories until its demise in the 1960s. The Senior Prom returned in the mid-thirties and the German Club dances continued to be as popular as ever. The students even petitioned Doctor Charlie for a "social hall" in 1937, and the president responded by calling the idea "a good one, if we only had the money."

Norman's had become the campus hang out of choice by 1935 but Jett's kept up the competition because "at Jett's, you could get beer." The Log Inn was the place for a special date or the ideal spot for the student to have Mom and Dad to take them out for a big dinner. A full course meal might set them back fifty cents, but as one satisfied student might have remarked, "it was worth it."

Orson Welles and his "War of the Worlds" caused havoc on campus too in the fall of 1938 as the students tied up campus phone lines for hours in their attempts to contact what was left of their world. They flocked to the Roanoke premier of "Gone with the Wind" in February, 1940, and noted with remorse the closing of the Confederate Veterans Home the year before. The students organized a campus dating bureau in 1936 and were attentive to the various "dating" and "co-ed" polls frequently run by the *Brackety-Ack.*

A big crowd turned out for the opening of the Salem Theatre at the corner of College and Main. (Courtesy Salem Times-Register)

The Lab-theatre hosts a matinee event.

A college drama from 1936/1937, "The Whispering Room."

The editors and writers of the student newspaper produced a superior product throughout the period. In an early April 1936 issue, the students were startled to learn that co-education had ended, and that the faculty had voted out the use of examinations as a means of evaluating student performance. What the students had unwittingly discovered, of course, was the paper's first April Fool's satire issue, which started a tradition that continues to the present. The *Brackety-Ack* covered campus news and issues with a vengeance. Through its "Observer Columns," the paper detected all that moved on campus. And with its connection with the "Associated College Press," the paper brought the students in touch with the larger world. It reported in 1937 that a cure for cancer had been found and in general kept a watchful eye on the deteriorating international scene.

Musically, the campus went from string to swing in the thirties. The students formed the RC Mountaineers, a string band, in 1935, and by 1940 the students and some townfolks had organized a swing band to reflect the national trend. The college orchestra, "The Collegians," continued to entertain and even had its own weekly radio program for several years. The Glee Club cut its first album in 1938, and the Sections sported not one but two radio stations by the spring of 1941, licenses notwithstanding.

The late thirties might have been the heyday of the classic battles between the Greeks and the "Barbarians," or non-affiliated students. Campus elections were always defined along strict Greek/non-Greek lines, and control of the student government or the new dorm council waffled back and forth between the two groups. The Sigma Chi's were the first fraternity to own their house and spent $4,500 plus an extra $350 on renovations for the privilege. The property on Market Street was home to the Sigs for over thirty years until they sold their house to the college and moved across the street into their present location.

There were always new clubs and organizations to dot the campus landscape. The "Engineering Seminar" appeared, as did a new English Club, an Economics Club, and "Phila"—a club for Jewish students; in 1937 the "Emergency Peace Youth Movement" started a chapter on campus. The Chemistry Club was "caught" discussing marijuana in 1938, while the "Peroxide Club" turned a few heads, so to speak, that same year.

Academic groups and honor societies also proliferated. The Harlequins was transformed into Alpha Psi Omega, an honor society of the theatre, and the Phi Society, an all-campus honor group, first inducted members in 1940. The academic year 1936–37 recorded several notable successes: the Blue Key chapter was voted the best in the country, the Sigma Chis had the highest scholastic average of any of their chapters in the nation; and a Pi Kap student was recognized as that fraternity's outstanding national scholar.

The Y's and Clericus continued their services to the student body: the "Student Hand-Book" was retitled "The Cherobiblos" in 1937, but the contents changed little. The Y's offered daily devotions throughout the semester but always noticed a certain upswing in attendance during final exams.

The Rats were never far from sight during the period. The shoe scrimmage at 4 A.M. was a regular pastime, and the Rat follies first went on from the back porch of the Ad Building in 1936. Female rats fared little better; a new ruling by the Rat Council in 1935 announced that they could wear no make-up but had to wear black hose until Homecoming in November. When the Administration reported to the *Brackety-Ack* in 1937 that the freshmen had tested well above the national average, the stunned sophomores demanded a recount.

The list of campus visitors was an impressive array of notable achievers. Senator Robert LaFollette, British author Sir Norman Angell, poet and biographer Carl Sandburg, economist Stuart Chase, cartoonist George McManus, and America's first Congresswoman, Jeanette Rankin of Montana, all delighted college audiences. First Lady Eleanor Roosevelt spoke in Roanoke and attracted a good following of students and faculty.

Poor Rat Betty Peters Moorman takes her dog for a walk; her sign says: "Love me, love my dog."

As if foreshadowing the impending doom of the world situation, students seemed more mindful of current events than ever before. Through the newspaper and several clubs, students debated the possibilities of war and once that had come to pass, whether the United States should or would enter the conflict. As early as 1936, students discussed **boycotting the Olympics staged in Hitler's Berlin and wondered if the United States had a moral obligation** to defend the Western Hemisphere. By 1940 and 1941, a more somber tone was evident across the campus and through the publications, almost as though the students knew that all would collapse shortly. An October, 1941 *Brackety-Ack* article reminded students that sixteen million Americans had been drafted last week and that "sixty-five Roanoke men stand ready to go." Pearl Harbor was just six weeks away.

On the sporting front, the late thirties were synonymous with the basketball triumphs of the five smart boys. Through three seasons and two post-season tournaments, the "five" amassed more victories and brought more fame to Roanoke than any sports team in the college's history to that time. After the state championship victory against Washington and Lee in 1938, the students celebrated with a rally on campus followed by a jubilant parade up High Street to the homes of the numerous professors who lived there.

Coach "Pap" White shows off his Five Smart Boys.

Baseball and football could not match the heroics of the five smart boys but did manage to account for their actions in respectable form, like the 1935 baseball team which lost only one game all season. Football fared less well during the period, but fan support and approval never waned. By 1941, popularity had reached such a point that the college introduced a second football team comprising men under the 154 weight limit. Six colleges fielded teams in the same classification for the season. Even the faculty got into the act in 1939 when they formed a touch football team to compete with the students.

It was life in the fast lane for Roanoke in the late thirties; for 15 cents, you could have this NIT program from New York City.

Football Captain "Rip" Patrone poses for this publicity shot from 1935.

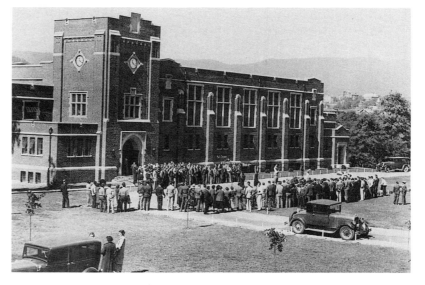

A pep rally outside of Alumni Gym. Go Team, Fight!

[T]he pentad of Robert Sheffield, Bob Lieb, John Wagner, Paul Rice, and Gene Studebaker in the late 1930's clearly put Roanoke on the map as a basketball powerhouse.

These legendary athletes are remembered as the "Five Smart Boys" and began Roanoke's climb to the top.

It was evident from the beginning of their careers at Roanoke that they would be a success. . . . When the "Smart Boys" finally jelled in the winter of 1938, Roanoke began attracting national attention by beating some of the nation's top collegiate teams. . . . Roanoke's only regular season loss was to N.C. State by two points and the team qualified for the National Invitational Tournament in Kansas City.

The Maroon's made it to the finals only to lose 45–30 to Warrensburg, Mo. . . . [R]eal recognition for the Maroons came on Jan. 11, 1938 when Cawthon Bowen—their sports editor for the Roanoke Times—referred to the quintet as the "5 Smart Boys." "It fitted them at the time," said Bowen. "They were the best five men on the team. . . . One game they were probably the most intelligent five players and without any previous thought I referred to them as the "Five Smart Boys."

To open the 1938–39 season Roanoke traveled to Lasalle and Villanova. After the Maroons opened with a one-point victory over Lasalle they were then six-point losers to a strong Villanova team. This would be their last regular season loss. The Maroons went on to win another state title as they cruised through the season. The dream had finally become reality. The Maroons qualified for the prestigious Metropolitan Basketball Writers Invitational tournament in New York [to which] the NCAA and NIT tournaments were then secondary.

In the semi-finals the Maroons were down six points with only two minutes to go . . . [but] came fighting back to earn a two-point victory.

However, the bubble was about to burst. In the finals against St. John's, in front of 14,443 Madison Square Garden fans, . . . Roanoke eventually lost 71–47 to a much deeper Redman team.

Though the five never accomplished a tournament championship, they began a legacy of strong basketball teams at Roanoke College.

From an article by J. Russell Hildebrand III in the *Brackety-Ack*, 20 January 1984.

The Maroon's grid iron brain trust: Head Coach "Pap" White and his assistant Buddy Hackman look things over in 1940.

By 1940, and in some ways reflecting the renewed academic code and structure adopted the previous year by the faculty, the athletic program was the subject of a thorough review and reevaluation. Doubtless, there had been excesses which had crept into the program, and the payments to students to play sports seemed hopelessly out of fashion to a school still trying to make ends meet. The faculty verdict, echoed by the board, was to scale back on the overall level of athletic competition, to limit the amount of aid which any student could receive to the cost of tuition, and finally to spend no more than ten thousand dollars on the entire athletic aid budget. The administration had imposed academic and financial order even if it meant athletic disarray.

Intramurals continued their strong tradition, and in 1940, women made their way onto the intramural badminton court. Soon they were playing basketball and competing in a host of other sports as well. Horse-shoe pitching became increasingly popular as the decade wore on, and hikes and field trips, to Natural Bridge and Endless Caverns, continued to excite.

As the clouds gathered by the late fall of 1941, Roanoke's innocence and determination would be taxed to their limit.

CHAPTER 14

"The real war babies,"
1941–1945

As if with a prophetic vision, the editors of the 1940 yearbook felt the impending doom of world order. They remarked that "the real 'War Babies' are just now finishing college. With but few exceptions, we of the class of 1940 were born into a war-wracked world and as if this pleasant fact were to follow us the rest of our days, we are ushered out into another."

On that infamous day of December 7, 1941, students clustered around the back porch of the Ad Building to hear the reports of Pearl Harbor. In shock and disbelief, the students must have wondered how their fragile little world would fare. The next issue of the *Brackety-Ack* was full of comment from students and administrators alike. Doctor Charlie headed the charge by announcing that the college was on "a full war basis" where self-discipline and economy were watchwords of the day. With a hopeful confidence, the president attempted to reassure his charges that all would be well. For many of the students, the moment proved sobering as the newspaper's editorial lamented "the darkness of war."

The faculty formed a Morale Committee for campus concerns and to give students an outlet for their fears and frustrations. On a broader scale, several faculty volunteered to join with town authorities to organize the Civilian Morale Committee to begin identifying Salem's response to war. A few other faculty members even helped to arrange the "Roanoke-Salem Intelligence Bureau" as war-time jitters and civilian uncertainties made fashionable the act of spying on those deemed subversive. By February 1942, the faculty agreed to cooperate further with the civilian defense effort by establishing a "Civilian Educational Service" with the purpose of furnishing the community with "information and training necessary to public discussion and understanding of issues of national defense." Former Dean and mayor of Salem Charles Brown headed the group of seven faculty and organized a speakers bureau, "a defense library," and a training center for the supervision of emergency classes such as first aid.

CLASS OF '40: THE REAL WAR BABIES

Some writer applied the term "War Babies" to American youth of twenty years ago, but the real "War Babies" are just now finishing college. With but few exceptions, we of the class of 1940 were born into a war-wracked world and as if this pleasant fact were to follow us the rest of our days, we are ushered out into another.

What effect all of this had on us, naturally, we can't evaluate, at least for another twenty years. But there have been certain influences playing on us during the past few years here at Roanoke College. Many of these are extremely local but powerful withal; social and economic currents have pulled and tugged at us without our asking.

There is no doubting that in a small measure our purely scholastic progress has suffered from a Golden Era in Roanoke College athletics. It was like hitting the jackpot on a slot machine. Without asking for it, the athletic department, starting with the magnificent football team of 1936, had fame and fortune and headache dumped in its lap.

We, the class of 1940, have ridden that bandwagon for all it was worth. We have stayed up all night to talk basketball; we set new records for cutting classes to celebrate the Five Smart Boys; we stole the bell and roped in classes who hadn't cut; we paraded the streets and indulged in every hysterical manifestation of which we had ever heard.

The war? We don't know; but then neither do our professors. We have followed it every inch of the way. We have stood, late to class, on the back stoop in the early morning and listened to Hitler from the car radios. We have met night after night with the faculty in little groups and tried to be intelligent. We know so little. On the whole our professors are more optimistic than we are. If anything, we are sick of hearing about it and tend now to shut ourselves away from it.

The tension has shown in our social affairs. Swing! We have eaten and slept with it. Twelve inch records, Benny Goodman, The Big Apple, truckin', Artie Shaw, juke boxes, Glenn Miller, many times more important than papers or quizzes were those who gave us music.

Somehow though, we leave with the feeling that we have closed an era. Perhaps all graduating classes feel the same.

Today toward the outside world the class of '40 is rather calm; perhaps, as a whole, too calm. Jobs aren't plentiful, but the College has been rather successful in keeping the wolf away from the door of its "babies." Many of us are rather stoical. We were born in a world of hysteria; we teethed on a golden ring and then had it snatched away and grew up in a world that was just plain hungry. We're pretty tough and more than a little resourceful. And above all thankful for the four years when we could sing and play and talk and read—unmolested. In this we have gathered fuel for the wintry nights.

Excerpts from an article by John Thornton, '40, in the *Roanoke Collegian*, May 1940.

"Up and at 'em?" The Sections is aroused at an early hour by the campus bugler in the spring of 1942. (Roanoke Times & World-News photo)

A view of the front range of buildings from Miller Hall on the left to Trout in the distance. Campus beautification and walkways would await another day.

Reflecting the national trend to preparedness, the students took it upon themselves, with administrative assent, to transform the campus and their routine into one of paramilitary order and training. The "student-army" renamed the Sections as "Posts" and, as a way of reorganizing campus life, gave themselves military titles, from privates to generals. Lights out came at 11 P.M., and reveille occurred at 7 A.M. Mandatory calisthenics followed and then a march to the "mess" in the Commons. High atop fifth Sections a student bugler sounded the appropriate calls. The attempt at military order might be regarded as a little silly today, or at least innocent, but at the time, the students considered it a good faith effort at preparedness. The *Brackety-Ack* lauded the concept, all except the titles, which it considered pretentious, and encouraged all male students to participate. All in all, student enthusiasm tended to wane after a few weeks; 7 o'clock came mighty early, and students ordering other students around was, even on a good day, difficult. An attempt had been made at least, and before Roanoke students could feel remorse, the war would turn their world into a far more serious affair.

A sterner President Smith reflects the more somber tone of the period.

A war time aerial view of the campus; the gym roof was painted with Civil Defense markings which it sported for years.

The photo carried the following caption: "J. E. ("Kentucky") Conley spins prop for cadet E. C. Jones, Jr., ready for his first solo flight."

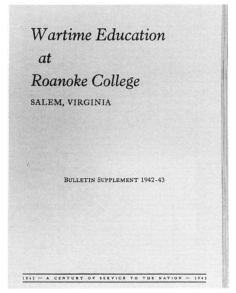

Wartime Education at Roanoke College

SALEM, VIRGINIA

BULLETIN SUPPLEMENT 1942-43

1842 — A CENTURY OF SERVICE TO THE NATION — 1942

The college was prepared to do its part too in fighting the war; an excellerated program of study was one of several features the school offered.

In some ways, the issue of war preparedness was not completely foreign to the Roanoke campus. As early as 1939, the college had hosted a unit of the Civilian Pilot Training Program sponsored by the Civilian Aeronautics Authority. The government-sanctioned program was made available at hundreds of colleges across the country to determine whether the students had an interest in flying. The student paid forty dollars and the government paid $275 to cover the cost of instruction and flight time. The semester-long course completed the requirements for a private license; as the catalog reported "it is left entirely up to the student whether he will continue his flying instruction in either the Army or Navy flying corps. It may be either an occupation or a hobby, for the decision rests entirely with the student." These "Maroons with wings," as they liked to call themselves, numbered 110 by the end of the spring semester 1942. Physics professor Charles Raynor headed the campus program that could boast that "the Roanoke College 'Dawn Patrol' is aiding vitally in the present war effort."

While the public could enjoy listening to "Good Bye Mama, I'm Off to Yokohama" and marvel at the news of Doolittle's raid on Tokyo in the spring of 1942, others in the government reasoned that the war effort would be anything but quick. As a result, a series of government directives were issued to encourage colleges to accelerate their course of study. Obligingly, the faculty decided in February 1942, to adopt a three year, three summer school-around-the clock calendar to facilitate the wartime demand. Accordingly, the college would also offer three commencements to accommodate the crisis.

Although they may have tried at times, the students had difficulty leaving the war behind. The National Anthem was now played before the chapel service; Professor Phinney's radio still received Hitler's speeches that he would dutifully translate for the assembled group of students; and the *Brackety-Ack* always carried a tearful letter of good bye from a departing student. Two students who were Austrian refugees kept a spotlight on Europe while two other exchange students from Venezuela confirmed the State Department's "Good Neighbor Policy" and helped focus attention on that realm as well.

Red Cross campaigns, United States Savings drives, and increasing efforts to conserve, all bombarded the students in the opening months of war. The board of trustees, reflecting the hysteria that captured much of the country, passed a resolution announcing that it would be "inappropriate" to consider any application from a person of Japanese ancestry.

THE FACULTY AND TRUSTEES

OF

ROANOKE COLLEGE

cordially invite you to attend the celebration of

The Centennial of the Founding

of

The College

MAY 29th to JUNE 1st, 1942

AT

SALEM, VIRGINIA

Although muted by the onset of war, the college still managed to celebrate its centennial, but in simpler fashion.

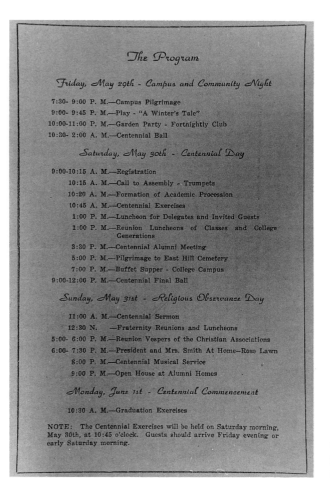

The Program

Friday, May 29th - Campus and Community Night

7:30- 9:00 P. M.—Campus Pilgrimage
9:00- 9:45 P. M.—Play - "A Winter's Tale"
10:00-11:00 P. M.—Garden Party - Fortnightly Club
10:30- 2:00 A. M.—Centennial Ball

Saturday, May 30th - Centennial Day

9:00-10:15 A. M.—Registration
10:15 A. M.—Call to Assembly - Trumpets
10:20 A. M.—Formation of Academic Procession
10:45 A. M.—Centennial Exercises
1:00 P. M.—Luncheon for Delegates and Invited Guests
1:00 P. M.—Reunion Luncheons of Classes and College Generations
3:30 P. M.—Centennial Alumni Meeting
5:00 P. M.—Pilgrimage to East Hill Cemetery
7:00 P. M.—Buffet Supper - College Campus
9:00-12:00 P. M.—Centennial Final Ball

Sunday, May 31st - Religious Observance Day

11:00 A. M.—Centennial Sermon
12:30 N. —Fraternity Reunions and Luncheons
5:00- 6:00 P. M.—Reunion Vespers of the Christian Associations
6:00- 7:30 P. M.—President and Mrs. Smith At Home—Rose Lawn
8:00 P. M.—Centennial Musical Service
9:00 P. M.—Open House at Alumni Homes

Monday, June 1st - Centennial Commencement

10:30 A. M.—Graduation Exercises

NOTE: The Centennial Exercises will be held on Saturday morning, May 30th, at 10:45 o'clock. Guests should arrive Friday evening or early Saturday morning.

A page from the Centennial program reflects the four day schedule of events.

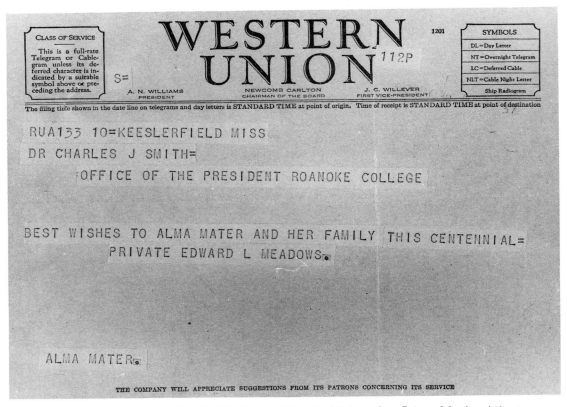

WESTERN UNION

RUA133 10=KEESLERFIELD MISS

DR CHARLES J SMITH=

OFFICE OF THE PRESIDENT ROANOKE COLLEGE

BEST WISHES TO ALMA MATER AND HER FAMILY THIS CENTENNIAL=
PRIVATE EDWARD L MEADOWS.

ALMA MATER.

All good wishes were appreciated, but Dr. Charlie especially prized this one from Private Meadows '40, at Keesler field in Mississippi.

A few events could continue, like baseball, which got a last minute reprieve, and the May Festival, replete with Queen and Court, as long as they could be done simply and not detract from the war effort. The long-anticipated Centennial celebration was modified as well. The "pomp and pageantry" would be replaced by a shorter ceremony that would be "dignified yet simple." The celebration was a success despite the troubled times. If the speakers and crowds could relish the moment and celebrate the college's first hundred years, they all felt, too, the uncertainty of the world scene and of the time in which celebrating seemed almost appropriate. They shared a common belief that Roanoke would have future times to celebrate.

By the summer of 1942, the war had made inroads into the college faculty. Six members of the faculty and staff, twenty percent in all, joined the armed forces; Professors Kolmer, Prufer, Steele, and Henderson, Coach White, and Admissions Director Ritchie all went off to war.

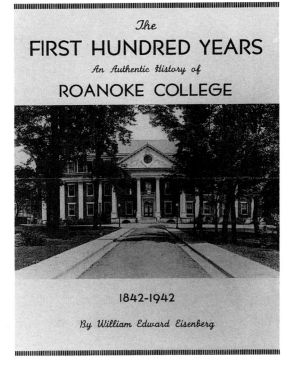

The
FIRST HUNDRED YEARS
An Authentic History of
ROANOKE COLLEGE

1842-1942

By William Edward Eisenberg

William Eisenberg's First Hundred Years *rolled off the presses in time for the festivities.*

The campus transformed. The Sections housed both Army and Navy aviation groups during the war.

Back on campus, enrollment surprisingly increased to almost record levels. A total of 370 students registered for fall courses including an all-time high of forty-six women. Residential space for the women was at a premium as Smith Hall was full to overflowing; the infirmary took in several others, and a vacant apartment in the faculty house became home to a few more. The men did not fare much better. The Sections were full to capacity, and the balance were housed in the Commons and the gym. Even President and Mrs. Smith took in four boarders in Roselawn. No one could have predicted the college's immediate good fortune.

A part of the college's bounty was the result of an army contract to house thirty soldiers on campus. With first Sections as home, the "Green Hornets" gave the students a real taste of military life. The army flyers stayed only half a year but had a definite impact on campus life. Another eighty-eight male students participated in a reserve officer training program. The group was divided into six companies: three navy air corps, one army air corp, one army, and one marine. In addition to their regular course of study, their programs included additional math and science and extensive physical conditioning. Upon completion of their studies, these men were automatically enlisted into the armed forces.

The academic year 1942–1943 promised to bring real change. But at first, students and faculty alike hoped to avert many drastic alterations. When some students questioned the legitimacy of ratting and "playing games" in a time of emergency, the faculty interceded to assure the students that having a little fun while they applied themselves diligently to their studies was permissible. As a result, the rat appeared once again; moreover, even a women's rat council restructured the program for the women. The "co-ed rat" was expected to wear her cap, carry candy, curtsy when approached, and make beds for the upperclass women.

Even football was continued. Although hamstrung by a small student turnout and limited competition from other colleges, the Maroons took to the field for what would turn out to be their last season ever. With a borrowed bus from a professional baseball team in Roanoke, the Maroons managed only a four-game season. In their only home game, the Homecoming festivities were allowed to continue only if the scale were modest and the decorations were "non-war related materials."

The campus clung to the hope that all would soon be over. Doctor Charlie was a constant source of inspiration as he exhorted his charges to do well and stay in school. The future needed leaders too, the president would say; and to convince them of his confidence, Smith often remarked that "God and Hitler were not compatible." The college made repeated efforts to adapt more and more of the course work demanded of students to the war effort itself. Still, general student performance and grades specifically took a turn for the worse.

The college kept Founders Day alive on 19 November 1942, David Bittle's birthday, and marked the first anniversary of Pearl Harbor with a special convocation. A "Campus Club" appeared which was designed to incorporate all the divergent elements on campus—the Greeks, non-Greeks, the reservists, and the military—into one united organization; the club worked pretty well for a time. The YMCA celebrated seventy-five years as a campus organization; from its founding in 1867, the group was one of the oldest and continuously operating chapters in the nation.

Never at a loss for words, Dr. Charlie converses with several students on the front porch of the Ad Building. The President's ability to remember student's names, both present and past, astounded all.

With the end of the fall semester in February 1943, the atmosphere on campus took on a more serious air. The college graduated nine students at mid-year, but that little group was paid the same tribute and given the same commencement ceremony of any graduating class in history. Indeed, when one student was given his notice to report before commencement itself, the

college even staged a special ceremony just for him. His former classmates assembled in the Lab-Theatre and watched in silence as the graduate crossed the stage and walked out the door into a world that was far less safe. The students sat quietly for a few minutes and, without a word being spoken, silently filed out of the auditorium.

Those nine were not the only students who disappeared in February. The Green Hornets had completed their training and had taken off for the front, and the two army reserve units on campus were also called to active duty. The student's "play army" of the year before seemed a distant memory to those remaining. Other students elected to enlist on their own, and despite Doctor Charlie's best efforts to the contrary, there was a ready trickle of would-be soldiers down College Avenue to the train station. A tradition developed among the students whereby on the eve of one's departure, the enlistee would be treated to a night on the town by his buddies; the next morning, he would be escorted to the station and have his lucky penny placed on the tracks to be flattened by the train as it pulled out of town. The penny would be retrieved by his friends and mailed to him as his good luck piece and as a symbol of his return to Salem.

Good luck, of course, was in great demand. The *Brackety-Ack* reported in increasing fashion about those students whose luck had run out. Almost hauntingly, the announcements of students killed, captured, or missing in action began dominating the paper. At times, there seemed little to cheer about and accordingly, in March of 1943, the college officially ended athletic competition "for the duration." The May Festival was cancelled as well,

and even commencement activities were cut short. The baccalaureate service was scheduled for the same day as graduation so that parents and guests might make the trip in a more rapid fashion.

IT'S ALL OVER NOW

When sports columnist Ozzie Worley used the headline *It's All Over Now* in his column *Sport-O-Data* in the November 20, 1942, issue of *The Brackety-Ack*, he was describing the football game played in Salisbury, North Carolina, the previous Friday against Catawba College. Little did he know then that it would be the last intercollegiate football game played by the Maroons. The following spring Dr. Charlie suspended intercollegiate sports competition for the duration of the war, and in 1946, the faculty would veto the return of the sport. It really was "all over now."

"But there was some real football played in Salisbury, North Carolina last Friday night. The majority of the sports fans who skimmed through the results of games played Friday night no doubt in a state of indifference just sighed deeply and declared that Roanoke College surely didn't play very well to get beaten as badly as 42-0.

"42-0? There was a story behind those headlines that wasn't revealed by the digits. . . . It wasn't a "win" victory for Coach Hackman's Maroons, but it was a lost game in which the Maroons cast aside excuses and played good, American football—the way it's supposed to be done. They hadn't done it against Hampden-Sydney, nor against Randolph-Macon, but they recaptured their fight against Catawba.

"The Indians weren't in our league this season. To use the trite expression—they had a powerhouse. The Roanoke boys knew what they were up against at the end of the first period. Still, they doggedly fought on . . . against three full Catawba elevens. At the half Coach Hackman said, 'Boys, as far as that scoreboard is concerned, I can't even see it. I don't care if they beat us by 100-0; you're playing football and that's all I ask.'"

The typical dilemma faced by many high school seniors—to go to college or to go to war. In this college public relations still, the school recognizes the problem but assures its reader that it is still patriotic to go to college first, and then make a better contribution to the war effort.

The west wall of the Lab-Theatre; the building was home as well to the English Department until the 1970s.

A common sight during the war years; another campus visit by your friendly local recruiter.

Black-out raids continued on campus, in case of emergency, and the *Brackety-Ack* apologized a few times for the "typos and other errors" that had occurred the week before. The newspaper staff had been caught short by a scheduled black-out and had not been able to finish checking the final copy of an issue. The paper reported the lowering of the draft age to eighteen in March, 1943, exhorted "co-eds" not to marry until the men returned from overseas, and explained the "College Registration Service," which the government made available to GIs by allowing them to keep in touch with college classmates once they were in the service. Intramurals did survive and provided an important outlet for those left behind. A track and field day was known as the "Relay Carnival," and a Saturday's contest in the pool was billed as "the Swimming Carnival."

Major campus news broke in March 1943 when the college signed an agreement with the United States Navy to house and to supply partial instruction to a group of its aviation cadets. Facing shrinking enrollments and an uncertain future, the college was delighted with the new program. By the spring, 105 naval cadets were calling the campus home. The college constructed both indoor and outdoor obstacle courses to assist in the physical training, and when the sailors were not studying or exercising, they could always stroll down to Main Street and catch Ronald Reagan in "Desperate Journey," which opened in Salem in May, 1943. The Navy "V" program was a fixture on the campus for almost the next year and a half. The cadets gave the school a real martial spirit as they trained both on campus and at Woodrum Field in Roanoke.

By the fall of 1943, the next academic year offered more questions than answers. Apart from the cadets, there were only fifty college men enrolled though a record 115 women. The college numbers were down by over 200 from the previous September. To ease the housing crunch for the women, the college renovated the Ferguson home on High Street, a social center for women since 1933, and turned it into a dormitory for eighteen women. For the first time in anyone's memory ratting was officially abandoned, although the caps remained as a symbol of status. Student government elections, postponed the previous spring over the uncertainty about which students might even return, were finally held in an attempt to restore some sense of order to the campus.

The *Brackety-Ack* was allowed to continue publishing and sported an all-woman staff—from editor to photographer. Even the naval cadets got into the act by writing for the paper a weekly column entitled "The Skywriter." The staff exhorted students to write their classmates who were off at the front and also implored the soldiers to write to the *Brackety-Ack*. A number of GIs obliged and the paper published their stories weekly. The newspaper still carried the unrelenting articles about the Roanoke men who had recently been killed or wounded. Haunting accounts of those classmates who were missing in action or captured by the enemy appeared all too frequently.

Some Naval aviation cadets get in some physical training on the college football field.

This photo was received by the Brackety-Ack *from two former students at the front, William Tice (right) and Charlie Gibbs '39. The article was entitled "Roanoke Men in Sicily." Gibbs' name is to be found in "Roanoke's Roll of Honor."*

On campus, signs of the war were everywhere. The students conducted Red Cross drives monthly, and the war bond booth became a school fixture. The "Battle Flag" flew from the front porch of the Administration Building with the number of Roanoke men, alums and present students in the armed forces emblazoned in the center. Rationing affected all Americans, and the students were no exception. By and large, the students recognized the sacrifice, but every once in a while, their frustration was made manifest. Some students complained of boredom and of their inability to get away. Gasoline coupons restricted private car use, and the Roanoke trolley was limited in both its schedule and its destination. Fashion reflected war-time conservation too as dress length got shorter to save additional material, and silk hosiery disappeared altogether.

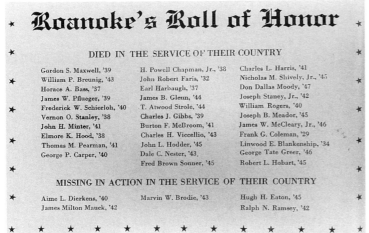

★ Roanoke's Roll of Honor ★

DIED IN THE SERVICE OF THEIR COUNTRY

Gordon S. Maxwell, '39	H. Powell Chapman, Jr., '38	Charles L. Harris, '41
William P. Breunig, '43	John Robert Faris, '32	Nicholas M. Shively, Jr., '45
Horace A. Bass, '37	Earl Harbaugh, '37	Don Dallas Moody, '47
James W. Pflueger, '39	James B. Glenn, '44	Joseph Staney, Jr., '42
Frederick W. Schierloh, '40	T. Atwood Strole, '44	William Rogers, '40
Vernon O. Stanley, '38	Charles J. Gibbs, '39	Joseph B. Meador, '45
John H. Minter, '41	Burton F. McBroom, '41	James W. McCleary, Jr., '46
Elmore K. Hood, '38	Charles H. Viccellio, '43	Frank G. Coleman, '29
Thomas M. Pearman, '41	John L. Hodder, '45	Linwood E. Blankenship, '34
George P. Carper, '40	Dale C. Nester, '43	George Tate Greer, '46
	Fred Brown Sonner, '45	Robert L. Hobart, '45

MISSING IN ACTION IN THE SERVICE OF THEIR COUNTRY

Aime L. Dierkens, '40	Marvin W. Brodie, '43	Hugh H. Eaton, '45
James Milton Mauck, '42		Ralph N. Ramsey, '42

★ ★ ★ ★ ★ ★ ★ ★ ★ ★ ★

During the war, the last page of the Collegian *always carried this sobering reminder of the real cost of war.*

As the men marched off to war, more and more women took their places. Here's a scene from the third floor labs of the Biology Department in the Ad Building some time early in the war.

Through the winter of 1943–44, as the war seemed to be improving, so too did campus attitudes and events. The students elected to go ahead with "Mid-Winters" although the women joked about whether there would be enough men to go around and that the "Stag Line" would stretch out the door of the gym. A radio club was formed and presented a Thursday afternoon program each week on WDBJ; the show featured campus entertainment, news and interviews. A Lutheran Student Association was begun as was the Womens Athletic Council to plan and to direct the spring's intramural program. Although the women's physical education instructor had departed in December to be with her husband, the college women were determined to press ahead. Even May Day returned as the social event of the season. By the spring of 1944, prospects seemed brighter all around.

And it would not take long for Doctor Charlie to find the rainbow either. His sights and energies were already turned to the post-war situation. More than ever now, he encouraged his male students to stay and finish; furthermore, the president began to outline his wish-list for future building projects— first a memorial chapel with the names of all the Roanoke men who lost their lives in the war inscribed on the walls, and secondly, a new library to replace the antiquated Bittle Hall. Smith, along with everybody else, could hardly wait for the war to be over.

LADIES PREFER BRUNETTES, NO KISSES ON 1ST DATE

With its tongue pocketed cushily in its cheek the Brackety-Ack held nothing sacred as it issued a questioneer in its first annual draft of co-ed opinion. There were several draft dodgers among Roanoke's chromatic co-eds, but strange as it may seem the Maroon ladies prefer brunettes 9 to 1 over blondes. For some its immaterial.

Only two coeds objected to their dates smoking, while 16 objected to their dates drinking. One young lady had no objections "if he doesn't drink more than I do."

Twelve coeds don't mind if their date wears a sweater rather than a coat on a date if the occasion is not formal. According to the Brackety-Ack statistical abstract a car means about 35 percent in the love life of the average Roanoke coed. With some it didn't matter; with others it was a decided asset.

Only one girl, according to the poll, doesn't object to a kiss on the first date even if the circumstances are right. The rest had objections. A checkup of boastful Maroon males should prove revealing.

One young lady is "surprised, but glad" if her date doesn't try to hold her hand on the first date. Fourteen are not disappointed if their date doesn't try to kiss her or at least to hold their hand on the first date. A few were bitterly disappointed.

One coed feels that a boy should date her a year before he can kiss her without fear of being offsides, while another said that until he could kiss her and mean it, it didn't mean a thing. With one, the lucky lad will have to wait for the kiss until he is engaged.

Only three around here would rather go steady than play the field, while one remarked that she would play the field until the right one came along.

"Home" is the favorite night spot of one Maroonette, while for most the Coffee Pot is the favorite night hangout with the Log Inn coming in a close second. Eight coeds believe that college will help them get married, five said they thought that college would do them no good in their matrimonial aims. "A lot of time will have been wasted if it doesn't," one Miss opined, while another was brazen enough to say "Who wants to get married?"

The *Brackety-Ack,* 28 February 1941.

In her royal regalia, May Queen Rosemary Dew sat for her official photograph in 1944.

Henry Hill posed for this photograph by war's end.

Remembering the boys on the high seas, this May Court dance has a nautical theme.

A member of the Semi-Centennial Class of 1903 had this offering for his fellows at the Centennial.

By August, 1944, the last of the naval cadet groups was called up to active duty and packed their bags for the last time in the Sections. The Navy had notified the college the previous spring that the program was to be discontinued and thanked the school for its role in assisting the campaign. College officials likewise expressed their gratitude to the Navy and privately recognized that the Navy school had done a lot to keep the college afloat during the war.

When classes began, student enrollment was also on the road back. A total of seventy-one males and a whopping 146 females enrolled for classes in September. To help accommodate the number of women, that bastion of male housing—the Sections—fell to the pressures of co-education as women moved into fifth. Sorority life continued its upswing with a new chapter on campus that semester and a total of twenty-eight women pledging the houses.

Ratting returned as well, and a new kind of GI appeared: the "vet," with his new ticket to higher education—the GI Bill—in hand. The first seven students enrolled with those benefits in the fall of 1944. Although the war was going well, it was, of course, a long way from over. Students still sold war stamps at dances, helped at Red Cross centers, assisted local farmers in picking apples, and donated cigarettes to the men abroad. The campus vets, their numbers increasing monthly, soon organized a club of their own to help each other in the transition back to civilian and collegiate life.

Franklin Roosevelt, running for an unprecedented fourth term, defeated Republican Thomas Dewey 80-78, on campus anyway; and more of the ritual and routine of college life was restored as the academic year wore on. The excitement and anticipation of victory and of the visions of the post-war world consumed the campus publications. The *Brackety-Ack,* the yearbook and *The Collegian* all prayed for a world of peace and understanding. By the spring of 1945, half of their dream had been realized, and before they would return to school in the fall, the world stood still and the guns were finally quiet.

CHAPTER 15

"From khaki to kampus,"
1945–1949

A popular column appeared in the *Brackety-Ack* in the fall of 1945 which underscored the transition that the college and the students were facing; "From Khaki to Kampus" represented the adjustment that hundreds of war-weary GIs would soon make. And the trading of a helmet for a rat cap was an offer that countless veterans were eager to accept.

The campus reflected the national mood and the atmosphere of the immediate post-war period. "Reconversion," the official government term for moving the economy and industry from war to peace, was in evidence at the college as faculty and administrators prepared for the influx of new and returning students. A new day was dawning which represented even more than victory over the country's recent foes. By the fall of 1945, a new-found spirit of confidence and optimism combined to produce an American attitude of enormous significance. Americans of 1945 had not only survived a war; they had beaten a depression too. Stored up in the process had been a generation's worth of waiting and longing. The country was prepared to embrace peace-time with all the energy and excitement that it had mustered to go to war. Failing was not even a consideration.

Change was underway on campus by the summer of 1945. Dr. Charlie grabbed the headlines by both celebrating his twenty-fifth anniversary as president and then announcing to the Board of Trustees his intention to retire. There were no dates set, but the president thought it was time for the board to begin the process of finding a successor. Dean Earl Broadwater elected to leave that summer and Edward Myers, Roanoke alum of the class of 1927, was appointed to replace him. Also leaving was long-time religion and philosophy professor Frank Longaker, who had been ready to retire in 1942, but who had delayed his decision until after the war, knowing that it would have been difficult for the college to find a replacement. Ready to take his place was Jimmy Rikard, who would double as philosophy and religion professor and college chaplain.

Henry Hill demonstrates the art of time-keeping for the photographer.

The view from High Street; campus plantings in the Back Quad began in earnest in the fifties.

In anticipation of the removal of the wartime caps on salaries, the trustees authorized almost five thousand dollars for faculty bonuses and further restructured salaries in the future with stipulations concerning rank and tenure. The board also recognized the unparalleled surge expected in enrollment over the next several years and, as a result, an unprecedented expansion of the faculty. Plans would be needed now.

The first wave washed ashore by the fall of 1945, but the anticipated return of the GIs had not materialized as yet. Of the 284 students enrolled that semester, only sixteen were veterans—seven of those former Roanoke students, and for the last time for a while women outnumbered men 180-104. By December, Dr. Charlie was predicting that by the fall of 1946, the college could expect upwards of more than a hundred new students, a fact which would boost enrollment over the 400 mark. At the extreme, Doctor Charlie advised, the figure could approach 500; that number would be the maximum number the college could expect to educate. By the following fall, enrollment had exceeded 600, and the president had a bit of explaining to do!

By the spring semester, the crunch was apparent to all. Over a hundred new students had registered for classes, eighty-five percent of them GIs. Five new faculty were hastily recruited to meet the demand. With Dean Myers's support, a faculty committee studied the complications of additional students in the future. The solution became known as the "afternoon college" concept in which as many as 200 students might be accommodated by taking courses in the afternoon and their labs in the morning. A modified version was adopted for the next year. Seizing the opportunity to make further academic changes before the crowd arrived, Dean Myers introduced the St. John's University "progressive plan for education in the liberal arts and sciences." The plan featured a number of new alterations to the curriculum and included a program of outside reading, to the faculty's delight and the students' consternation.

Religion and philosophy professor Frank C. Longaker moves class outdoors to the Front Quad—a popular move with students of any era.

Students are hard at work in the newly refurbished biology labs; students and faculty labored there until 1971 when the Life Science Building opened.

It must be Halloween! There goes Henry Hill's bell again. Who are those hooded creatures in the organdy ruffled curtains? Are they students? Or could they be (as rumor had it) Chaplain Rikard and Dean Myers?

Constance Moser and Barbara Hendrick strike stunning poses for the May Day review in 1947.

Peacetime Salem looked happy and serene in this college admissions photo. That's the Longwood home in the background.

The year 1945–46 brought changes to the students' lives as well. Students celebrated the end to "war time"; the national daylight savings schedule which had been in place since Pearl Harbor. Students had complained about needing flashlights to find their way to their eight o'clock classes. Ratting—suspended during the war—was back in force, and a new school tradition of a picnic in Roanoke's Fishburn Park on Halloween signalled an end to Rat season. A giant bonfire would conclude the night's festivities as the freshmen tossed their caps into the flames.

The *Brackety-Ack* continued as the student conscience. In one editorial, it berated the administration for the lack of "a co-ed recreation center" where students could gather informally for sodas and snacks. Further, the paper demanded that the women be removed from fifth sections. On the international front, it urged students to pity Germany less and remember more the suffering and pain that Hitler had inflicted. To that end, the college held a special memorial service in memory of the thirty-three Roanoke men who died in their country's service.

The paper kept up on the social scene as well. It offered its first music column reviewing recently released records, "Disc Data," and covered the big event of the fall, The Harvest Dance, with unnerving accuracy. A Barbarian Club organized before the fraternities could shake off the cobwebs, and the three sororities garnered forty-four pledges in the fall. A Pre-Med Club was formed; Alpha Psi Omega, the acting society, tried to put a few plays on but could not; and the Chemistry Club listened to a talk on "The Atom Bomb" in November, 1945. Norman's (now in Jett's old quarters) was still the place to be and now you could even call ahead to get food to go—that number again: 318-J!

Athletics were also resurfacing. Intercollegiate basketball reappeared in this first year as did baseball by the spring of 1946. An even bigger campus sensation was caused by "The Freak Game" when several women—"The Smart Girls"—challenged the men's basketball team to a grudge match. The only catch, though, was that the men would have to play by women's rules, plus a few other stipulations: wearing dresses (hula preferably), make-up, and boxing gloves. Whether the guys were still that good, or maybe because the women spent the majority of their time laughing, the men triumphed 19-15. The story and photos were picked up by newspapers as far away as Guam.

Intramurals returned with a vengeance; even football was played as a spring sport to get the students ready for its return in the fall. But in March 1946, the administration dropped its own version of an atomic bomb. A faculty committee had vetoed the return of a football team. The students were stunned; the alumni were outraged, and Doctor Charlie took off running. No decision of his administration caused him more distress than the flap over football. The president would spend a good deal of his remaining three years defending the college's decision. Doctor Charlie was not opposed to the sport per se; he was opposed to the ever increasing costs for scholarships and for maintaining the program. The president stated that if a suitable competitive arrangement could be found, wherein the emphasis would be on scholastic ability first and gridiron prowess second, the college could still have a team. Considering Roanoke's financial restraints at the time, the president stated that "Roanoke could be a good college or have a good football team. We can not be both."

By the fall of 1946, the real onslaught of GIs hit campus. Defying the best college prognosticators, the projected enrollment of between 400-500 students passed the 600 mark in September. Of that number, half were veterans and three-quarters of them had been former Roanoke students. Campus facilities were taxed to the breaking point; the Sections housed three hundred students, and bunk beds became the

rule of the day. Still, there were over fifty students who could not find college housing, and the faculty approved their living in town wherever they could get accommodation. The nineteenth century notion of the boarding house returned briefly to the school.

The academic resources of the college were pressed to the limit as well. No fewer than eighteen new faculty, several of those part-time, had been recruited to meet the demand. Long-time faculty and staff members Homer Bast, Fran Ramser, and the Snows—Frank and Lucile—were among the group to make their appearance that fall. At the other end of the spectrum, Harry Johnson, chemistry professor since 1919, elected to retire. Although the "afternoon college" concept was not officially embraced, the school utilized almost every available time and space on campus; classes were routinely scheduled until five in the afternoon.

Booming enrollment meant a dramatic increase in faculty too. This, Dr. Charlie's last photograph with his faculty on the front step of the Ad Building. Look for those fresh new faces of Zeb Hooker, Fran Ramser, and Homer Bast, to name a few.

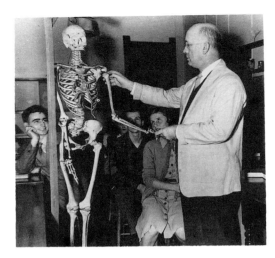

"The shoulder bone's connected to the . . ." Long-time professor George Peery illustrates anatomy with the help of a friend.

When it opened in the fall of 1947, the Cavern was quite the campus hangout.

The academic year featured the new look curriculum with its reading component of "outside" additional books. Students were expected to complete their reading, both required core texts and others recommended by their disciplines, and then take examinations on a Pass/Fail basis. The year also noted the addition of two new majors—psychology and education—and the further broadening of elective credits. The English department introduced courses in public speaking, journalism, and play production. A course in photography also found its way into the catalog for the first time. The major academic battle for students over the year was the dispute over a college attendance policy which forbade "cuts" in any particular course. The students reasoned that they were adults, would be responsible for the material in any event, and that their honor code was predicated on the notion of mutual trust and respect. In time, the faculty agreed, and by early 1947 the newspaper celebrated the student "victory;" all seemed won until several recalcitrant professors started imposing daily quizzes in their classes. To this tactic, the students cried foul but to no avail.

Physically, the campus had more plans than funded projects. The trustees still talked about a new memorial chapel, a library, a new science building, and a dormitory or two. But progress on this front was slow. The students' pleas for a recreational center were met in October with the opening of the Cavern; this "swank, posh joint" featured a jukebox, a soda fountain, and seating for forty. The Cavern was an immediate hit with the students; the only complaint heard was that it was always so crowded. The college agreed to run the Cavern on a non-profit basis and soon introduced other items to be sold besides the meals and drinks. The old store, long operated by the Monogram Club in the gym, was closed, and its merchandise of pennants, jewelry and snacks was incorporated into the Cavern's operation. With their recent good fortune, student leaders next turned their attention to a call for "a student union run by students."

The campus celebrated Henry Hill once again on the occasion of his seventieth birthday and his thirty-fifth anniversary of service to the college. Apart from the other presents and testimonials, the college presented Henry with thirty-five silver dollars as a token of its appreciation. At a special ceremony, Henry reminisced about how he was the first person to greet Doctor Charlie on campus when he came as president in 1920 and how "there hasn't been a frown between us ever since."

The administration attempted to modify the rat system in the fall of 1946. Although hazing had not been a persistent problem of late, the faculty reasoned that a few well-intentioned changes would result in a stronger system for the future. The most controversial element of the reform became the college proscription against "acts of service" demanded of the lowly rat. Henceforth, the freshmen could not be ordered to perform various duties for their "masters." The sophomores were outraged at this treatment and demanded a reasonable settlement. After a month, the administration relented and agreed to restore most "acts of service." Ratting survived the challenge.

The campus fraternities returned to life for the 46-47 year. During the war, the KAs, the Pi Kaps, and the Sigs had fallen to less than a handful—to two, four, and one respectively. The Sigs were even forced to rent out their house on Market Street. Now, the three groups were prepared to start over. The Pi Kaps obtained quarters above a store on Main Street; the Sigs reclaimed their house, while the KAs could only muster dorm space as a starter. The three sororities kept pace with an additional 44 new pledges. For the opposition, the Barbarians gave way to the Monadelphous Club for alternative programming.

Students formed other new groups as well: the Future Teachers of America, a new radio club, a Newman Club for Catholic students, and the Wesley Foundation for the Methodists. Over 500 students stood in line for flu shots, enjoyed informal dances in the Lab-Theatre on almost every Saturday night, engaged in a major uproar over the student government, and participated in another Halloween with a half day of classes, picnic, parade, and follies.

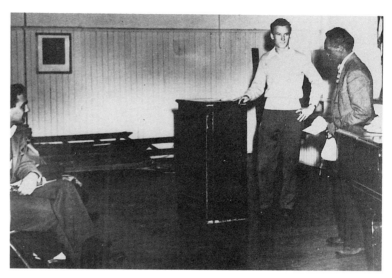

Happy Birthday, Henry! The students surprise Mr. Hill one more time.

The basement of Miller Hall became home to a number of "student hams" in the late forties.

A front campus walk looking west past the Faculty Apartments, the Infirmary, and Smith Hall in the distance.

Making a recording for speech class.

As expected, the big controversy of the fall was the lack of football. The *Brackety-Ack* took turns between pleading with the administration and berating it. School spirit was the real loser, the editors felt, not to mention the end to the Homecoming tradition. The president reiterated his pledge to play again if suitable competition was forthcoming, yet increasing numbers of students felt that that was only a polite way of saying "no." Homecoming might be salvaged by attaching it to a home basketball game, and if the lack of a fall sport affected school spirit, then another sport might satisfy the demand. Or at least the students could hope.

The spring of 1947 marked the beginning of women's intercollegiate sports at Roanoke. With coach Fran Ramser at the helm, the "Maroonettes" hit the hardwood for their inaugural basketball season and finished with a respectable 3-3-1 record. Men's basketball returned to its winning ways; baseball played a full season, and Homer Bast, released from the classroom, debuted as the track and field coach.

Intramurals enjoyed increasing popularity. New competitions included shuffleboard and co-ed soccer, and the old stand-bys continued to entertain. Women's intramurals, begun only in this decade, grew and expanded. In general, women had become more assertive and confident during the war with the absence of the men. Now that the males had returned, many women were not in any way interested in resuming the older positions and attitudes. Many males commented that the campus women "displayed more personality than they should." Even the nicknames of the women's basketball teams suggest a certain coming of age: along with Lena's Hyeenas and Kilroy's Girls, you could find the Rough & Readies, the Spikers, the Hellraisers, and, of course, the Amazons.

By the spring of 1947, seventy-one new students joined the ranks as enrollment hit an all-time high of 613. Fifty-two seniors graduated, dutifully taking the Graduate Record Examination as a pre-condition to commencement. As a fond farewell, the faculty produced the first "Faculty Follies" in May to the delight of the packed house in the Lab-Theatre. College life had begun to settle down.

For the fall of 1947, enrollment again exceeded the 600 mark. The crunch of new student applications forced the college and admissions committee chairman, D. R. Carpenter, into a series of difficult decisions. The faculty limited the total of entering freshmen to 150 and had over five times that many applications. The committee prioritized with veterans first, children of alumni second, and regular high-school graduates third. Thirty-eight percent of the incoming class, as a result, were veterans and exactly half of the entire student body were former GIs. The *Brackety-Ack* had this to say on the new registration system in place for the first time that semester: "the line stretched to the Courthouse."

Eight new faculty were added to the ranks, including one Zebulon Vance Hooker, and the college bade farewell to long-time Librarian Janet Ferguson. Trustee chairman and former Congressman James Woods further saddened college hearts with his death in July 1948.

Congressman James P. Woods presided over the Board of Trustees for years. He was a faithful friend and benefactor of Roanoke's until his death in 1948.

The new and improved Miller Hall in 1947. The building housed the physics and mathematics departments until 1970.

New physics professor Ray Brown lends a hand in the new Miller Hall basement labs.

The first physical expansion since Pearl Harbor had taken place over the summer. Miller Hall had tripled in size at a cost of $65,000 to make room for new physics labs and classrooms. The college also leased space from the Methodist church in the Chalmers Fellowship building; and with an eye on future expansion, the college began its long march up High Street with the acquisition of the Bowman property behind the Sections.

Renowned British historian Arnold Toynbee paid a visit on campus at the invitation of Dean Myers, and Doctor Charlie celebrated his sixty-fifth birthday while reasserting his intention to retire as soon as practical. The curriculum received a bit of pruning

with the removal of the extra reading requirement; student whining and faculty grumbling had doomed the experiment almost at the onset. The faculty sponsored a series of "job lectures" for would-be graduates and joined the students in marvelling at Roanoke's huge, new neon star high atop Mill Mountain.

The students enjoyed jitterbugging in the Cavern and reading about the adventures of the "Free State of Wheby" in the paper. The students were shocked when a rat was found innocent in rat court—"the first time ever"—and celebrated the mystery horseman on campus. Somehow, every time Tex Ritter got loose, so too did the bats in Fifth Sections.

Students organized a new debate club, raised money for a community fund drive, hosted the Student Congress of Virginia Colleges, and watched 525 of their fellows line up for their TB X-rays. The *Brackety-Ack* worried alternately between an imposed ban on student parking on campus in December, 1947 and by February, the alleged presence of "Commies at Roanoke."

The Greek system was slowly rebuilding. Twenty-eight students pledged the fraternities, and the Sigs celebrated the Diamond Anniversary of their founding on campus in 1872. Cabin parties officially returned only after administration demands had been met; the women could attend only if they signed in and out of their dorm, did not engage in drinking, and made certain a chaperone would be present at all times. Somehow, the students still managed to have fun.

Students could still not accept the fall without football. Even though soccer debuted and women's field hockey along with it, there was an emptiness that the students found hard to accept. Spirits improved substantially, however, during the winter; the Maroon basketball team finished the season 16-1 and claimed the state title for small colleges. After news of a big victory at Hampden-Sydney reached Salem, there was an impromptu campus pajama party outside Morehead Hall as the women left their dorm to join the revellers on High Street. The team accepted a faculty challenge to meet Dr. "Swish" Smith and his "Fabulous Five" for campus bragging rights. The spring's track team did the cagers one better by going undefeated and winning another state title.

The academic year 48-49 dawned with record numbers once again. Six hundred thirty-three students and seven more faculty settled in for the new semester. To help reduce the housing crunch, Hildreth Hall, long the home to Buildings and Grounds, was refurbished as a men's dormitory; the college had purchased a surplus quonset hut which it constructed below Hildreth Hall near the athletic field to serve as the new maintenance facility. That summer the college opened its outdoor pool which would refresh visitors for the next thirty years. The campus finished other renovation projects too: a new phone system, florescent lights, a buzzer system for Morehead Hall, and "even the library went modern with an electric clock." The Christmas star was rediscovered after being misplaced during the war, and was rehung for the season on the front of the Ad Building as it had since the thirties.

ANECDOTES FROM THE EARLY DAYS
OF DRAMATICS AT ROANOKE COLLEGE
by Sam Good '50

In the Laboratory Theatre . . . the stage had a proscenium opening of 24' and a depth of about 13'. The grid above the stage was 13' above the stage floor. Wing space was at a premium so we hit on the idea of putting our huge, resistance dimmer on a balcony above stage right . . . another balcony held our "fly gallery" above stage left. The resistance dimmer got very hot during the run of a show, especially when the lights were on a dim setting. During one season which was particularly warm outside, the light crew was in the habit of pouring beer on the dimmers to cool them off!!

The "Lab" had a bat living in the attic area above the auditorium. It became a looked-for occurrence for the bat to make his appearance during the intermission of a show and circle over the heads of the audience. . . . indeed, he became a good omen and was applauded for his appearance since it signalled a successful show!!! Nelson Bond, Showtimer's Writer in Residence, named him "Myotis Subulatus" and wrote a "Requiescat in Pace" on the occasion of his death in 1958.

When the Rialto Theatre closed, Showtimers bought enough seats to fill the Lab Theatre (about 250). The Rialto had been a "cowboy" movie house located just behind the old Colonial American National Bank on Campbell and Jefferson. . . . For Betty (Ross) Garretson's production of *Murder In The Cathedral*, I was cast as First Knight and George Kegley was Fourth Knight; Charles Swecker was Becket and David Thornton was one of the Tempters. During the show, I was to suddenly burst thru the swinging doors that separated the small lobby from the auditorium and march to the center of the house and up on stage. During one performance, I blasted through the door and on to the center aisle followed by two knights but not by the fourth, George Kegley. . . . The gales of laughter from the audience focused our attention on him standing by the door, holding it up. . . . I had knocked it off its hinges with my grand entrance!!

Students could be found playing bridge in the Cavern at any hour and still complaining about football. Water battles were increasing with regularity as one survivor from the "Floating Fourth" reported to the *Brackety-Ack,* while other students signed a petition for a greater emphasis on sex education in campus programs. Cardinal Key, a national honor society for women, was established, as was Phi Mu Alpha, a women's group dedicated to knitting. A little something for everyone. The *Chicago Tribune* was right after all, if it meant to report the campus election of 1948: Dewey defeated Truman handily 210-130. The campus fraternities formally joined the Inter-Fraternity Council and promptly compiled the fifth best scholastic record of the 152 chapters across the nation.

The athletic program boasted two new cars for 1948–49—the ones retired had a quarter of a million miles between them. Roanoke's track team went undefeated again, while the swim team managed its first victory in three seasons.

Above all, the year 1948–49 will be remembered as Doctor Charlie's last as president. By April, a successor had been named, and President Smith announced that this commencement would be his final one. He warmly accepted the invitation to be the graduation speaker to the class of ninety-two members, the largest in the school's history.

His speech was full of memories, of joy and tears. He applauded this class that had entered in adversity and had triumphed in the end. He invited them to do the same in life. For this "child of Roanoke," it was a bitter sweet day. He would rest, but he would not go far.

The KKK Strikes in Salem; Paint Rikardmobile

In the darkness of the midnight hours last Tuesday night, a benevolent gang of student painters visited the Rikard residence, with the result that the now famous Rikardmobile took on the new look.

Responding to a call sent out through all the men's dormitories and fraternity houses, an army of hooded creatures, composed of almost fifty students anxious to befriend the College chaplain, met at a designated hour in front of the college gates to begin their helpful mission.

Instigated by the YMCA the move got underway as a part of the Hallowe'en festivities two weeks ago, but the plans were postponed until a greater number of students could participate and a more masterful job to be completed.

When word came from "spotters" posted at strategic places that all was in readiness, the masked horde descended upon the Rikard residence where they found the antiquated flying comet awaiting renovation. By some mysterious silent power the notorious automobile started speeding down High Street and across the campus. It came to rest finally behind the Sigma Chi house where special lighting had been provided to facilitate the work of the elves, the nomes, and fairies, who are accused of carrying

out the feat.

Several minutes after the jobs of sandpapering and paint-mixing had been completed, the actual painting began, and in an amazingly short time a freshly attired new car came into being—a shining black machine with Chinese red trimmings. As a crowning touch to the evening's accomplishments a bomb was placed under the hood and attached to a spark plug so that a column of smoke would be emitted upon any attempt to start the engine. The famous car was then returned to its regular bed in front of the Rikard home.

When questioned about the incident, Prof. Rikard stated that he was very much pleased with the wonderful change, and to those who made it possible, he said. "I thank you." Comments from the Rikard children were somewhat different, however. Susan, the chaplain's youngest, merely ejaculated, "Whee!" Sally wanted to know, "What is it?" and Peter immediately shifted the blame with, "I didn't do it!" The Rikard dog came up with a strictly canine comment—"Yeow!" and passed the incident off lightly.

The *Brackety-Ack,* 18 November 1949.

The Ideal College President

Who better to suggest the qualities of the "ideal college president" than the man who had filled those shoes for 29 years? Here from the President's Page of the December 1948 *Roanoke Collegian* is Dr. Charlie's recommendation.

"If I were responsible for the choice of my successor (which I am not) I would pick me out a strong, honest, fearless, and good man who can be trusted. I would lay the College both on his shoulders and on his heart in full confidence that the "know how" will be acquired as he wrestles day by day with problems that are never new. I would rather take my chance with a man who has the capacity to grow up with the job rather than with one who is already grown and therefore, entirely too confident that he has all the answers.

I have only one first qualification for an ideal college president. In my book he must be interested primarily in the intellectual, cultural, and spiritual development of his students. If he thinks of his college either as a country club or as a football factory or a tavern on the highway of life, he will serve well neither his college nor his country. In these critical hours for humanity when the destiny of all mankind lies in the balances, our great nation must be furnished men and women of insight who combine great faith with great courage. Whence shall come the good citizens who shall keep our country great unless from the colleges? In a very faulty way this has been my own guiding star. For the many failures that have been mine I am truly penitent. But I still yield none of my faith that the ultimate glory of Roanoke or any other college will derive from the young Americans who leave it better than when they came, alumni, we call them, but always men and women who above all else are strong and true, and good."

Chas. J. Smith
President

"On the job" was the original caption to this college publicity still from 1948 as the president makes a phone call.

CHAPTER 16

"The Roanoke College
family,"
1949–1955

The new president and first lady Sherm and Charlotte Oberly.

The sixth president of Roanoke College, H. Sherman Oberly, assumed duties in 1949.

Sherman and Charlotte Oberly moved to Salem in the summer of 1949 and took up residence in Rose Lawn. After almost three decades and for as long as just about anyone could remember, the president's home had become synonymous as the Smith's residence. Now, all of that had come to a close. Doctor Charlie might have been leaving the president's home and office, but he was not leaving the college; the board of trustees had seen to that. After so long—through depression and war—the thought of facing the future without the good doctor was not an idea that gave comfort to the trustees. Instead, they created the new post of Provost and elected the venerable Dr. Smith to fill it.

At the age of fifty-one, Oberly possessed the experience and dedication necessary to follow in Charlie's footsteps. Trained in psychology, Oberly was the college's first president with an earned doctorate, although he wisecracked in an interview with a student reporter that he "learned more psychology driving a cab than in a classroom." After a career in teaching, Oberly had moved into administration and most recently had been the Dean of Admissions at the University of Pennsylvania. That experience would be sorely taxed soon after his arrival.

The predictions had proven correct. With the passing tide of veterans coupled with the lower birth rate during the Great Depression, colleges across the country were prepared for bad times. The incredible expansion of students and faculty immediately after the war would dissipate about as quickly as it had all begun. By the fall of 1949, those eventualities had confronted Roanoke. Total enrollment numbers fell to 528, over a hundred fewer students than the year before. The number of veterans dwindled to a mere 150 compared to 248 in 1948 and 321 in 1947. Yet that was only the start; the beginnings of the Korean conflict in 1950 made further inroads into the college age pool. By the fall of that year, enrollment had slipped to 464 and by the spring semester of 1951, down to 412. Further erosion occurred in the fall of 1951 as college numbers shrank to 364, the lowest peace-time level since the thirties.

Former admissions director Oberly was prepared to wade into the fight. With his new admissions director, Homer Bast, the two men planned their strategy. First, recruiting visits to the secondary schools should be attempted; second, a "College Day" for area high schools might interest increasing numbers of local students; and third, Julius Prufer was pressed into action as the college's new alumni director with a principal charge of revitalizing alumni chapters across the country with an eye on the alumnis' children as potential students. Accordingly, professors Bast and Prufer hit the road, and the college hosted its first College Day. Bast canvassed 125 high schools in a couple of months and Prufer covered as much territory. By the fall of 1952, the downward spiral had been checked. Enrollment moved up to the 400 mark plateau, and by 1953, 454 students made their way to Salem for classes. The crisis had been averted, and by mid-decade, growth had replaced retrenchment as the key to the future.

Along with Oberly came a host of new faces. Dean Myers had resigned and the president tapped English professor William Bartlett to move into the chief academic office. Clarence Caldwell was promoted to Business Manager in 1949, and David Thornton became Director of Development in 1950 after the sudden death of Stewart Hanks. With Bartlett's desire to return to the English Department by 1952 and the arrival of Perry Kendig as Dean, the college had assembled the leadership group that would preside over college affairs for the next quarter century. Kendig, Caldwell, Thornton, and by 1956 Don Sutton, became the management team Sherman Oberly hired to bring the college into the modern era.

The sun-lit Back Quad from above.

The college's new dean and English professor William Bartlett. His tragic death in 1954 prompted college officials to name a future dormitory in his honor.

The young Perry Kendig came to Roanoke in 1952 as dean of the college and professor of English. Eleven years later, Kendig became president. Kendig is flanked by professor and Chaplain Jimmy Rikard and Dean of Women Helen Hobart.

OUR TRIP TO TEXAS
(pronounced Takes-us)

8:50 PM
Thurs. 1-27-55

Dear Mrs. Dooley:

"And after this dream of being in a magic wonderland, where my dream of Texans (pronounced Takes-us) with Stetsons, cowboy boots, bright shirts, jeans—and a "Takes-us stride"— and instead of "Yes, thank y'all"—it is "Yea-us"—!! Well I was a goin' to express it all this-a-way, but I guess I should express it that-a-way—and as George Gobel says—"so here I am, and there you are!" I'm afeared I shall wake up!

Charlotte and I have just returned from dinner with Mr. & Mrs. Hedrick. Turning in early, because tomorrow is a busy and full day and our theme song shall be—"Cross over the Bridge"— that is we plan to fly to Anacachio Ranch . . . and then drive to Eagle Pass and go to Piedras Negras (Mexico) for dinner, etc. But—let us go back!

Phoned residence of Lawson W. Cooper '35, and talked with his wife—a Texan. . . . She gave me the phone number for her husband. . . . Cooper was surprised, but when I asked if I could see him, he gave directions . . . to CONVAIR. Security is the keyword there. I saw some dozen B-36 bombers under repair— and what looked like dozens of B-36 planes at the Carswell A.F. Base—they are 4 motors and 2 jet jobs! Tremendous!

We had a fine lunch—T-Bone steaks, etc.—of course! But, with regret we broke up. Cooper, I believe, really got a lot of pleasure out of this. In fact, his top man insisted that Cooper use the car of the boss to take me to the Hotel (NOTE for Clarence— thereby saving $3.00 taxi!).

I have rented a 16" movie projector for two weeks so as to be prepared to show movies here in Fort Worth—and along the way.

SUMMARY after one day: Our alumni are interested, and really flattered and pleased to hear from the campus. This job is well worth the time, expense and effort—on a long range program.

TO THOSE AT HOME—remember the hours of planning in the office, and my planning, plus the energy required to meet each new situation!

Frankly, I'm right "tard" this evening!

Best—

HSO

The "movers and shakers" of the trustees enjoy a bit of chit chat in the early fifties. From left to right are Leonard Muse, Henry Fowler, Socks Kinsey, Fielding Logan, Sagen Kime, and Stuart Saunders.

Financially, the college established its employee benefits package in the early fifties. It debuted its first retirement plan, joined the federal Social Security program, introduced life insurance, and offered its faculty a tuition remission program for their children both at Roanoke and at scores of other institutions. The college joined the Virginia Foundation of Independent and Church-Related Colleges in 1952, a source of increasing revenues over the subsequent decades, and launched a one million dollar campaign drive in 1951.

Physically, the campus received some much needed sprucing up during the period. The Sections had its floors refinished and new tiles placed in the bathrooms, and to comply with new Virginia fire safety regulations, a sprinkler system was installed. New furniture was purchased as well, featuring "Hollywood beds" and new desks and dressers. Even the students got into the act; Blue Key adopted a program called the "Clean-up Drive" in which they completely repainted Smith Hall and also purchased trash cans and ashtrays for campus use. The Administration Building saw some internal improvements and Trout Hall received a major face

lift; the old second story porch and outside stairs were removed from Trout, and an interior staircase was added to the ground floor. Chaplain Rikard's offices were carved from the old chapel and thereby left a more compact rear section for services and programs.

The campus sported new asphalt walkways, and a new flag pole was erected facing the gate to the Back Quad. Morehead Hall was closed briefly for repairs but reopened in 1953, and the Lab-Theatre saw a series of improvements both to the structure and to the technical capabilities of the facility. The college invested heavily in the "war surplus" market for everything from vehicles to file cabinets and, in part because of student complaints, leased the Commons and Cavern operations to a management firm. A recent *Brackety-Ack* poll had listed Commons complaints as "not enough milk, too much grease, and that the dishes weren't clean." Students also thought that "dinner music" might aid digestion. The new firm did not offer music but did give the diners a television to watch over meals, which was a good public relations move at least; good will was soon shattered when the Cavern hiked prices on cigarettes from 20 cents to 22 cents a pack.

Morehead Hall glistens in the snow. This structure had served as a women's center and residence hall since the 1920s. It was razed in the late sixties to make room for Antrim Chapel.

The old Methodist Church came into college hands in the early fifties and was used by the college as a chapel until Antrim opened in 1970. This area is now the front lawn of the campus at the corner of Clay and College.

A final tribute. Henry Hill is honored at the dedication of his bell tower in June, 1954. Dr. Charlie is seated next to Henry as Sherm Oberly stands behind. Henry Hill died just a few weeks later.

The major acquisition of the period was the purchase of the Methodist church property in the front of the campus bordering Clay Street and running between College Avenue and High Street. For $115,000 the college acquired the old church, its education building (Chalmers Hall), and the parsonage. The college used the church for the next twenty years as the college chapel, and the parsonage became the Deanery for Perry Kendig. The education building was long studied by the college as a possible library until those plans were shelved and the building was adapted to a combination dormitory and office building, its same function forty years later.

A final project was indeed the most sentimental: a resting place for Henry Hill's bell. The college's long-time guardian had suffered a heart attack in November of 1953; seven months later on Alumni Weekend, the college dedicated a bell tower in his honor. Looking frail and tired, Henry accepted the thanks from students, alumni, and his colleagues for his dedicated service since 1911. Henry Hill died just three weeks later.

President Oberly and his growing faculty in 1951/52.

Academically, the faculty experimented and adjusted to life in the post-war world. The curriculum saw the addition of a science requirement and an orientation course, and the elimination of the Graduate Record Exam as a part of graduation. The college added majors in nursing and medical technology and new minors in sociology, psychology, physical education, and drama. A host of new classes ran the gamut from thermodynamics to remedial reading, home economics, and "creative writing, adopted for female interests." Ties with Hollins College were strengthened in the fine arts area, and the faculty eliminated Saturday classes in 1951. The college opened its first language lab in that same year and introduced a new advising system for students. Meanwhile tuition advanced from $12 to $15 per credit hour. The college petitioned unsuccessfully for an Air Force ROTC unit on campus.

Roanoke celebrated the Christian Education Year with great aplomb. The college rededicated itself to its Christian tradition and sponsored a pep rally with 400 in attendance and a campus dinner for 225. The United Lutheran Church in America pledged $100,000 in additional college support. The college hosted a major campus event in the fall of 1951—a symposium entitled "Developing Human Resources"—which attracted 2,500 visitors for the weekend conference.

Long-time professor and Registrar D. R. Carpenter, on the faculty since 1909, and English professor Charles Dawson retired. The campus was shocked by the tragic death of William Bartlett. Miss Vivian Cronk, for thirty-three years the secretary to Roanoke College presidents, died suddenly in October, 1953. But all faculties are reborn too. The year Dawson retired, two newcomers took up residence in the English Department—Matt Wise and Bill Deegan, who before they were finished would amass over sixty-six years of service between them. Sam Good joined the faculty in 1954 and treated audiences to his productions over the next four decades, both on campus and in town through "The Showtimers," a group he helped found in 1951.

Campus visitors included the likes of Dr. C. W. Mayo, a founder of the Mayo Clinic, and United Nations President Carlos P. Pomillo, on campus to help celebrate "UN Week" in 1952. Doctor Charlie, never a stranger to campus, survived a cerebral hemorrhage in 1950 to help Salem celebrate its Sesquicentennial in 1952 and also to preside over graduation in Oberly's absence the following year.

Faculty follies were an annual hit for both faculty and students. That's President Oberly hamming it up in the back row.

Heading into the old Methodist Church, the graduating seniors march for a special convocation. The building on the right across the street is the old town hall; it was built in 1871 and razed in 1967.

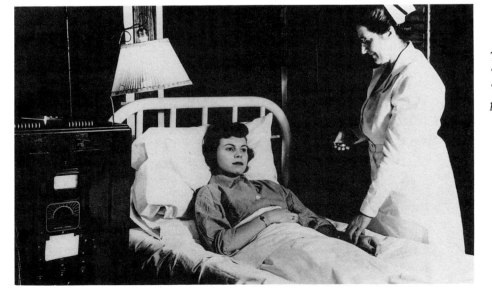

The college's infirmary offered "tender-loving care." The "afflicted" student posed for a publicity still.

There would be little disputing the fact that the major topic of conversation on campus in the early fifties was Korea. For an America that prided itself on its isolationism and non-interventionist tradition only a generation before, it must have seemed a cruel dream to this new generation of students to be at war again after only five years of peace. Still, this new world order demanded commitment, and the students of Roanoke stood ready. The government announced that no student would be called up during the academic year and mailed special packets informing the students of their situation. The college helped by administering the Selective Service College Qualifications Test, and the *Brackety-Ack* kept students posted as to developments in Asia. One newspaper poll asked the students if they felt that the war would be over in six months; eighty-two percent answered "NO." Another survey questioned future relations with the Soviet Union, whether the two countries would enjoy a peaceful relationship; only three percent said that chances were "good," 27% said "Fair," 54% answered "Poor," 12% stated "No chance." Four percent were uncertain. Support of the UN action waned after a time as a 1954 editorial showed students "How to Beat the Draft."

With the antics of Senator Joseph McCarthy, the peril of domestic communism was made real to the students as well. The *Brackety-Ack* published "A Primer on Communism" and polled students with regard to "avowed Communists being allowed on college faculties." Nine per cent responded "Yes" while 85% felt that to be an unwanted situation. When asked about "former members of the Communist Party" and their right to be on a faculty, 45% said "Yes" and 39% responded "No."

Students effected changes in the class attendance or "cuts" policy after months of negotiating with the faculty in 1950. The number of cuts depended upon the student's overall GPA, with the poorer student getting none and the honor student as many as twelve in a semester. Students complained that they were not treated as adults by the administration and protested that the recently hired night watchman was really just a "college spy." The honor system underwent another review but survived, as did the name *Brackety-Ack* in a paper contest to change the name.

The "Steering Wheel" became a campus feature in 1951; the first of these "campus forums" examined the relationship between students and faculty, and concluded that "more informal meetings" were the key to better understanding. The administration ban on student cars on campus was lifted after a compromise was worked out; Blue Key came to the rescue with a plan for parking, permits, and "a counterclockwise traffic flow" to the Back Quad. No freshmen were allowed to have cars on campus nor were students who were on probation; alas, neither were women.

Other topics remained taboo, as this observation from the 1951 *Rawenoch* makes clear:

> Upheaval reigned on the campus last week when Prof. Guts of the biology department announced that it was a scientific fact that there really were two sexes. The dean's office immediately branded this as a lie, saying that boys and girls are alike, and that there is no reason why boys and girls should be attracted to each other. This restored peace and order on the campus, and was backed up by the administrations order that celibacy for campus students will be enforced. Thus the humdrum routine of campus life was restored. Dates are now taboo, as are figs.

With their bobbed hair, longer skirts, and home perms, the women enjoyed a chance to have a snack at Normans, a movie at the Colonial, or an evening out at the Coffee Pot. The women had their own student leaders, the WSGA—Women's Student Government Association—and participated in May Day like never before.

A view of the fashionable formal parlor in Smith Hall. The men could call for the dates here, under the watchful eye of the housemother across the hall.

The pageantry continues! Another magical moment from May Days in the fifties.

GIRLS' SPORTS PROGRAM OFFERS CHANCE FOR PARTICIPATION TO ALL

For Roanoke girls the Women's Athletic Association offers a full sports program. On the varsity level two major sports are offered—hockey and basketball. These activities permit a girl to earn a major sports letter. The teams play many games at home and also make extended trips to other colleges throughout the state. Knowledge of the sport or previous participation in it are unnecessary and anyone who wants to learn to play is heartily welcomed.

Intramural activities are conducted in two parts: team sports and individual sports. The team sports are hockey, volleyball, basketball, swimming and softball. The teams are made up of the respective classes and competition for honors is heavy. The members of the winning team of any of these sports besides class glory, receive pins and W. A. A. points. Individual sports include: tennis, badminton, table tennis, shuffleboard, and arch-ery. The winners of the various tournaments receive pins representing their sports and points in W. A. A. Everyone who enters a sport is given a basic number of points and according to her class standing, is given extra points. By accumulating enough points a girl may earn her letter.

In the Spring a mammoth May Day program is given by the W. A. A. The participants display their dancing ability in this program which is a part of the school wide celebration.

The sports program enables girls to participate in relaxing athletic activities and also to become acquainted with other girls who have similar interests. It likewise gives one a chance to support her class. If you can't play a sport come out anyway and support your team!

The *Brackety-Ack*, 22 September 1950.

Rats enjoyed a new-found ally as the sophomores inducted new president Sherm Oberly as "Rat Emeritus" in 1949. New Dean Perry Kendig was treated to a similar fate three years later. Ratting continued as always, with many of the old gags and rituals and enough new wrinkles to keep everyone guessing. Along with the parade and follies, an official "rat trap" debuted and in 1951, the first "tug-o-war" between the rats and their masters. A noteworthy event occurred in 1950 which the *Brackety-Ack* chronicled as "the bitter struggle for power between the Rat Council and the Rebels." A rat uprising was staged and promptly resulted in several sophomores being dumped into the pool as the freshmen announced their "United Crusade for Rat Freedom." Needless to say, the rebellion was suppressed.

Greek life continued to amass academic honors throughout the period. The Inter-Fraternity Council ranked Roanoke College number one in the nation on the basis of their over-all fraternity grade point average. The Sigs were voted their organization's best scholastic chapter in Virginia four years running. Of course, the Sigs were not always in the library; the long-standing campus event "Derby Day" first took place in 1951. The Kappa Alpha's became the second fraternity to own their own house when they purchased a home on High Street in 1950. A fixture in the *Brackety-Ack,* "Greek News," was first run in the early fifties under the heading "Fraternity-Sorority Chatter." Rushing and pledging continued on the upswing, and the big topic of conversation in 1954–55 among the sororities was the question of "going national." By the spring of that year, the Sphinx, the oldest of the local sororities begun in 1930, was rechartered as Phi Mu. The other two present sororities, Delta Gamma and Chi Omega, would follow in the fall.

Always in good humor, President Oberly graciously accepts his citation making him "Rat Emeritus."

RAT EMERITUS

Amidst the colorful fanfare of a military ceremony, Dr. H. Sherman Oberly, new president of Roanoke was officially installed by the Rat Council and the freshman class as "Rat President" of the class of 1953.

The award of a certificate entitling the new college head to "all the privileges and honors bestowed upon 'Rats' at Roanoke College," was made by a special, though somewhat belated messenger from Jefferson Davis in Richmond, who was Randall Taylor disguised as a Confederate colonel.

The bearded and decrepit colonel dramatically entered the quadrangle, where all the "rats" were dutifully lined up in ranks awaiting the special messenger. He galloped up to the excited campus-people astride a chestnut horse, relating that he had been somewhat delayed in his journey which had begun in 1863.

After brandishing a sword to prove that he had accepted General Grant's surrender just three days before, the jovial southern colonel explained in his crackling drawl that he had "stopped by to see that the new president was properly installed by one of the South's greatest institutions—Roanoke College."

With a roar of approval from the "rebels," the Colonel's Confederate color guard waved their flags, while the Colonel read to the gathering the proclamation he bore. The scroll read:

It is hereby decreed on this 17th day of October that Dr. H. S. Oberly is formally installed as "Rat President" of the class of 1953. That he is entitled to all the privileges and honors bestowed upon the "Rats" at Roanoke College, and as "Rat Emeritus" has the distinct privilege of continuing and perpetuating the high crime of "Ratting" on all future students who matriculate in Roanoke College.

By Order of Rat Council
Gilbert A. Robinson, President

As a true "rat" Dr. Oberly was presented with the traditional white rat hat, and an extra-large rat tag, so that he could be identified. Dr. Oberly even bowed down toward the East and praised Allah in the traditional manner when the upperclassmen cried "ROANOKE."

The Colonel then dubbed Dr. Oberly "Rat Emeritus" and rode away in all the splendor due so eminent an individual.

The *Brackety-Ack,* 21 October 1949.

Life in the Sections could be pretty snappy too, at least in this PR photo. Check out those socks!

More Rat antics; at least they seem to be smiling.

The student activity fee moved from $40 a year in 1950 to $50 by 1955; some students grumbled after the increase, especially when the Student Government officers announced that they were off to Kansas City to attend the "National Student Assembly." The officers dismissed the complaints by announcing that they had "learned a lot." The college Glee Club had performed live on an NBC television broadcast to over "two hundred stations coast-to-coast." The Physics Club survived another get-together: "The Physics Club held their annual picnic and party at Fishburn Park in Roanoke last week, with refreshments consisting of ex-lax, milk of magnesia, and lemon water. Commissar Raynor announced that this purge of the party would have dire consequences. New members are now being recruited." The club sponsored its own ham radio operation from the basement of Miller Hall; with call letters W4SPW, the students could chat with other operators around the world, at least when their generator, powered by the remains of an old Jeep engine, would let them. Time had to be saved too for taking rides in the building dumb waiter which officially transported materials between the basement and the third floor.

'TWAS THE NIGHT BEFORE

Twash the Night Before (hic) Furlough
And all through Wells Hall,
All the bottles were empty.
But that isn't all.

The kegs were all hung
Out the window with care,
In hopes that the morning
Would still find them there.

And Steve in his long-Johns,
A jug in his lap,
Had just settled down
For a little night cap.

When out on the quadrangle,
There rose such a clatter,
I sprang out of my sack,
To see what was the matter.

Away to the porthole I flew
Like a flash,
Tripped over a bottle
And fell with a crash.

The moon in the sky
On that night of all nights,
Shown down from above,
Like a great spotlight.

When what to my bloodshot
Eyes should appear,
But a ten ton truck,
And a batch of reindeer.

With a little old driver
So lively and silly,
That I knew right off bat
It must be Dean Willie!

More fast than jet planes,
His reindeer they came,
And he screamed and he shouted
And called them all names.

Now Percy, now Algy,
Now Shmoe and now Vixie,
On Rudolph, on Beauregard,
On Blockhead and Trixie.

And then in a twinkle
I heard on the roof,
The stomping and stamping
Of hob-nailed boots.

As I fell back inside
And staggered around,
Through the window Dean Willie
Came with a bound.

He was dressed all in clothes,
From his head to his foot,
And his gun was all blackened
With carbon and soot.

A bundle of bottles
He had flung o're his back,
And he looked like a bootlegger
Just opening his sack.

His eyes were all bloodshot,
His dimples like any,
His cheeks like four roses,
His nose like a cherry.

He was short and round,
A right funny old elf,
That hiccuped when he spoke,
In spite of himself.

A wink of his eye
And a twist of his head,
And before I knew it,
His bottle was dead.

He spoke not a word,
But went right to his work,
And left a new shaft
For each little jerk.

Then laying his hand
Aside of his roan,
And giving a burp
Willie left us alone.

He piled in his truck,
Cranked up in a jiff,
Then shot off the roof
Like a bat out of Smith.

But I heard him shout
'Fore he drove out of sight:
"Merry Christmas to all,
Turn out that d _____ light!"

The *Brackety-Ack*, 14 December 1951

"Dad" Strudwick was gone but his bench was a constant reminder to the Rats of their subservient status.

Alumni Day was bigger than normal in 1950 as the association celebrated the fiftieth anniversary of the annual event. Over 400 alumni came back to Salem to help with the revelry; the administration got more than it bargained for when a dedicated group of alums turned a part of the festivities into an impromptu forum on football. College officials just listened!

Students were up to numerous pranks and projects. None who were involved have forgotten the bricking up of the rear entrance to the Ad Building in the spring of 1955. There were, of course, constructive pursuits too. Students raised money each year for the March of Dimes to fight polio, and raised $767 to help erect a new chapel in 1950. They helped host the Western Virginia Science Fair, and once again answered the questions from the army of census takers that hit the campus in 1950. For the election of 1952, the students clearly liked Ike a lot more than they liked Stevenson, 235-87.

One of the oldest student organizations merged with another in 1949 as the YMCA and YWCA became the Student Christian Association. There were a host of denominational groups on campus in 1950 including the BSU (The Baptist Student Union), the Canterbury Club (Episcopal), and the Lutheran Student Association. Clericus continued its long tradition. By 1953, the *Brackety-Ack* reported that the religious organizations were fading on campus and that only prompted the "Religious Emphasis Week" to be organized in the following year. The Fortnightly Club began serving refreshments to beleaguered students during final exams in 1950; the practice continued until 1953 when the women stopped the contribution because students' conduct and complaints overshadowed the expressions of appreciation. Like everyone else, the students could mess up a good thing.

By the early fifties, the memories of football had begun to fade; time, and the college, had won out. Almost a decade had passed since the last home game against Randolph-Macon in 1942. The *Brackety-Ack* reported by 1951 that "school spirit had never been higher" and students looked ahead confidently to future sporting successes. Although designed to fill the void left by football, soccer had not quite measured up; students were dumbstruck with a soccer victory in 1953—that coming after eighteen straight losses.

Baseball enjoyed a rather checkered history during the time, not only in wins and losses but also in whole seasons when the team did not even materialize. Students complained about the lack of enough athletic fields and the need for more tennis courts. The college responded in 1954 with the addition of two new asphalt courts laid out next to the older clay courts. With the advantage of new facilities, the college brought back tennis as an intercollegiate sport the following year, and Professor Frank Snow agreed to supply the pointers. An Appalachian Trail Club was formed to provide students an outlet for weekend expeditions. And a popular pep band was organized, which saw duty at numerous contests over the years.

Basketball and Coach Buddy Hackman enjoyed continued success with several Mason-Dixon conference titles and even more "Little Six" state crowns. Hildreth Hall became an athletic dorm in 1950 as the basketball team moved in; a couple of months later, it survived a run-in with a renegade Coke truck with hardly a scratch. Fran Ramser and her field hockey and basketball teams continued to amass victories in women's sports.

But final kudos are reserved for the Roanoke track men of the times—the "Bast Boys." With cross country and both indoor and outdoor track, the teams won numerous state and conference titles for their mentor, Homer Bast. No one could catch our cross country runners for a period which extended three years and a string of twenty meets in a row.

Soccer was introduced in 1947 to help allay student complaints about their missing football program. These Roanoke booters from 1949 did their best to make students forget.

ROOM SERVICE

When it was learned that the basketball team would occupy Hildreth Hall for the 1950–51 session, many were heard to say, "Well, it certainly will be a relief to get rid of those rowdies who have been raising the roof of Hildreth for the last two years. At last we will have a group of men who are ready, willing, and able to make full use of the peace and solitude of the 'Little White House' and devote many hours to quiet study and solemn meditation."

Perhaps such moments were justified, for since the beginning of its use as a men's dormitory two years ago, Hildreth has compiled a terrifying record of thrills and excitement. It has been said that criminals, gamblers, and vandals have passed through its gleaming portals to seek new fields of conquest and adventure within its mysterious walls. Last week, however, a new visitor completely ignored the gleaming portals and just passed through one of Hildreth's mysterious walls.

Due to the acute shortage of milk in the commons, the guests of chateau Hildreth arranged for a startling innovation; room service at Roanoke College. Probably through an over-zealous effort to push their product, the coke people made their first delivery rather abrupt. By quick calculation, they figured out how many long trips it would take them to carry all those cases of coke into the building, and decided that such a course was far too strenuous and time-consuming.

Picking the softest looking opening (as a matter of fact, the very window through which showers of blue ink rained down on last year's Hildreth guests), the coke man sought to deliver the whole load in one fell swoop. Actually, however, the only thing which fell was the side of the building. Approximately one-third of the cargo was actually delivered, but the remainder of the order was left conveniently outside the window, within easy arm's reach.

Just about the time the truck began lumbering toward Hildreth Manor, the Korean-minded occupants decided that it was some new kind of enemy secret weapon and quickly raised the white flag of surrender which may be seen in the front center of the accompanying photograph. As the picture proves, however, the ruthless and determined coke man was set on doing his job, through rain or snow, wall or window. It may be truthfully said that the mid-afternoon coke party was a smashing success.

Article by Joe Baldwin in the *Brackety-Ack,* 22 September 1950.

"Tennis anyone?" Wearing the latest in tennis fashion, these students head off for a few sets.

CHAPTER 17

"A growing Roanoke,"
1955–1963

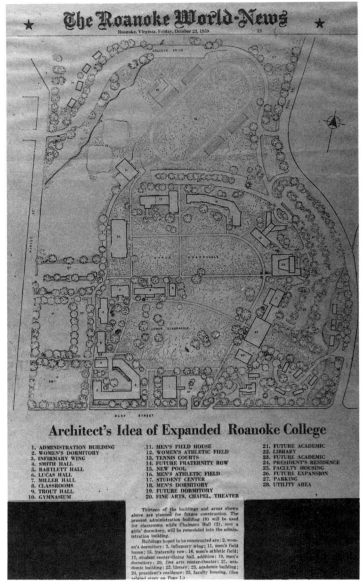

Architect's Idea of Expanded Roanoke College

1. ADMINISTRATION BUILDING
2. WOMEN'S DORMITORY
3. INFIRMARY WING
4. SMITH HALL
5. BARTLETT HALL
6. LUCAS HALL
7. MILLER HALL
8. CLASSROOMS
9. TROUT HALL
10. GYMNASIUM
11. MEN'S FIELD HOUSE
12. WOMEN'S ATHLETIC FIELD
13. TENNIS COURTS
14. FUTURE FRATERNITY ROW
15. NEW POOL
16. MEN'S ATHLETIC FIELD
17. STUDENT CENTER
18. MEN'S DORMITORY
19. FUTURE DORMITORY
20. FINE ARTS, CHAPEL, THEATER
21. FUTURE ACADEMIC
22. LIBRARY
23. FUTURE ACADEMIC
24. PRESIDENT'S RESIDENCE
25. FACULTY HOUSING
26. FUTURE EXPANSION
27. PARKING
28. UTILITY AREA

Thirteen of the buildings and areas shown above are planned for future construction. The present administration building (8) will be used for classrooms while Chalmers Hall (2), now a girls' dormitory, will be remodeled into the administration building.

Buildings hoped to be constructed are: 2, women's dormitory; 7, infirmary wing; 11, men's field house; 14, fraternity row; 16, men's athletic field; 17, student center-dining hall, addition; 19, men's dormitory; 20, fine arts center-theater; 21, academic building; 22, library; 23, academic building; 24, president's residence; 25, faculty housing. (See related story on Page 1.)

Planners of the late fifties envisioned a different Roanoke; this one featured a faculty row of houses, new buildings on Clay Street and a missing High Street.

The college's only Rhodes Scholar, Frank A. Reid, '08, served on the Board of Trustees from the 1920s until the fifties.

If President Sherm Oberly had spent the first seven years of his administration preparing, restructuring, and assembling a new management team, the last seven years of his presidency were marked by the execution of the biggest construction boom since the Back Quad expansion of 1910. The contours of the modern Roanoke would take shape by the late fifties and early sixties.

As important as the physical expansion was the adoption of planning procedures to help the college identify and prioritize its needs and concerns for the future. The first campus "Master Plan" was approved in 1959, and it projected "a new Roanoke for a new age." The plan depicted a greatly expanded campus both in terms of acreage and building additions. A college "Ten Year Plan" was formally adopted in 1962 as the first comprehensive accounting of overall college projections and planning considerations. If expansion and growth were to be the buzz words of the sixties, the college had to be in position early enough to anticipate the demands. Already by 1962, the school envisioned a student body of one thousand by 1970. For that to become a reality, land would have to be purchased, buildings constructed, and money raised. The stage was set for the decade which would see more change and development than any other in college history.

Financially, the college retooled to put itself in a stronger position. The board of trustees adopted more aggressive investment policies with the college's endowment in 1956, and witnessed the first balanced budget in that same year, beginning a string which has not been broken since. The college pursued federal money in a way never before imagined. The Federal Housing Administration awarded a $425,000 grant in 1957 to assist in the construction of two new dormitories, Bartlett and Fox; and the National Defense Student Act of 1958 provided, in time, hundreds of thousands of dollars in financial assistance to enable more and more students to attend college. Sputnik and the Cold War had more than their share of educational benefits.

The board of trustees moved its annual meeting to the fall for the first time in 1960, departing from a tradition that dated back to the days of Julius Dreher and the nineteenth century. They soon discovered, however, that they were meeting in the spring about as often as they would officially convene in the fall; the volume of business and the increasing pace of college affairs demanded more constant attention and decision-making.

Fund-raising was never far from the top of college priorities. With Dave Thornton's steady hand, the college launched its most ambitious campaign in history—the two million dollar "Anniversary Challenge" to be met by 1967 at the college's 125th anniversary. The school's "Living Endowment Fund" continued to thrive, and fund-raising techniques truly hit the media age with its first film production in 1960; other prospective donors were offered a set of slides and an accompanying tape recording for the comfort of home viewing.

The trustees appointed a special committee in 1958 to reexamine the relationship with the Lutheran synod in Virginia. The church and college had slowly drifted farther apart over the last twenty years, and the nature and future of that relationship needed to be addressed. By 1960, a preliminary report suggested that the two groups might indeed rededicate themselves to each other. The synod expressed hope in being able to support the college on a more regular and substantial basis in the future, and to underscore that hope, pledged $100,000 to the construction of a new college chapel. In response, the college dropped its boilerplate motto about the school being "broadly Christian, not narrowly sectarian" and prepared to consider a new age of church relations. The church donation turned into more good will than good money, but at least a dialog had been established.

With the death of long-time trustee and benefactor A. M. Bowman, the college received a bequest of $100,000 to put to the expansion projects of the period. Tuition jumped from $480 a year in 1957 to $540 by 1958 and to $650 by 1962. But still there was never enough money. To meet the ever-increasing demand of student enrollment, the trustees were forced to consider borrowing the much needed capital. Twice the board went to the brink, once to borrow $250,000 for renovations to the Sections and again in 1960 to ask for $600,000 for a new residence hall, but stopped just short. Only in 1961 did the trustees succumb when they felt obligated to borrow $300,000 for an expansion project for the Commons.

Clearly the demand for greater facilities was brought about by the spiralling student enrollment. With 529 students registered for classes in the fall of 1955, the figure moved steadily upward. By 1956, 585 students were present, followed by 633 the next year and 695 by 1958. By 1960, the 700 mark had been eclipsed for the first time, with 722 students officially enrolled. If the growth rate was remarkable, it was still only a fraction of what it might have been. For the freshman class entering Roanoke in the fall of 1960, the college received over 700 applications for the 175 available positions and the 89 additional late-comers were told not even to bother to apply. In the student body, males still outnumbered females two to one, 421 to 248; there were thirty-five students on the Korean GI Bill; and the first of a new category of military dependants, seven children of soldiers killed during the Second World War, made their way to Roanoke. The religious preference of students was evenly split in 1960: 121 Baptists, 120 Methodists, 100 Episcopaleans, 98 Presbyterians, and 86 Lutherans were the principal denominations represented.

By 1961, enrollment hit 761; the comprehensive fee for tuition, room and board was $1,400; the percentage of local students began to drop perceptibly, and for the first time in history, women outnumbered men in the freshman class, 142-133. By the following year, the 800 figure had been passed.

The old KA house could be found at the end of College Avenue next to the Deanery. The frame structure had been built in 1874 and stood until the college tore it down in 1957.

Ready for the big dance, two couples meet in a fraternity house parlor for final preparations.

To accommodate the student onslaught, the college's physical plant was taxed to the breaking point. The older buildings were routinely reconditioned and renovated to help face the crunch. Bittle Hall was spruced up with new paint in 1960; Smith Hall had all new plumbing installed; the old Methodist Church's Education Building was rededicated as Chalmers Hall in 1958 and renovated as both office space and a women's dormitory. A new parking lot appeared behind the Sections and a general campus landscaping plan was first implemented. Bartlett Hall, a dorm for women, and Fox Hall, a men's residence and the "Sixth Section," both came on line in 1958. By 1962, plans were ready for another dormitory that two years later would open as Crawford Hall.

With the additional numbers of residential students, seating space in the Commons was at a premium. One solution was the change from student waiters to a cafeteria-style operation in 1957. Overcrowding persisted, and by the summer of 1961, construction began on an extension which connected the Commons building to the original gym, now the Lab-Theatre. The connecting piece allowed the Commons to expand its seating from 160 to 358. Downstairs, the Cavern tripled in size from 44 chairs to 150. The Lab-Theatre benefited too with additional backstage space for its construction shop and dressing rooms. And the first college bookstore found a home in the basement as well.

The Cavern continued to be the campus hot spot of the late fifties.

HODGES KEEPS SCHOOL IN SHAPE FOR 25 YEARS

As we all know, there is a great deal of work connected with keeping an institution the size of Roanoke College in such an eye-appealing condition. Naturally there are many small things that come up throughout the school year such as broken windows, light bulbs burning out, and broken locks which all have to be repaired.

The man in charge of this tedious and everlasting work is Mr. Harry Hodges, who has been with Roanoke College since 1934. At present Mr. Hodges has a staff of eighteen men and women under him; however, this was not always so. Joining the Roanoke College staff in 1934 Mr. Hodges worked as a carpenter until 1938 when he was promoted to Foreman of the Maintenance Department. He served in this capacity until 1943 when he was again promoted, this time to Superintendent of Buildings and Grounds.

From 1945 until 1950 the school had a Director of Physical

Planning but once again Mr. Hodges returned to the top as Superintendent.

There are many jobs which seem endless such as grass cutting, raking leaves, and shoveling snow during the winter months.

During the past summer many other jobs were performed such as refinishing floors and repainting the chapel, inside and out.

To me it seems that Mr. Hodges does almost everything around here except teach.

Being a Salemite, Mr. Hodges at present resides in his home town at 220 Market Street with his wife and two children. With the exception of a two week vacation period he works a nine hour day all year in keeping the school in the fine state that it is so we may enjoy it.

The *Brackety-Ack,* 25 September 1959.

THE NEW COMMONS

As he swung open the front door, a sophomore found himself in a foyer, facing a walnut-paneled wall. From it he let his glance wander over the cinnamon-bright paint of adjacent walls, up to the soundproofed ceilings and modern lights.

"I see it," he said, "but I don't believe it."

The best was yet to be, for he had stepped only into the entrance of the renovated and enlarged Commons building; his astonishment would grow when he hit the dining room proper.

Many on campus "saw it but didn't believe it" as the new Commons opened this semester. . . . It culminated last year with wails of agony from everyone, including students who had to stand in rain and snow, waiting to eat, faculty members who had to schedule long breaks in classes because of the time it took to feed resident students, and members of the Slater Food Service

Management, Inc. charged with responsibility to serve inviting meals under conditions that made it virtually impossible.

The College population had outgrown the dining hall, there was no other way to put it.

One day of work was lost to mother nature, when a skunk holed up in an area that is now a ladies' restroom but at the time was only an open square space in a maze of pipe and timbers.

The efforts of workmen to extricate the little black animal without undue exposure to its retaliatory measures raised quite a flap before it was over; everyone was in on that act, including the local newspaper and television cameramen. As the skunk finally emerged under forced draft, one workman had to go home and bury his overalls.

Excerpts from an article in the *Roanoke Collegian,* Fall 1961.

"Operation Bookswitch" in action; the whole affair went off with military precision.

Finally, the major project of the period was the new library. Ordered by the Board in 1958, plans and funds were ready by 1960, and the cornerstone was laid in November, 1961. At a cost of $750,000, it was by far the most expensive project the college had ever undertaken. When it was finished, Don Sutton stood ready, bull horn in hand, and Operation Bookswitch was underway. When the dust had settled the students had transported the library's collection from Bittle Hall to its new home across High Street carrying 30,000 volumes in 2 hours and 13 minutes: a new world's record! Clifton Fadiman, a well known author and literary critic, was on hand for the formal dedication and the unveiling of the 600 pound bronze plaque which hung in the foyer with the names of the 900 donors who had contributed $150 or more to the cause.

Academically, the expansion of the faculty matched the record numbers of students. From a total of thirty-six professors in 1950, the number became fifty-seven by 1963. The names of new faculty and staff from any given year are impressive; the year 1956 was no exception. Listed in alphabetical order, they read like a who's who of college affairs over the next several decades: Charlie Bondurant, Elinor Coleman, Bob Coulter, Pat Gathercole, Robert Lorenz, Harry Poindexter, Tex Ritter, and Don Sutton.

"OPERATION BOOKSWITCH"

To the roar of a fraternity cannon and the rasp of a bullhorn in the hands of Donald M. Sutton, director of the student activities who planned it, "Operation Bookswitch" got underway in the bright afternoon sun of September 13, at 1:45.

When the cannon boomed again at 3:58, the last book to leave Bittle Memorial Hall was carried over the threshold of the new library.

In the hectic 2 hours and 13 minutes in between, nearly 400 students had moved 30,000 books across the campus and onto the shelves of the new $750,000 building. They promptly laid claim to the title of "world collegiate champions," throwing out a challenge to any other student body that wanted to try to duplicate their feat. No takers are expected.

By a very conservative estimate, they had moved over 7 tons of books. By actual count they had consumed 756 cups of soft drinks and walked a shattering 2,240,000 paces.

Clad mostly in shorts and shirts, the brigades moved out at near dog-trot in the first half-hour, wearing down to a more conservative walk as the 90° heat began to take its toll. Book dyes ran off on sweat stained shorts, putting many students in rainbow hued outfits by mid-move.

Divided into special units and teams, men and women of all classes, members of the faculty and staff and even a couple of Salem neighbors, made long lines that snaked between the two buildings.

As they picked up numbered loads, carriers passed specially posted guides who directed them to the proper lines for floor destinations.

Once inside the new library, they were met by teams that helped unload the books in the proper order on pre-numbered and waiting shelves.

Co-eds who made the mistake of starting without socks soon raised blisters and shoes began to appear in piles along the line of march as the women stayed in line bare-footed rather than drop out.

Occasionally someone missed his place in line and was called back in again by whooping companions.

The voices of guides grew progressively more hoarse as the afternoon wore on and finally some just pointed their directions.

It was a hard, hot job and students carried it off with a festive air that left everyone gaping and gratified. Just for the record, the title of the last book in was noted: "Banned Books: A Study in Censorship."

The *Roanoke Collegian*, Fall 1962.

The newly-finished library in 1962.

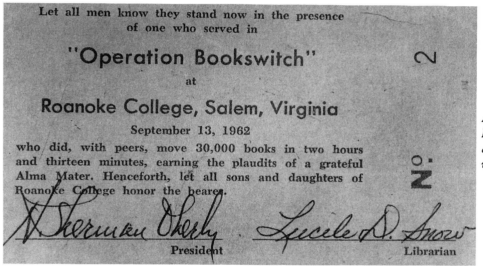

Let all men know they stand now in the presence
of one who served in

"Operation Bookswitch"

at

Roanoke College, Salem, Virginia

September 13, 1962

who did, with peers, move 30,000 books in two hours
and thirteen minutes, earning the plaudits of a grateful
Alma Mater. Henceforth, let all sons and daughters of
Roanoke College honor the bearer.

Sherman Oberly
President

Lucile D. Snow
Librarian

N°. 2

*All survivors of "Operation
Bookswitch" were issued this
authentic certificate in
recognition of their labors.*

Of course, the college lost several celebrated faculty and staff to retirement as well. Professor Evans Lindsay retired in 1956; former dean Charles Brown and bursar Happy Mann stepped aside in 1958. The following year George Peery decided to end a career at Roanoke that had begun in 1906; he had labored faithfully in the Biology Department, most of that time as its chairman, and served on the college faculty for fifty-three years—longer than anyone else. Dean of Women Helen Hobart ended her long association with the school in 1963.

The academic program moved ahead with a number of changes designed to update the college curriculum. Required minors were deemphasized in 1961 as the faculty encouraged students to select from a broad range of elective courses to underscore the advantage of liberal learning. A major in Sociology came about in 1959, and a host of new courses, including Russian, made their way into the college catalog. Professor Miles Masters led the way to Europe on numerous off-campus expeditions, while back home the college introduced its evening program in 1961.

The faculty received its first official "Faculty Handook" in 1960 which detailed the rights and responsibilities of faculty members. Dean Perry Kendig created a new committee in 1960 to enable faculty to help in the process of reviewing and evaluating other faculty—the Faculty Personnel Committee. The whole administration endured another "self-study" or reaccreditation examination that same year.

Professor Jimmy Rikard, complete with beach chair, engages some students in discussion. Chaplain Rikard offered "TRC" (The Reading Course) to a generation of Roanoke students.

Dean Perry Kendig takes a moment to chat with a couple of students.

The faculty voted to end a new system of freshman orientation in 1961 because it tended to "coddle" rather than instruct the students in the rigors of academic life. The orientation course was allowed to remain, but it was stripped of academic credit. More testing was performed and administered by Chaplain Rikard to establish psychological profiles of the students and guidance information for the college. The English Department still required its minimum proficiency exam, and in 1956 the faculty introduced a new grading system; in the future, failing a course not only brought the student no credit, it counted as a minus one on the quality point scale. "WP" and "WF"—withdrawal passing and failing—appeared that same year, as did a ban on classroom smoking. Classes were back to being taught on a six days a week basis, and a continuing tradition, the Honors Assembly (now a special banquet each spring) was first staged in 1960 to recognize some of the college's best students.

The faculty still busied themselves with matters like a dress code for students. Dean Kendig routinely reminded all those enrolled that no student could marry during the semester without his permission; failure to do so resulted in automatic suspension! The Rat System came under increasing faculty and administrative scrutiny by the early sixties. At one point, the faculty had virtually passed a resolution demanding an end to the system but then compromised by expressing a hope that the practice would be "deemphasized."

In the ever shrinking world of post-war America, the students of Roanoke expressed an interest in and a concern about world affairs that was unprecedented. Clearly the majority of the students felt as Marshall McLuhan said in 1960 that the earth had become a "global village." And no event sent a shiver down the country's Cold War spine faster than Sputnik did in the fall of 1957. In an editorial published a week after the Soviet satellite was launched, the *Brackety-Ack* exhorted students to redouble their efforts in their studies in defense of America. The paper called upon the faculty to increase the science requirement to make future graduates more fit in the battle for survival against the "Russian menace." In the opening laps of the space race, the *Brackety-Ack* interviewed students in a story entitled "What would you do if?" you were the victim of a "fatal attack of atomic poisoning." More than a few students, sensing their patriotic duty, signed up for a test the National Security Agency offered on campus in the spring of 1958. Convocation topics like "Fall Out" were not uncommon, and by 1960, the college formed the "Survival Committee" to develop and implement the college's civil defense plan. Professor Ron Walpole of the Mathematics Department served as campus warden and had installed a special switch in his office which activated the college's official air raid siren on the roof of Miller Hall. Every student and faculty and staff member was assigned space in a designated shelter in the basement of some college building. When Crawford Hall was built, its basement was designed as a reinforced concrete bunker replete with "radiation showers" and the works. Civil defense supplies—food, water, and other essentials—were maintained by the college for years. All faculty were assigned to the college's library; someone figured that all the books present would give the faculty something to do for the next two thousand years. With the first Soviet cosmonaut in space in the spring of 1961, coupled with the Cuban missile crisis in the fall of 1962, the *Brackety-Ack* each time called for students to make ready.

First in line but last to eat, the Rats form their famous gauntlet for the upperclassmen.

A couple of Rats give the grass a little brush up. In case you're wondering, yes, that is Sociology professor Janice Saunders on the right.

As Cold War tensions intensified, individuals and institutions across the United States in the early sixties prepared for the worst—nuclear attack from the Soviet Union. Civil Defense plans were devised, fallout shelters were stocked and made ready, and assignments were given to willing hands. Roanoke College, too, prepared its staff and students for the possibility of war, or at best the threat of fallout. Students were advised the following:

What can we do?

1. Do not panic. We cannot jump in our cars and run away. There is no place to go and the roads will be blocked. We will certainly be killed if we try it. Remember that evacuation is not a solution. Stay where you are in as good cover as possible. If you go to a private shelter carry a gun. You may need to kill some crazed person. There will be no policemen.

2. Follow eagerly the plans on campus for air raid drills and shelters. Remember we are all in this together.

3. The women should be taking courses in first aid. Do not wait to be asked but ask Dean Hobart how you can do this.

4. Study as though this were the last year of schooling for you. It may well be.

5. Learn to pray. Most of us are very much indifferent to religion. Maybe that God will save this nation if enough of us ask him.

What is the worst to expect?

We may have to remain in shelters for a week or more. There may be no electricity, no heat, no sanitary facilities and no hot food. The water here can be gotten from the pool. There will be enough to keep us alive. We will eat canned food. We cannot cook since we must conserve oxygen. Can we take it?

National politics captured increasing attention. In 1956, the Young Republicans traveled to Richmond to hear President Dwight Eisenhower on a campaign stop. Back on campus, Ike swamped Adlai Stevenson again in the student election 262-82. Four years later even greater excitement occurred when Vice President Richard Nixon came to Roanoke; over a hundred students traveled to the airport for the rally and campaign speech. The students staged a series of discussions and debates reflecting the added national interest in the election. Unlike the national decision, Nixon won a handy victory over John Kennedy on campus.

With respect to civil rights, the editors of the *Brackety-Ack* maintained a cautious conservatism. Although at first applauding the Supreme Court decision to integrate the public schools of Little Rock, Arkansas, the paper found little sympathy in supporting an attempt to integrate the University of Alabama the following year. While there were no blacks at Roanoke, several students felt proud at least to play against other schools that allowed blacks to attend and to participate in athletics. Catholic University, a school which did both, was barred by state law from playing in Virginia with an interracial team; consequently Roanoke travelled to Washington to compete.

A timely float rolls down the street in the 1961 Homecoming parade.

The *Brackety-Ack* continued as a legitimate student forum. In 1958, the paper's staff won a "first class" rating in a national competition sponsored by the Associated Collegiate Press. When another year's staff tried to kill a popular gossip column "Scratching the Surface" because it was not worthy of a good paper, the student outcry made the staff reverse itself; a new column appeared to take its place: "The Brackety-itch Yak." Classified ads appeared for the first time in 1957—at five cents a line—and the satire edition continued to confound and amuse.

The paper loved conducting polls of student opinion, some serious topics and some silly. A 1958 survey which asked students "what to do about the overcrowding on campus?" discovered that the overwhelming response was to "limit the number of women allowed in." A poll taken two years later about equal rights for women concluded that they should have some rights but certainly not all. A telling response came in a 1957 poll about abolishing the honor code; a solid majority, 271-94, felt the system did not work and should be discarded. Although some faculty agreed, the administration's decision was to keep the code and make the students even more accountable. That meant the passing of an "honors test" to be administered to students on the provisions of the system. A grade of 90 was necessary to pass; on the first testing, 183 passed while 105 did not. Testing one's honor only made the students grumble more.

The college had its own weekly television show in the fifties. Channel 10's studio offered the latest in state-of-the-art camera equipment.

"My Sister Eileen" entertained audiences in the Lab-Theatre in 1957.

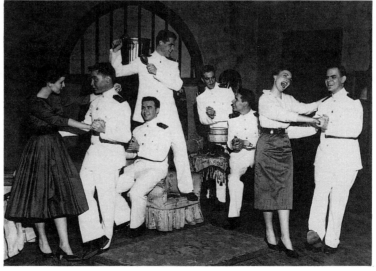

The Commons moved from its traditional student waiters to a cafeteria-style service in an effort to accommodate more diners.

May Day festivities continue to offer musical reviews into the sixties.

An old-fashioned barbeque in 1961 attracts a crowd; just in case things got a little too hot, the fire truck is at the ready!

Campus life afforded the usual array of good times and bad. A new radio station appeared, WROC, and in 1958, the first official "Student ID" cards were issued. Students complained about the new five dollar charge for registering their cars, and just to make sure that the students were impressed with the seriousness of the new campus parking regulations, the college had the Salem Chief of Police on hand to recite the rules and the fines.

During the better part of one academic year, the clock in the Alumni Gym's tower was removed for repairs; students conveniently cited its departure as the reason for their chronic tardiness. The crafty faculty doubtless saw through the conspiracy. When a new college viewbook appeared in the late fifties, students enjoyed hearing the official version of life at Roanoke and wondered why the photos did not show the "decaying state of the Sections."

Unlike "Tide" the laundry detergent, while the Commons was "new" in 1961 thanks to the recent expansion project, as far as the students were concerned it was certainly not "improved." In a major show of solidarity, over two hundred students protested conditions by boycotting dinner one evening. The protest worked as the administration agreed to meet with students and to discuss bettering conditions. An accord was reached which entailed the hiring of a new chef, the installation of a suggestion box, and other meal-time improvements. The student dress code, coat and tie for the men and flats or heels and gloves for the women, was relaxed as well. A women's student government request in 1960 that they be allowed to wear "bermudas" on campus at certain times was flatly rejected.

Socially, the campus witnessed the continuation of the two oldest festivals, the May Court and Homecoming, and saw the advent of numerous others. The May Day celebration continued as a moment of pageantry under the able direction of Fran Ramser. Homecoming underwent more change but remained a popular weekend each fall; in 1956, the Homecoming Queen was retitled "Miss Roanoke" and in subsequent years, the title became "Miss Roanoke II," "Miss Roanoke III" and so on. The campus was home to other royalty as well; along with the May Queen and her princesses, there was the Rat Queen and the Apple Blossom Princess.

There was always new programming; the student Social Committee saw to that. A "costume ball" was staged in 1955; a Spring Weekend debuted in 1957, and the first Fall Festival by 1959. The 1960 fall event included a soccer match, a parade, dinner, a bonfire, and a dance. The college "Parents Weekend" also appeared for the first time in the spring of 1960, and officials were delighted to have 150 parents in attendance. The students even had a chance to celebrate after lining up for their polio shots in 1956; the college physician Dr. Russell Smiley delighted them by taking all of the money they had paid for the shots and treating them to a party and dance in the gym.

Social activities inevitably spilled into town too. No place was more popular than The Brook Club when it opened across from the GE plant, and the Salem Record Shop always had a crowd. Spring break and Ft. Lauderdale became increasingly popular as the fifties progressed; when snow closed the college for two days in February, 1960, there was serious faculty discussion about taking two days away from spring break. The student firestorm of protest gave Dean Kendig only one recourse—he told them to drive safely.

Greek life flourished during the period with record numbers and additional houses added to both the fraternities and sororities. In 1959, a local fraternity known on campus since 1947 as Lambda Kappa Psi, went national to become Pi Lambda Phi. Alpha Phi joined the ranks of the sororities a couple years later. The Inter-Fraternity Council was reorganized in 1955 to act as the clearing house for the male greeks; the IFC moved rush to the spring in 1962 and raised a few faculty eyebrows when it eliminated a minimum GPA needed for rush in 1960. The Sigs celebrated 1,000 chapter meetings in 1956 with the KAs not far behind in the following year. The KAs hosted their first Old South Ball in 1959, and the Delta Gammas sponsored their first Folk Festival in 1963. Only the Pi Kaps spent official time in the dog house when they incurred the wrath of the administration in 1961.

The Rat System came under increasing scrutiny but somehow survived, thanks mainly to the vigilance of the sophomores. The Rats were expected to memorize the plaque to Doctor Charlie on the front of the Ad Building along with their usual assortment of chores and rituals. Faculty and students alike enjoyed the serialized story "The Diary of Anne Ratt" when it ran in the *Brackety-Ack* in the fall of 1958.

The three college fraternity houses presented in this composite photo from the early sixties.

The Rats and their beanies head into the chapel for another meeting.

There were a myriad new academic groups formed as well. A Model United Nations Club came to order in 1960, a new English Club in 1956 (and another in 1962), and the Goodwin Society—a group dedicated to meaningful discussion and the publishing of their literary magazine, *Reflections*. The Biology Club reorganized itself as Tri-Beta in 1958. A new debate club appeared, a glee club in 1960 and "The Bards" and "The Belles," two groups of student singers. The French Circle was formed in 1962 and offered the college's first foreign films series that same year. The RoCo Grotto, students interested in cave exploring, was organized in 1957 and appeared live on national television when NBC's Today Show came to Roanoke in 1958.

The Honor Council continued the struggle to uphold its standards. The students proposed doing away with the library fines policy and running the library on an "honor basis," but the librarians were not as confident. "Quiet Hours" during exams were a council proposal in 1959. The enforcement function of the Honor Council was reassigned in 1961 with the birth of the Judicial Board. Henceforth, honor violations, dorm infractions, and charges brought by the women's student government would all be tried by the "J-Board." The Dorm Council was established in the late fifties to give students more power and responsibility over their own affairs. In 1961, the forerunner of today's "Resident Assistant" program was introduced as the dorm council recommended "Proctors" on each dormitory floor.

The "Cherobiblos," published by Cardinal Key after 1956, was still the student's bible, and the college boasted its first language lab in 1960 on the first floor of Trout Hall. "Health Services" superceded the "Infirmary," and the college's Placement Center increasingly prepared students for the "real world." Students annually contributed to the "Campus Chest"—a part of the Community Chest—and averaged 150 pints of blood each year for the Red Cross.

On the sporting front, baseball went the way of football by the mid-fifties. Lack of a suitable playing field coupled with declining student interest and administrative support doomed life on the diamond. Basketball remained with some success. The college added a swim team in 1956, a golf team the following year, and even a bowling club in 1960. The tennis team of 1961 finished the season with an 11-1 record while the Roanoke "mermen" showed improved style in the pool. Men's soccer continued to get better as well. Women's athletics still offered only two sports: field hockey and basketball.

ROCK WASHERS WANTED FOR BITTLE'S BOULDERS

Rock washers, no experience necessary, are being sought at Roanoke College. Their job will be to help clean nearly three tons of rocks found here last summer.

The rocks are a part of a vast collection begun over a century ago by Dr. David Bittle, founder and first president of the college. This collection was part of Bittle's dream of making Roanoke College an outstanding educational institute. It was started with the purchase of the Hayden collection in 1857 which gave Roanoke College the most valuable "mineral cabinet" in Virginia.

When Bittle sought financial aid for his unendowed school, he instructed friends to send a rock for his collection if they couldn't make a donation. Rocks began to trickle in from every state and as far away as Mexico, Peru, Japan, and India. Additions were also purchased for the collection until, in 1893, the Bittle rock collection numbered some 12,000 specimens and occupied the entire west end, main floor, of the administration building. About 1900 the stones were packed into open boxes and stored away, and from this time on silence surrounded the once famous collection.

Then, last summer, Mrs. Grace Bosworth, Director of Public Relations, read of the missing Bittle collection, and she and Sam Good, Director of Admissions, set out to discover if the rocks were still around. Their search uncovered box after box of gray, dirty rocks in both the basement of College Hall and the attic of the Chemistry Building.

Sixty years of neglect had left a big cleaning job for Mrs. Bosworth and Mr. Good. Another tremendous problem would involve classifying the individual rocks by name and location of source.

This fall, Pete Ely, a junior at R.C., volunteered his services for the clean-up job. Pete, who hails from Connecticut, plans to make a career of geology and, the opportunity to examine these rocks is more joy than burden.

As yet, only a part of the original Bittle collection has been found, and it is suspected that much of it remains concealed in various buildings on campus or as doorstops in offices.

An article by Barbara Lubinski in the *Brackety-Ack*, 20 October 1961.

A photographer captures some of the
artistic wizardry of Maroon
basketball of the early sixties.

Fran Ramser and her 1957 field
hockey Maroons. Women's
intercollegiate athletics debuted in
the fifties.

Again, running was Roanoke's strong suit during the period. The cross country team continued to impress, one year finishing seventh in the nation. But Elwood Fox's track team compiled an even more remarkable accounting; between 1953 and 1958, the track and field men won thirty-eight consecutive meets without a loss. Their string of conference and state titles was equally impressive.

Twice the students considered either changing the nickname "Maroons" or adding a mascot. Both times, in 1957 and again in 1963, they decided against tampering with tradition. Already they were asking the question "What is a maroon?" The students of 1910 had the answer: it was simply a color. While other colleges changed their nicknames and added mascots, Roanoke never did. It should be proud of that.

In the spring of 1962, Sherm Oberly surprised more than a few people by announcing his retirement. In a year, he would turn sixty-five and felt that the time had come for a younger successor. He had been at the helm for fourteen years and had guided the college well through the enrollment emergencies of the early fifties to the bounty of the early sixties. He had managed the institution's affairs wisely, both financially and academically. He established the process and had hired the people who would get Roanoke ahead through the next generation. Oberly, moreover, had maneuvered the college into a position that would enable it to reap increasing dividends and a remarkable expansion in the immediate years to come. In short, he had left the college in better shape than he found it, the measure of any steward.

Homer Bast and his runners compiled an amazing record during the period. Here is the 1955 team.

The ultimate shutter-bug, Sherm Oberly, is caught in the act on the porch of Roselawn. Homer Bast, listening to conversation, is framed in the middle.

"A new man
for a new age,"
1963–1969

The year 1967 marked Roanoke College's 125th anniversary since the days of Bittle and Baughman on the hills outside Staunton. The year was marked with special events and testimonials celebrating the accomplishments of the college. A Founders Day was reintroduced, and Roanoke City, Roanoke County, and Salem—in a rare expression of unanimity—all honored the school with a "Roanoke College Week" in October. On hand too was the Secretary of the Treasury, the Honorable Henry H. Fowler, already the college's most famous son, to bring greetings and congratulations. The anniversary's theme placed the student at the heart: "A New Man for a New Age." The women apparently would have to wait for another age.

When Sherm Oberly announced his intention to retire to the board of trustees in the spring of 1962, the board routinely prepared for a national search to find the next president. Through the fall and winter, names of candidates appeared and interviews were held, but none of those captured the heart or the imagination of the trustees. By the spring of 1963, attention was slowly shifting back to campus and increasingly centered on the man who had faithfully served at Oberly's side for the previous eleven years—Dean Perry Kendig. With the board's election, President Kendig became only the second Roanoke chief executive to be selected from within the college ranks, the first since Julius Dreher was tapped in 1878.

The Secretary of the Treasury, the Honorable Henry H. Fowler, fields questions from the media at this college press conference.

Through the first six years of Kendig's presidency, the college would build more buildings, purchase more property, and raise more money than at any other time in its history. A true campus transformation occurred with the construction of three new dormitories, four fraternity houses, and work underway on a chapel and a massive science complex. Campus acreage doubled during the period to make way for the expansion and to provide for new athletic fields and stadium. It was a remarkable revolution.

To prepare the way, the board of trustees began to streamline its operation when in 1963 it authorized its executive committee to act on behalf of the full board. As if anticipating the rapid pace and decisions that the college would face in the immediate future, the trustees felt that requiring the formal action of the full board would only hamstring the college at critical junctures. Further, the investment committee of the board was given additional latitude in making its financial decisions. By 1965, the board established two new vice presidencies—finance and development—and promoted Clarence Caldwell and David Thornton respectively to fill them. The modern college's cabinet system was taking shape.

When Perry Kendig changed positions and became President in 1963, he and Ginny also changed their campus residence from the Deanery to Roselawn.

This peaceful view of the Ad Building almost denies the rapid change that came to the campus during the decade of the sixties.

The ever-expanding campus. Crawford Hall was finished and housing women students by the time this aerial shot was taken in the spring of 1965. (Warren Gilbert Photography)

College fund-raising hit heights never before imagined. With a goal of two million dollars, the 1967 anniversary challenge had been launched with some trepidation. Yet by the time of the celebration, the fund had exceeded the two and a half million dollar mark. David Thornton, never one to kill a good thing, announced an extension to the challenge and set a new measure of 6.9 million dollars as the goal; already by 1968, 4.1 million was safely in the bank. In 1965, the board had mandated additional efforts in the college's public relations program and also recommended a "major gifts" component to future development strategies. By 1969, the college introduced its "Associates Program," a special designation for those benefactors who give a thousand dollars or more each year to the college.

Relations between the college and the church took a major step forward in 1965 with the signing of a reaffirmation agreement which brought the two bodies more closely together. The first such

document in forty years, the statement embraced the principle of mutual interest and cooperation. The Synod of Virginia again pledged continued financial assistance; the college responded by appointing a director of church relations to compliment the college's first full-time chaplain, Pat Keister, who had started his campus labors in 1963.

The board pledged higher faculty salaries and benefits in 1966 and 1967, and even ordered administrative cuts to ensure better faculty pay. The trustees, eager to protect their rapidly expanding physical plant, ordered an insurance appraisal in 1968 to make sure that the five million dollar building and $880,000 contents coverage was enough in case of some emergency. The trustees also approved, with Tex Ritter's able hand, a new seal for the college in 1964 and the creation of the Roanoke College Medal in 1968 to be awarded to special friends of the college.

The college saw two of its alums honored with Time *magazine covers in the space of two and a half years. Henry Fowler, '29, leads the way.* (Time-World, Inc.)

College President of the Board Stuart Saunders, '30, headed the merger of the Pennsylvania Railroad and the New York Central in one of the decade's most heralded corporate take-overs. (Time-World, Inc.)

Enrollment continued to grow during the period, and applications materialized on an even faster pace, allowing the college to be increasingly more selective. For the freshman class of 1963, the college received 791 applications; two years later, 1,167 forms made their way across Admissions Director Sam Good's desk. General college enrollment moved upwards from 833 in 1963 to 916 in 1964; the college hit its target of 1,000 students by 1970 a year early with the academic year 1968–1969. The fall figures included 330 freshmen, 90 transfers and 676 returning students for a total of 1,096 students—eclipsing the millennium mark for the first time in college history. College charges for tuition, room, and board escalated right along with enrollment and the increasing inflation of the late sixties.

Physically, the campus grew up and out in every direction. First, Crawford Hall, a dormitory for women, was completed in 1964, and long before that

was finished, a new residence hall for men was being planned. The result was Bowman Hall built beyond the Sections on longtime trustee and benefactor A. M. Bowman's land. The college acquired the property and a $100,000 bequest at his death in 1963. By 1964, Clarence Caldwell had hit the sidewalks around campus, bag of money in hand, buying up property as quickly and as quietly as he could. And Clarence could be as quick and as quiet as anyone. By the end of that year, the college had moved west of Market Street for the first time and acquired the property for four future fraternity houses and the largest parking lot on campus. The college moved south to Clay Street with another acquisition and in time east, up High Street, and finally north along the old creek bed to Hawthorn Road.

*The college choir
practices in the chapel.*

As early as 1965, the college began planning two major building projects: a science center and a religion-fine arts complex. Both were regarded as essential components of the new Roanoke and fund-raising went forward in earnest. The site selected for the science center caused two immediate problems: the building and its parking lot would eliminate the college track and stadium and a good part of its athletic fields, plus force the relocation of the college shop and maintenance facility which was located along side the field. To accomplish the former, the college acquired title to the land north of campus and

proceeded to regrade and improve the fields. The creek was placed in a conduit running under the new stadium, and concrete stands were constructed along the west side of the new site. To accommodate the college shop, Caldwell decided to leave campus altogether and to purchase a vacant 7 acre warehouse site about a mile from school at the other end of College Avenue. The three quonset huts and office gave ample shop room and storage space. The old "playground," first purchased by the college in 1885, and the home to every major outdoor sport ever since, had seen its last victory.

*The first plans for
what would become
Antrim Chapel and
Olin Hall. These
buildings never got
off the drawing
board.*

THOMPSON AND PAYNE
ARCHITECTS AND ENGINEERS

THE RELIGION-FINE ARTS CENTER
FOR ROANOKE COLLEGE

The Center will consist of a gracious quadrangle flanked by the Chapel, the Auditorium with its Music and Drama Wing, and the Fine Arts Building.

The new *Chapel* will seat 150 with offices for the Chaplain and facilities for counseling, small conferences, and symposiums. The new *Auditorium* will seat 1250 with a completely equipped stage including a movable altar for large religious services, an orchestra

pit for concerts and musicals, and special sound and lighting facilities for all types of presentations. Estimated cost: $1,515,717.

The new *Music and Drama Wing*, located at the east end of the Auditorium, will provide two floors with acoustically designed studios for teaching vocal and instrumental music, for groups and individuals, as well as rehearsal halls and workshops for dance and drama instruction. Estimated cost: $890,867.

The new *Fine Arts Building* will have four large studios for the arts, a hall for exhibitions and recitals, as well as lecture halls, classrooms, and offices. Estimated cost: $437,390.

Plans for the religion-fine arts facility did not more as readily. With the 2.7-million-dollar price tag for the science complex and a 1968 temporary federal funding freeze, the college was unprepared to attempt two colossal expansion projects simultaneously. However, a gift of $250,000 by the Antrim family in memory of their son gave the college the reason to go ahead with the first phase of that project and in the spring of 1969, ground was broken for Antrim Chapel.

The first of the fraternity houses finished was the Pi Lam house, a bit up Market Street from the official fraternity quad, which opened in 1965 at a cost of $212,000. The three other houses followed in 1967—the new homes for the Pi Kaps, the Sigs, and the KAs. The college purchased the older houses of the fraternities in return.

The last of the residence halls to be erected coincided with the closing of Marion College, a two-year Lutheran school for women in Marion, Virginia. The financially troubled institution closed its doors in 1967, and Roanoke accepted its students and agreed to construct a new residence hall and name it in honor of the college. The Marion College property and other assets would be sold, and Roanoke would use those funds to pay for the construction of the new facility. Marion Hall opened in 1968 and was formally dedicated in the spring of 1969 with scores of Marion alums on hand for the celebration. Marion was air-conditioned, fully carpeted and featured semi-private bathrooms. To the Roanoke College student used to fans, hardwood floors, and a trip down the hall, Marion was soon dubbed "The Hilton."

MARION COLLEGE

In 1873 Marion College was founded as a Lutheran institution for young women, receiving its accreditation as a junior college in 1913. In 1967 it closed its doors, leaving behind a long heritage, many memories and a host of faithful alumnae. In 1923, while on the search for endowment, Elmer T. Clark wrote a short pamphlet—"Why Discriminate Against the Girl?"—in hopes of helping the Marion cause.

"There is a strange inconsistency in man's dealings with women. Always he has professed, and truly so, to venerate her above all else. But always he has discriminated against her and suppressed her. . . . Socially and sentimentally he has bowed at her feet and acknowledged her as his superior; but in every other sphere he has deemed her as his inferior. Here is a strange and anomalous situation.

"But the strangest element in his situation is the fact that we have carried this discrimination into the field of education—the very field in which women render their greatest service. . . . Yet it is more difficult for the girl to secure an education than for the boy. There are fewer scholarships for her. There are fewer opportunities to work her way. Her colleges universally have smaller endowments.

One might conceive of such an attitude on the part of the secular world, but surely the Christian Church would not adopt it! Women support the Church more loyally than men. Surely the Church would not discriminate against its girls! But the Church does! . . . Discrimination against the girl in her higher education is unjust, unfair, unworthy. And in a Christian Church, which would go out of business but for women, it is likewise folly. It ought to cease.

Give, then, your support in unstinted measure to the Christian College for women. . . . Marion Junior College stands for equality of educational opportunity for girls. The ideal of its founders was to provide for girls liberal education under Christian influences and environment. This ideal is cherished by the College and its entire program is fixed around this ideal as a centre.

Marion College was a Lutheran two-year school in Marion, Virginia, which closed in 1967. Roanoke accepted its students, and funds from the sale of its campus and its endowment were used to build Marion Hall.

Physically, the college was not finished yet. When John Fishwick, the president of the Norfolk and Western Railway, decided to sell his house, the college paid him a visit. By 1968 and for a tidy $63,500, the college purchased the residence destined to be known as "The President's House" at the far end of Market Street. Roselawn, the traditional home of the presidents since it was built in the teens and newly refurbished in 1964, was scheduled for demolition. Fortunately, it was decided that the new fine arts center would be built further north along High Street and venerable Roselawn was spared.

There were, of course, numerous renovation projects throughout the period. The Deanery was claimed by the development staff as office space for fund-raising, alumni affairs and public relations. College Hall contained the infirmary on the first floor for a while before the business office decided to annex the property. The upstairs served as sorority suites for almost twenty years. Bittle Hall saw continued improvements, including the addition of the campus post office to the south of the building. For faculty and students alike, each year began with an attempt to refamiliarize oneself with the campus directory. Psychology moved to Roselawn, History and Political Science to Trout, English from the Lab-Theatre to the Sections, and the Fine Arts jockeyed for position where they could. And the academic musical chairs were only beginning.

President Perry Kendig's inauguration took center stage in the spring of 1964. On a cold April day in the Back Quad, four hundred faculty and dignitaries processed, representing 235 colleges and universities. The thousand guests and spectators enjoyed the festivities and were treated to the first of many presidential addresses delivered by Perry in his own inimitable style. With the dean becoming president, there was an obvious job opening which President Kendig was prepared to fill. First he asked Physics professor Lee Anthony to serve as acting dean until a full search effort could be mounted; in the spring of 1965, Kendig settled on his choice—Edward Lautenschlager.

Kendig pledged his support for a stronger, more professionally active faculty. The number of faculty with Ph.D.s rose from around 40 percent in 1964 to over 50 percent by 1969. The first faculty sabbatical leave was granted to Professor Ron Walpole in 1966, and four additional research grants were awarded in the following year. In 1967, the college helped support Biology professor Harry Holloway and a Roanoke student, Ron Campbell, who would win a National Science Foundation grant for research in Antarctica. The two spent three months with the United States Research Program collecting data for its study of "Endoparasites of Antarctic Vertebrates." The college also debuted the *Roanoke Review* in 1967—a professional journal dedicated to literature and literary criticism.

The college acquired this property in 1967 and designated it the new President's Home, ending Roselawn's reign which had begun in the nineteenth century.

Integration came to Roanoke in 1964 when Virginia Maxine Fitzgerald registered for classes; by the summer of 1966, the campus was home to an Upward Bound program, and segregation officially became a thing of the past.

The college library boasted more than a collection of books during the decade. It was the site of numerous art shows including the annual faculty-student exhibit begun in 1962. The building hosted a permanent local history exhibit of the Roanoke Valley Historical Society, and became the political nerve center of the campus as well since it housed the Board Room for the trustees. The faculty and the student government met in the same room. The library signed a cooperative agreement with Hollins College in 1967 which entailed, in part, the sharing of each school's card catalog. The Roanoke staff doubtless celebrated in October 1968 when the final book was reclassified from the old Dewey Decimal System to the new Library of Congress System.

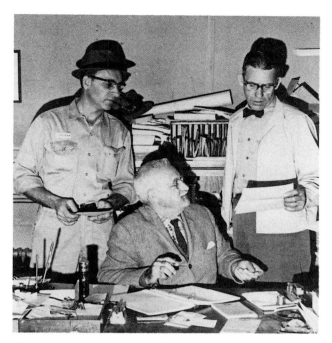

The task of maintaining the college's physical transformation of the sixties fell to these gentlemen; Harry Hodges, seated, worked at the college for half a century; Charlie Perfater, on the left, served for over thirty years; Homer Johnston is standing on the right.

The faculty and staff pose with their new chief, Perry Kendig. Flanking Perry are Acting Dean Lee Anthony (left) and Registrar Homer Bast and Business Vice President Clarence Caldwell (right). (Don Hall Studio)

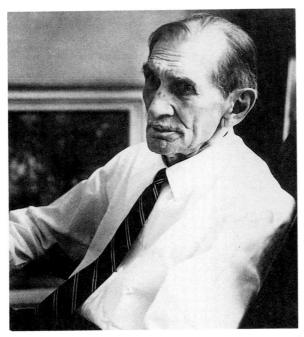

Salem native Walter Biggs was a renowned artist who taught painting at the college for a number of years.

The Commons and the Lab-Theatre were officially joined in 1962 creating additional space in the dining hall and the Cavern. President Kendig was inaugurated in the Back Quad on a cold April day in 1964.

Academically the faculty continued to review and revise the course of study. A new degree was authorized in 1964, and the first Bachelor of Business Administration was graduated the following year. In 1967, the faculty first awarded degrees with distinction: cum laude, magna cum laude, and summa cum laude. A Psychology department was added in 1963, and Jimmy Rikard was still administering personality tests to all incoming freshmen. President Kendig offered additional support for student counseling when he observed in 1965 that "many students lack motivation and application and as a result need orientation and vocational guidance."

The faculty ended Saturday classes, to the delight of the students, in 1967 and revised the traditional "four week reports" on every student to "mid-term grades" for freshmen and those students having difficulty in a particular course. The faculty granted "competency" for the first time in 1964 for students who had tested out of a certain class, and further revised the grading scheme with the introduction of "AB," "IN," and "SP" in 1967; the days of the simple A, B, and C were gone for good. The evening program continued to expand, as did foreign travel under Professor Miles Masters's watchful eye. The faculty reached a new decision regarding the "cuts" policy in 1964 which essentially included henceforth only freshmen and those students on academic probation. And if there were any questions about who was on probation, the faculty revised those measures in 1967; the college established a series of escalating measures—from 1.2 to 2.0—which the student must reach or be placed on probation.

Certainly, the principal work of the faculty of the late sixties were two studies: one, to review the college semester calendar and to see if there were alternatives; and second, to reconsider the college's curriculum. The former evaluation was concluded first, and in the 1968–1969 academic year, the new 4:1:4 calendar debuted. The students would take four courses in the fall and spring terms and one course in the "Interterm" during the month of January. The new curriculum would appear in the following year.

It is not a great journey. The old campus is four miles away as the crow flies. But a man doesn't go often.

You go back to meet, in the cool, sometimes smelly chemistry building, a pleasant man named Andrew (Buck) Murphy.

Murphy is associate professor of chemistry at Roanoke College; a tickling Irish humor about him and the holder of a teaching talent which touches people and causes them to remember Murphy and the periodic table of elements as well.

Years after the fact of Murphy, chalk-dusted and lecturing in the auditorium, you find people who remember.

Years after, they remember the loss of a little of the freshman's dread when Murphy hauled into the lecture auditorium with the first quiz of the season. Hauled in and exclaimed: " 'Buck' Murphy rides again! We'll cut through the valley by way of Red Gap and cut them off at Eagle Pass!!"

Remember, too, a fellow named Eustace Peevey from Botetourt County, who showed up on multiple choice tests.

A brilliant fellow named Thud Snodgrass intrudes himself into Murphy's lectures and it is the tragedy of Eustace Peevey's career that he thought up most of the theories and concepts of chemistry long before the people who get credit for them in the textbooks.

"It's not to be a stand-up comedian," said Murphy, "it's to keep the attention of the class."

Murphy's vocabulary and the way with the strategic joke came to Roanoke College in 1947. He has a bachelor's degree from Erskine College in the Roaring Twenties. He got the master's in chemistry from the University of North Carolina.

Murphy can quote Thomas Wolfe among the test tubes; can keep the Thud Snodgrasses and the Eustace Peeveys doing their part for the learning process year after year. He can, after some study, condense a portion of the way he feels about teaching.

"We are constantly striving in the attempt to develop a respect for accuracy and the ability to distinguish theory and fact or opinion and fact . . . through chemistry you can stress that."

They learn their chemistry from Murphy and remember the man—the chalk-dusted Murphy who could, and can, say "Due West, South Carolina" and get a laugh out of the way he says it.

They have dedicated the yearbook and the freshman manual to him.

They are all glad that "Buck" Murphy still rides in a warm world containing Eustace Peevey, Thud Snodgrass, and a rare technique for touching the mind where it matters.

Excerpts from a column by Ben Beagle, Jr. in the *Roanoke Times and World-News*, reprinted in the *Brackety-Ack*, 14 February 1964.

Faculty work was not always weighty. A 1963 decision about faculty parking in assigned spaces caused pandemonium, and a faculty committee in 1965 about maintaining the faculty lounge and exploring the possibilities of a faculty club found more problems than solutions. And nothing caused a greater uproar than a 1966 *Brackety-Ack* threat to conduct and publish its own faculty evaluations. Concerted faculty pressure brought that attempt to naught.

The passing of time saw the retirements of Julius Prufer in 1965, after forty-three years of dedicated service; Helen Hobart in 1968, the college's first dean of women in 1941 and later a Sociology professor; and beloved Chemistry professor Buck Murphy in 1969. Death had claimed Ashley Robey in 1965. To honor its retired members, the faculty recommended and the trustees approved in 1968 the creation of the rank of "faculty emeriti" and elected three former faculty as the first recipients: Julius Prufer, Charles R. Brown, and Helen Hobart. Sadness struck the campus twice in sixteen days during the spring of 1967; while on campus celebrating his 85th birthday, Doctor Charlie Smith succumbed in the place and amidst the friends he held so dear; a short time later, Sherm Oberly died in Richmond with Charlotte at his side.

The new president, Perry Kendig, chats with some students under the bell tower.

The view down Main Street.

The Commons sported a new "country club" awning and entrance through much of the era.

After the tumultuous summer of 1968—of demonstrations and convention protests—at the fall board of trustees meeting, one trustee asked Dean Edward Lautenschlager if there had been any "unusual behavior by the students;" Dean "L" did his best to allay any trustee suspicions that Roanoke was coming apart. To be sure, there were no dramatic showdowns or confrontations but on the other hand, "the times, they are a changing." Student attitudes between 1963 and 1969 changed about as much as did the campus's physical plant. If the *Brackety-Ack* began the period by analyzing the advantages and disadvantages of "Red Rockets, Torpedoes, and Buzz Boards"—all favorite types of campus skateboards—it finished the decade with headlines like "Life at RC Induces Paranoia" and "Students Must Educate Faculty."

The campus in 1963 saw the arrival of smocks, shifts, and weejun shoes, the first "Keep off the Grass" signs, student folk groups, and discussions of the Test Ban Treaty, and was stunned by the news from Dallas in November. In the following years, the student body became increasingly more aware. There were scores of articles in the paper and numerous "open discussions" on campus about integration and civil rights, "Sex and You" and birth control, lowering the voting age and promoting social action. Students formed a "freedom movement" in 1965 and two years later organized the "League for Progressive Ideas." The hip *Brackety-Ack* announced in 1964 that "conformity is bad news" and a headline recorded "World's Fate Dim as 67 Begins." The students organized a "Vietnam project" in 1966 which sent food, clothes, and supplies to a Catholic orphanage in Saigon run by a Roanoke alum; students collected funds too in 1968 for "Biafra Relief."

Spiro Agnew paid a visit to campus during the Nixon-Agnew campaign of 1968.

Increasingly, the war in Vietnam occupied more student time and thought. If the war and the draft were at first an annoyance, by 1966 the *Brackety-Ack* had a single word answer to the problem: "Canada." By the following year, various students and groups called for the end to the draft, and the paper reported on how the Defense Department had a plan to draft militant students first. The *Brackety-Ack* printed an HEW memorandum on "How To Stop Student Unrest," called for Muhammad Ali's release, and authorized an editorial supporting the SDS—Students for a Democratic Society.

Interest in national and international affairs was reflected too in a newfound campus activism. Students protested the college alcohol policy in 1964, and the paper encouraged students to "demonstrate on campus problems." Noting that "responsible dissent is essential," the students challenged the faculty and administration on a number of fronts. The Commons, a frequent target of scorn, fared no better by the end of the sixties; the Slater System, the contracted operations and inventors of the "Slater

Mystery Meat Supremes," received a weekly tongue-lashing from the students. Mandatory weekly chapel ended in 1967. Student dress and conduct codes underwent serious revision, and the separate women's dorm rules were relaxed in the same year. Students celebrated dorm visitation hours two years later; the men's dorms could be open to "visitors" from 7:30–11:30 P.M. on Friday and Saturday evenings and on Sunday afternoons from 2 to 5 P.M.

It would be foolish to think that all students were committed to change or that college life was so dramatically altered that little of the old remained by 1969. Tradition and conservatism were persistent themes as well. In the campus election staged in 1964, Barry Goldwater defeated Lyndon Johnson 278-265. A thousand onlookers packed the gym in 1968 to cheer Vice-Presidential candidate Spiro Agnew on a campaign stop; Alabama Governor Wallace had addressed a crowd twice that size the year before in the Back Quad.

The festivals continued as well. Homecoming with Miss Roanoke College was always popular, and the May Court with its Queen and Princesses still attracted real interest. The college sponsored the "Prettiest Cheerleader Contest" and even hosted an annual visit from a *Playboy* "Playmate of the Month." Social events attracted big crowds too. Judy Collins, the Platters, Wilson Pickett, and Richie Havens all made it to campus during the period. Alumni Weekend was moved to earlier in the spring in 1969, and for the first time since 1900, it was not a part of Commencement week. Parents Weekend was shifted to the fall to balance the college calendar.

The Rat was still on campus, but the official "ratting period" was down to just a couple of weeks. The old Rat Council had been updated and renamed the "Traditions Committee," but many of the old features and the follies survived. A new tug-o-war over the Roanoke River provided a keen photo opportunity in 1965. Students could play off campus too. Bryce Mountain Ski Resort opened in 1965 "designed with the student in mind;" for those students unable to travel down the valley, Commons trays came in handy on the Bowman hill during a 1966 snow fall. Spring break was bigger than ever and students no doubt were bemused when Ft. Lauderdale City Manager mailed copies of the city's "Rules and Regulations" to student newspapers across the eastern United States; the *Brackety-Ack* did its "civic duty" by publishing the statutes.

May Days with their courts entered the period but did not survive the turbulent sixties.

Greek life weathered the times rather well. The fraternities celebrated their new homes and succeeded in getting the administration to allow "combos" and beer in their houses. Rush moved to the spring, and the Pi Kaps celebrated fifty years on campus with a special dinner and dance in 1966. The Pi Lams purchased a fire truck for "special events" and the KAs managed to set fire to the pole vault pit with their cannon in 1967.

Academically, the students still maintained their honor council and participated in faculty affairs like never before. Students were given seats on several faculty committees studying both the new calendar and curriculum. A student proposal for "a reading day," a break between the end of classes and the start of exams, was adopted by the faculty in 1966. New honor societies were formed in physics and psychology, and the Cinema Club organized in 1968 promised to offer "stimulating films." A new radio station WRCR, went on the air in 1968 first from the Sections and later from its new "studio" on the top of Trout Hall. The college sent a team to New York to appear on GE's College Bowl, and the debate club won several tournaments. By 1969, the History Department became the first on campus to allow students to attend and vote on departmental business.

On the playing field, the "Skullbashers" first strapped on their helmets as a club team in 1965; by 1966, lacrosse was here to stay. Basketball returned to its winning ways by 1966 and the arrival of Coach Charlie Moir in 1968 ushered in a new age of basketball prowess. The "Moir Miracle" of that year resulted in the best team in thirty years, finishing 22-8 and winning the Mason-Dixon tournament championship. Frankie Allen, the college's first black athlete, started his career on that team on his way to numerous individual records. The newly opened Salem Civic Center would be home to the Maroons for the next decade.

The men's swim team enjoyed an impressive record with several state titles to its credit. The women added a swim team too in 1965; because of a lack of competition, the women held only two meets—both with Lynchburg College—and the Roanoke "Marmaids" managed a split. By 1968, the women garnered a 7-2 season.

Clearly, the big winners of the time were Coach Andy Moson's soccer teams. After a dismal 1-8-1 start, the club improved to win state and Mason-Dixon titles in 1965, 1966, 1967, and 1968. The '68 team finished 10-1-1 and was ranked by the NCAA as the best small college team in the South and thirteenth nationally.

"THING-GATHERING"

A few weeks ago the big news on campus was the purchase of a fire engine by the Pi Lambda Phi fraternity. Although a fire engine hardly seems practical it reflects the prevailing campus fad around the country for groups and organizations to have certain bizarre objects to raise morale and spread publicity. Sure enough, another fraternity at Roanoke College had announced plans to buy a Sherman Tank from Army Surplus to raise spirit, provide transportation, and presumably, with inter-fraternity rivalry being what it is, to run over that Pilam fire engine.

However, think for a moment. Can you imagine what would happen if this good-natured "thing-gathering" got out of hand? What would happen if the organizations on campus stepped up their competition to get larger, wilder and kookier things than ever before? A future *Brackety-Ack* article might read something like this:

Roanoke College is agog at the actions of the Greek organizations and the screwy purchases they have been making to add to their fraternity "thing" collections. The race has reached fever pitch and the campus is becoming so crowded, academic life is becoming jeopardized.

The Kappa Alpha fraternity first purchased a Greyhound Bus, which could be seen tearing across the quad. Pi Kappa Phi

acquired a new model steam shovel which it promptly painted in fraternity colors. Pi Lambda shot back by pooling the funds of its members and buying the Salem Town Hall for a fraternity house. Not to be outdone by its fellow Greeks, Sigma Chi showed tremendous originality by purchasing the entire Bronx Zoo and transferring the contents to Roanoke. (This may explain the mysterious disappearance of various faculty members.)

From then on, things got quite out of hand. Pi Kappa Phi, determined not to be outdone, wrested the Library of Congress from the U.S. Government. Sigma Chi, positive of getting the "thing" to end all "things", has recently purchased the Rockette Corps from Radio City, while the KA's and Pilams in a joint effort have bought the entire Democratic Party, planning to use them in their rush program. Panic reigns on the campus.

Caution and better judgement is thrown to the wind. In a last ditch effort, Kappa Alpha bought the Norman Luboff Choir, and are reportedly teaching them fraternity songs. Sigma Chi is bidding against the Pi Kaps for the purchase of the American Ballet Company.

Mr. Sutton has since declared Roanoke College a disaster area. Can nothing be done to salvage sanity of thought at Roanoke College. The Campus comments: "Help!"

An article by Morris Dearing in the *Brackety-Ack,* 10 January 1964.

A final note to the chapter can be added. A campus wag observed in 1969 that "when a student went to see the Dean, we used to ask what the student had done. Now we ask what the Dean has done!" By any measure, the sixties could indeed be characterized as a time of "unusual behavior by the students."

Cage action in Alumni Gym; it was always cozy, for both players and crowds; when the Salem Civic Center opened, the Maroons played off campus for more than a decade.

A courageous Fran Ramser instructs her archery class from in front of her students!

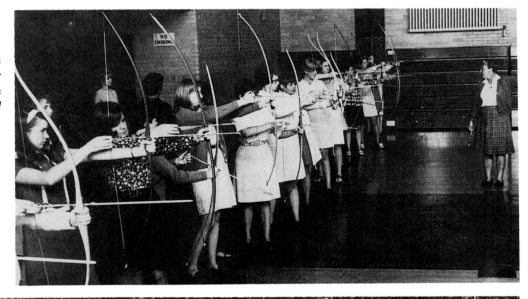

Soccer crowds picked up as the Maroons amassed more victories and championships.

CHAPTER 19

"New priorities,"
1969–1975

President Perry Kendig rebounded from a mild heart attack he suffered in the fall of 1968 to lead the college into the decade of the seventies. By contrast to the incredible change and expansion of the 1960s, any decade would pale in comparison. For Roanoke, the early seventies were a time of ready adjustment, review, and reflection. The physical and spatial additions now demanded assimilation and incorporation. In short, Roanoke identified some "new priorities" as the seventies began.

For the first time in twenty years, enrollment became less a question of fate and more a product of management. The confidence and optimism of the sixties had lulled college officials into a false sense of complacency with regard to the pool of college applicants. For two decades, enrollment had been a problem of too many rather than too few. Imposing limits and quotas on the numbers of students had been an annual process, and programming the college's enrollment expansion had been a principal avocation for years.

College enrollment continued upwards for a while. In 1969, the number of students passed the eleven-hundred mark, and in the following year, the student body numbered 1,180. In 1971, the twelve-hundred barrier had been pierced. President Kendig, half-seriously, commented on the wisdom of a system which mailed 15,000 catalogs over 75,000 miles to produce 1,300 applications to get 450 new freshmen of whom 61% would graduate. The board of trustees was uncertain as to a future course in 1971 as far as enrollment was concerned. Pondering the course of future expansion, the board hesitated and decided to postpone any far-reaching decision.

By the following year, the wave crashed, and the college recorded its "first decline in enrollment in memory." When classes began, 1,127 students could be counted; by 1973, the numbers slipped below the 1,100 mark. In 1974, after concerted effort and even the adoption of an 800 phone number to facilitate prospective student calls, enrollment rebounded to 1,268. College officials were pleased, but the optimism had been shattered. Moreover, there was considerable erosion in that number because, by the spring of 1975, only 1,202 students remained. References to national predictions forecasting declining applicant pools for the balance of the decade only made prospects seem gloomier. From a time of buoyant excitement, the college was fast moving to a state of anticipated retrenchment.

The trustees moved into the seventies by restructuring their system of governance and by liberalizing their interaction with both the faculty and the students. President Kendig had called for more individual contact between the board members and the various college constituencies in 1969. By 1970, the student body president was the first student formally to address the board in college history. By 1971, a number of faculty and students participated in several trustee subcommittees, and in 1974, the Student Government Association president was made a permanent, non-voting, member of the board. Another student recommendation was adopted by the board in 1973: to appoint a recent graduate to the trustees. The board obliged by nominating James Stump, Class of 1972, to join its ranks. In the same year, the trustees also agreed to share all financial information with the entire campus at the same time that they first viewed the statements.

The college signed a new covenant with the Virginia Synod of the Lutheran Church in 1970; both the college and the church pledged their mutual support and respect and hoped to work more closely together in the future. Additional discussions with Hollins College were initiated in the early seventies to consider possible cooperative ventures. The budget report of 1974 celebrated twenty consecutive years of being in the black. The trustees saluted numerous college friends and servants on the occasion of their retirements, and none were more touching than the resolution to "Miss Bessie" Dooley, a secretary for forty-four years to seven deans, one registrar, and two presidents.

Fund-raising continued at its record-setting pace. By 1972, the college had collected more than thirteen and a half million dollars during the previous ten years. Even the election of Development Vice President Dave Thornton to Virginia's State Senate in 1970 and the additional responsibilities that entailed did not slow the continued dollars. As the Anniversary Challenge culminated with its 6.9 million dollar goal, another campaign was ready to take its place. "New Priorities" was launched, not with an eye on physical expansion but with a renewed dedication to improving the academic program and faculty development. Having supplied the college with an impressive array of new facilities, the new emphasis for fund-raising focused on what went on within the brick and mortar. Faculty salaries were considered the principal concern, and professional development received increasing attention. Instructional support and student financial aid were also seen as "new priorities." Funds continued to roll in while Thornton cautioned students that their "mature conduct would lead to a greater fund-raising potential." Major leadership gifts, from the Crawford and Hunter estates, for example, spearheaded the college campaign. In 1974, Roanoke ranked fourth in the nation in the percentage of alumni giving to the college.

The new decade saw the opening of the science center: the physical science building in the fall of 1970 and the life science complement a year later. The site of the complex proved better suited to a football field than a massive five-story, three-building center. Constructed in an old creek bed, the limestone soil proved more porous, and indeed downright cavernous, than anticipated. The physical science building, today's Trexler Hall, is a fifty foot structure resting on a seventy foot header. Yet that inconvenience to find bedrock was nothing compared to the problems encountered by Life Science; by the spring of 1970, after a year's construction, the whole building began to settle. The project became a nightmare both for the college and for the construction company. The elevator shaft buckled

and snapped and the entire building had to be resecured. Thousands of cubic yards of concrete were pumped back into the caverns beneath the foundation in an attempt to stabilize the structure. So much concrete was forced downward that the grout emerged from pipes and toilets as far away as Broad Street. The cleanup became as big a nightmare as the construction; the building was finally salvaged and belatedly opened in 1971.

Looking west from the Science Plaza. Despite construction problems and delays, the three building complex of Trexler, Massengill and Life Science opened in 1970-71.

Chairman of the History Department Harry Poindexter does a little last minute advising during registration.

With the completion of the science complex, the stage was set for an Oklahoma-style land rush across the rest of the campus as the different academic departments jockeyed for position and attempted to lay claim to the properties vacated by the science faculty. Up for grabs were chemistry's Lucas Hall, math's and physics's Miller Hall, biology's third floor of the Ad Building and psychology's Roselawn. When the dust had settled, the social science and humanities faculty were clustered in new digs like never before. English moved out of the front of the Lab-Theatre and its space in Sections to its new home on the top of Lucas Hall. Foreign Languages pulled its scattered offices together and centered them on Lucas's main floor while the Religion-Philosophy Department congregated downstairs. The departments of History and Political Science, on the road for years with stops in Trout, the Sections, and the old Deanery, were delighted, along with Sociology, with their new offices on the third floor of Miller Hall. Business Administration took up residence on the main floor in Miller. Fine Arts finally got better accommodations too; theatre got more space in the foyer of the Lab-Theatre while the art faculty moved to the top of the Ad Building for its studios, work areas, and dark room. Music inherited Roselawn as the final movement of the piece.

If the college did not add new buildings in the early seventies, it certainly invested great time and money renovating the older ones it had. Along with the major overhauls of Lucas and Miller halls—both buildings were completely refurbished and air conditioned—the college renovated the Lab-Theatre, the Commons, and the Cavern. The school ended its contract with the Slater System in 1970, and Dick Phelan arrived to manage the Commons operation, an assignment he has held ever since.

With the opening of Antrim Chapel in 1970, the old Methodist Church was expendable, and in the spring of 1972, a demolition crew arrived to raze the structure. A new campus master plan was adopted in 1969 which projected a Roanoke of the future. The plan envisioned a string of "Bowman Halls" extending up High Street, a faculty row and loop drive across the northern face of the campus, and a new administration building along Clay Street at the entrance to the campus. The plan also called for the destruction of Wells and Yonce Halls—the oldest of the sections. When the trustees approved the razing of the old Sections in 1974, it sparked a controversy both on campus and among the alumni. The *Brackety-Ack* published "the Death of Sections" and questioned the college's commitment to its traditions and past. The students presented a petition to the trustees asking them to spare the venerable old dorms. The trustees accepted the remonstrance and announced that there were no immediate plans to proceed with the demolition. The Sections had been spared.

Spatially, the campus had grown from 28 acres in 1959 to 65 acres by 1970. Still, there remained two major building needs that the college entertained: the first, a fine arts center, and second, a student center. The proposals and planning continued, but the necessary funding would not materialize until mid-decade.

The modern interior of Antrim Chapel; the building was dedicated in 1970.

Math professor Bill Ergle waits for the right answer.

The Rommel Plan of 1907 called for a Market Street orientation; by 1970, at least the Science Center looked to the west.

High atop the Life Science building was a new greenhouse; botany professor Phil Lee was never happier.

Academically, the college introduced a new curriculum in 1970 to go along with its new calendar. The new academic program offered a "distribution" system which featured a series of subject areas from which the student would select a given number of courses. The curriculum offered choice and flexibility for students in the best liberal arts tradition. A special feature was an interdisciplinary course requirement which ideally put students and faculty together to investigate a topic from a variety of vantage points.

Reflecting the same sentiment, a faculty committee proposed a liberal arts major in 1970 to emphasize the broad advantages of a general course of study. The faculty voted to reject the proposal after considerable discussion; even the *Brackety-Ack* had labeled the program "a farce." Three years later, however, the faculty did approve not just a major but a new degree—the Bachelor of Liberal Arts. It embraced the same philosophy and required the student to take five courses in each of three separate disciplines.

The faculty added other components to the catalog as well. New majors in education and physical education debuted in 1970 followed by the college's first interdisciplinary major, urban studies, in 1972; two years later, criminal justice made its appearance. New courses were always being introduced, and independent study and internships were utilized as never before. Television production went on for the first time in 1970, and Italian was spoken for credit in 1972. The college's extension office offered new and exciting alternatives as well; a course on flying airplanes took off in 1970 and three years later, a course on jumping out of airplanes followed.

The faculty survived another self-study in 1970, wrote a new statement of purpose in 1971, and authored a paper on academic freedom in 1974. Relations with the administration and the trustees hit the skids in 1973. Faced with declining enrollment and worse prospects, the administration felt compelled both to reduce the size of the faculty and to impose limits and quotas of tenured faculty for the future. Needless to say, the faculty was not overjoyed. Some compromise was achieved, but the quota system stayed in place for over a decade.

Faculty-student relations reflected the spirit of the times rather squarely; there were disagreements and the occasional showdown but in the end, the students recognized in the faculty their kindred spirits. One such flap began in 1969 over the issue of faculty evaluations filled out by students. At first, the faculty had balked and Dean Lautenschlager encouraged them "not to participate" in another round of surveys sent out that fall. Within a year, however, enough faculty agreed with the students that the dean announced that the evaluations were "optional" for faculty wishing to use them. A few years later, faculty evaluations were a requirement for all professors.

The honor system went the way of ratting and the May Court by 1970. The year before, a student referendum had indicated that the system did not work and that the responsible students wanted it changed. Faculty resisted that sentiment and requested that the students try again. By the following year, it was clear to all that the system had failed. Consequently, a new "proctor system" was designed whereby the faculty would supervise exams and students had to "pledge" their work on assignments. An Academic Integrity Board was designed to serve as the system's tribunal. A regrettable, if realistic, decision had brought an age to an end.

Vietnam had proven a testing point for both faculty and students. With growing turmoil at home as well as in southeast Asia, the faculty increasingly agreed with student comments and petitions. In response to a student request for the cancelling of classes in October, 1969, for a national moratorium on the war, the faculty willingly obliged. As a result, hundreds of students participated in a campus forum on the war, handed out pamphlets at local shopping centers, and engaged in a candlelight march through the streets of downtown Roanoke. With the bombing of Cambodia in the spring of 1970 and after the shootings at Kent State and Jackson State, campus activism reached new heights. In light of the national march on Washington scheduled for the middle of May, student leaders petitioned the faculty to suspend the semester and cancel final exams. Surprisingly enough, the faculty agreed, with the stipulation that all remaining work should be made up in the fall.

Going . . .

going . . .

gone! The old Methodist Church falls in 1971 to make way for the new campus entrance sign and lawn. The college kept the church's education building (Chalmers Hall) and parsonage—now the Faculty House.

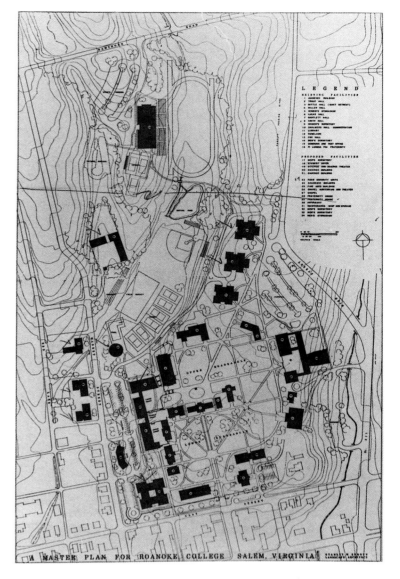

Another "Master Plan" for Roanoke. This called for the elimination of the Sections and construction of a whole string of "Bowman Halls." The beginnings of a Fine Arts complex can be found across High Street.

Students requested of faculty additional roles in college governance, and during the period, students won the right to participate in numerous faculty bodies. The Student Life Committee, the Planning and Development Committee, and even the Admissions Committee all saw student membership.

Even the faculty meeting itself fell to student pressure by 1973 as the student government president, the *Brackety-Ack* editor, and two other students were allowed to attend. By 1975, the number of students eligible to attend had risen to eleven.

Financial aid continued as an ever increasing concern. With tuition keeping pace with inflation in the seventies, the need to assist more students with more money was never greater. The percentage of students on financial aid rose dramatically between the early sixties and mid-seventies. By 1974, a third of the student body was receiving financial assistance. A new scholarship program appeared in 1972 named in honor of the college's first president David Bittle. Five incoming freshmen were named Bittle Scholars and each was awarded five hundred dollars yearly. Two years later, the number was doubled to ten but the award remained constant. Today the college has 42 Bittle Scholars enrolled with an annual scholarship award of over $200,000.

On the lighter side, the faculty was still grappling with the parking issue, and being reminded that the coffee and donut fund in the faculty lounge—always run on the honor system—was chronically coming up fifty percent short each week. The faculty committee in charge had a simple solution: Eat less or pay more! Other faculty blamed the shortage on the students!

Charlie Perfator inspects the college's latest acquisition to combat Old Man Winter—a new snow plow.

Faculty were still asked to help recruit students by passing along potential names to the Admissions Office and by paying visits to prospective students. The faculty were likewise encouraged to eat in the Commons to develop closer associations with the students. Faculty adjusted to the Educational Privacy Act of 1974, complained about President Nixon's wage and price freeze in 1971, and no doubt sheepishly admired the brick masonry skills of several students when they sealed up Professor Jesse Thompson's office door on the top floor of the Ad Building.

Campus life at Roanoke reflected the national trends of the times. Clearly there was a dedicated group of students eager to question and, if need be, to challenge; another group of students typically not engaged or preoccupied by other personal situations; and probably a sizeable majority of students in the center prepared to adopt some causes and to ignore others. All such groups and subgroups were evident in the student record of 1969–1975.

For those students bent on change, there were substantial battles and significant victories on both fronts, social and academic. A 1969 *Brackety-Ack* article entitled "Are you getting your $2,600 worth?" set the tone for many. As far as campus life and policies were concerned, there were lots of targets for the students. Soon, out the window went issues like "dress codes" and separate rules and regulations for the women and the men. Alcohol policies were rewritten, and if dorm visitation was a victory in 1969, it was soon eclipsed by "open dorms;" by 1972, the cause had become "co-ed housing." The college relented and two years later, the first co-ed dorm opened for the fall semester. Having won that fight, by 1975 the ever-escalating demands took on the issue of off-campus housing and the students' right to live where they wanted. Again, the college compromised and allowed seniors the option of living in town if they chose.

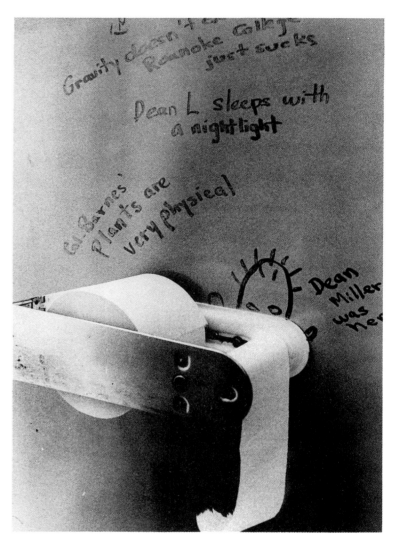

Assorted campus graffiti from the early seventies.

The night the Obelisk went up. Determined to create a memorial that would last, the students dug down to the water pipes before they poured their concrete. They dedicated their monument to Sections janitor Ed Jackson.

The Front Quad, looking little different than it had at the turn of the century.

Social issues existed beyond campus too. In 1970, students formed the Social Action Committee to address questions like "world hunger and campus waste," and in response to Earth Day, several students organized the Pollution Committee to help. Vietnam continued as a major topic of conversation, and the students started the Information Action Committee to disseminate news about the war, the Pentagon Papers trial, and a Chicago Seven forum at UVa, and to collect money for the Kent State student defense fund. The *Brackety-Ack* embraced conservation and the legalization of marijuana, and even printed a form letter that students could sign and send to their congressman in Washington protesting the SST, the ill-fated supersonic transport that the United States contemplated building in the early seventies.

Academically, many students were just as committed to reform. Along with their campaign for a share of college governance, students wanted more professors, better elective courses, a higher calibre of entering freshmen and the elimination of the language requirement. The Interterm was fast losing popularity even by the early seventies; students announced that "the reality was different than what the administration had promised" and that "inexperience and poor planning" had doomed the term. By 1973, the Interterm had simply become "a bore." Even the advent of the "Free University," a collection of courses taught by students and faculty for fun, could not salvage true excitement.

Every student's nightmare—registration! Early morning hours, long lines, and closed classes often combined to frustrate even the most patient of students.

Chemistry professor Ben Huddle came to Roanoke in 1969 and soon had a new home when Trexler Hall opened the following year.

Between 1960 and 1970, the campus acreage had doubled and the building space had tripled. The modern college had taken shape.

In 1971, the eighty-four sociology majors rallied in support of additional staffing in their department; they met with Dean L and complained that three sociology professors were simply not enough. The dean remained unconvinced. When reading day mysteriously disappeared from the calendar the next year, another student petition was directed at Registrar Homer Bast; Homer decided to put it back.

The campus had its share of visitors during the period. Civil rights leader James Farmer, CBS News commentator Douglas Edwards, and an Iroquois tribal group, the White Roots of Peace, all engaged campus audiences. Popular television personalities, "Bewitched's" Agnes Moorehead and fresh from "Green Acres" Eddie Albert, entertained college crowds as well.

The period sounded the death knell for several long-standing college traditions. No longer "relevant" were the old practices and pageants of ratting, the May Court, Homecoming, or Miss Roanoke College. By 1972, they had all passed into history. An attempt in 1975 to bring back Homecoming and to select a queen caused an immediate protest and was promptly labeled as "sexist."

Good times could still be had of course. On campus, the Allman Brothers and Steven Stills saw to that. The Flamingo, across the street from the ballfields past Longwood Park on East Main Street, became the campus hot spot. "Weekends" became the thing in the early seventies; the college hosted a parents, an alumni, a fall, and a spring weekend officially, and an impromptu, unofficial weekend which first appeared in 1973: "Jungle Weekend"—a time of strange behavior and bamboo collecting. And like every other college campus in America during the spring of 1974, Roanoke had its share of "streakers."

Campus fads come and go. Years back, swallowing goldfish and squeezing people into phone booths were the "in things to do." But today, at colleges throughout the nation, streaking has become the latest craze.

All week long streakers, those who run nude through public places, have been spotted around the Roanoke College campus. Spurred by continued news reports of mass streaks throughout the country, and prompted by warmer weather, students have shed their clothes to "run nude".

Times and techniques of Roanoke College streakers vary. Monday night, three men streaked in front of Crawford Hall, as Deans Lautenschlager and Miller watched.

Tuesday, the warm evening prompted about thirty men to streak around the fraternity houses. A large cheering group, estimated at 250, lined Market Street to watch others streak by. Students used bikes, motorcycles and car-tops as they passed the crowd in their birthday suits.

Three men were arrested by the Salem Police, when they ventured too far on motor vehicles in the buff.

These men were joined by one young co-ed who bared her chest as she was driven by in a sports-car. Later, a van pulled up, about fifteen nude men hopped out, circled, hopped back in and took off.

Streakers have not only appeared on campus at night, but have also been spotted running during the daylight hours. Confirmed reports say that one male streaker emerged from a car on the road behind the Infirmary, dashed in front of Marion Hall, and then headed into one of the fraternity houses on Tuesday afternoon.

The *Brackety-Ack,* 8 March 1974.

The Greeks suffered through a time of declining interest and numbers. By 1972, of the 170 beds in the college-owned fraternity houses, only 106 students were in residence. Those numbers prompted college officials to announce that unless occupancy reached 95 percent, the fraternities could lose their houses. That threat has loomed over the fraternities' heads ever since. On a happier note, the Sigma Chi's celebrated their one hundredth anniversary since their initial establishment on campus in 1872; the Delta Gammas followed suit the next year as their national organization turned the century mark. With the addition of the science center, a new feature to the fraternities' bid's day debuted in 1974: "The Run." The prospective pledges would take off running from the Back Quad, head down the stairs around Massengill Auditorium, and across Market Street to their choice among the fraternities. The Saturday event became an increasingly popular campus spectacle as the decade progressed.

Back in Halcyon days of yore, otherwise known as Freshman year, depending upon point of view, sections was a bona-fide big deal. (No pun intended). While Section six contained many freshmen, 3rd, 4th, and 5th Sections contained the elite of the campus, if one considers this to be the higher orders. Many of the inhabitants of this zoo have passed into legend, from Tex Ritter's Cow, to Ackley's Harley-Davidson (built from the wheels up in a suite in 5th Section) to Tom Bonuara's all semester parties. Having been weaned on a diet of sections fable it is sad for me to report sections imminent demise. The death knell of Sections was struck from the desk of finances because Roanoke needs money, or rather, they don't want to lose their government grants for Bowman and the Houses because of lack of residents. Sections was ordered closed because of lack of residents. Sections was ordered emptied of students conditionally for next year. Of course, 5th Sections had already surrendered with scarcely a blow, to the girls. True, it did go out in grand style, with graffiti on her walls, a chrome plated john and a green telephone, but nevertheless it was lost. Now 3rd and 4th may be going the way of economic necessity. That will close forever the history books on the Sections Traditions—the days when the guys were as close as brothers, when Dean Segner reigned and no one ruled, have passed. Long live the new order!

When guys gather in smoke-filled rooms to think fondly "far outs" are spoken, and many happy hours of hanging out are remembered, the conversation, if coherent at all, often turns to 5th Sections greatest hour of glory, "Jungle Weekend" when the tall dorm was festively decorated with bamboo shoots from top to bottom, when music filled the quad and frisbees filled the air, along with numerous colors. The dorm, with all doors open, boasted a keg on every floor, and produced several memorable parties. During the day, since it usually coincided with Spring Weekend and Alumni Day, the crowds gathered around the steps, to listen to music and watch the alumni have their picnic, throwing frisbees or playing kickball. Getting into your own act was the order of the day, and pretending to be degenerate seemed to be the favorite pastime. Reports of the class of '24 swooning en masse while walking by are not too exaggerated. What this comes down to is that, what with Alumni Weekend starting, and it being waterfight season and all, and there will never be another jungle weekend—it could happen in fourth section—there's plenty of space, lots of graffiti, some nice steps to hang out on, and bamboo down by the pool. The beer is in the Cavern. But does anyone feel in the spirit? Tomorrow will tell.

The *Brackety-Ack,* 27 April 1973.

The changing face of Roanoke; blacks were first admitted in the 1960s.

Hal Johnston cuts the net after Roanoke defeated Biscayne College in the 1972 finals of the NCAA South Atlantic Regional Basketball Tournament. The Maroons went on to win the national championship against University of Akron. (Tim Ribar '74 photo)

Academic clubs and organizations flourished during the times. Students began the Politics Forum in 1970, the Heuristics Society for "people who like people" in 1972, and the Salem Flying Artillery Memorial Society—a group of history students using the name of Salem's most famous Civil War unit. The college was honored with a Chapter of the American Chemical Society and new honor societies in mathematics and french. Interest in the outdoors saw the formation of a Bike Club, a Ski Club and the First Aid Club; communing with nature was a goal of the Meditation Society of 1971.

The United Black Students first organized in 1972, a new literary magazine—"The Natural Child"—came off the presses in 1970, and students formed a Bicentennial Committee in 1975. Radio station WRCR was still broadcasting, a chess club began playing, and the Young Republicans and Young Democrats started arguing all by 1975. The Collegium Musicum offered an outlet for those musically inclined, and theatre productions continued to impress. In 1970, the first student opera went on, and in the following year, the rock opera "Tommy" had its campus premier.

The sporting news of the period was dominated by the celebration of the college's first national championship—the NCAA Division II basketball crown in 1972. With stars Hal Johnston and Jay Piccola, Coach-of-the-Year Charlie Moir guided the Maroons to a 28-4 season. Even without all-time leading scorer Frankie Allen, who had graduated in 1971 with 2,780 points, the Maroons could not be stopped. During the period, the cagers went to four straight NCAA playoffs and won the Mason-Dixon Conference title six times in seven years.

If basketball was enjoying the glory, soccer—the dominant sport of the sixties—went from good to bad. From a state title in 1969, the soccer club of 1974 failed to win a match. Men's teams in golf, tennis, swimming, and track and field all compiled successful years. The cross country team of 1972 finished its season undefeated, and the college swim team in the following year was the first co-ed club in Virginia. The other major sport on the rise was lacrosse. Growing interest and fan support boosted the lax men to their first national top ten ranking by 1973, and in 1974, the Maroons finished the season ranked seventh in the country.

"An NCAA Title"

The Maroons flew to Evansville on the afternoon of Tuesday, March 14, in time for a work out in preparation for their NCAA Finals appearance. Joining Roanoke in Evansville were Akron, Tennessee State, Eastern Michigan, Missouri-St. Louis, Southern Colorado, South-Hampton, and Assumption.

In their three games at the Nationals, the Maroons defeated their opponents by a combined total of 63 points—an NCAA record. And Roanoke's victims had a combined enrollment of 48,000—almost 40 times larger than our enrollment of 1250. Another interesting note—the Maroons were behind only once in three days, by the score of 3-2 in the Missouri-St. Louis game; a situation quickly rectified by five straight Roanoke baskets.

Most important of all, however, was the team play of the Maroons. Other teams surely had more talent but the Roanoke guys were able to get it together when it counted. Hal Johnston's leadership was never more evident, and the unselfish play of the whole team paid off in the end.

The University of Akron made it to the championship game by defeating number one ranked Tennessee State 81-79 in overtime.

But the Maroons again displayed confidence in one another and won the title game 84-72 before a crowd of 5233.

After cutting the nets and receiving their championship wristwatches, the Maroons saw two of their own selected to the All Tournament Team. Senior guard, Hal Johnston was named Outstanding Player and was joined on the honor squad by team mate Jay Piccola, a sophomore forward. Also on the team were Len Paul of Akron, Lloyd Neal, and Len Robinson of Tennessee State.

Returning to Roanoke Saturday morning the team was met at the airport by a crowd of well wishers and were treated to a motorcade through Roanoke and Salem.

Later in the week Johnston was named First-team Little All American and Piccola Second-team by the Associated Press.

Coach Charles Moir was named College Division Coach of the Year by AP and the National Association of Basketball Writers.

Roanoke definitely had its most outstanding season in 1972. All the honors reflect on the high quality of the basketball program at Roanoke College; one all students and area residents can reflect upon with pride.

Excerpts from an article in the *Brackety-Ack*, 31 March 1972.

Hail the conquering heroes! The victorious Maroons celebrated their 1972 NCAA basketball crown with a parade down Main Street. (Ray Petrea photo)

First a club sport in the sixties, lacrosse gained major acceptance by the seventies.

Women's athletics truly blossomed by the early seventies. Women's teams were added in golf, volleyball, and lacrosse, and the Maroon women enjoyed titles in most of the continuing sports. Field hockey finished 9-1-1 in 1969, the swimmers were 7-2 in 1970, and the women's basketball team ended 1971 with an 11-2 record. Even the new sports produced winners. The 1974 golf team won the state title and the first year of volleyball competition boasted an undefeated season.

Long-time coach and athletic director Buddy Hackman retired in 1971, the same year the college established its Athletic Hall of Fame. Today, the room which commemorates the inductees is named in his honor, a fitting tribute to the man who guided Roanoke College athletics through five decades of the twentieth century.

CHAPTER 20

"The margin
of difference,"
1975–1983

Retiring President Kendig greets Norm and Jo Fintel in 1975.

When Perry Kendig announced his intention to retire to the board of trustees in the fall of 1973, he set in motion a presidential search that would take a year and a half. By the summer of 1975, Norm and Jo Fintel, fresh from the Mid-West, arrived to take residence at 535 North Market Street.

Perry Kendig was handing over a college almost twice as big as he had received. The physical boundaries of the campus had doubled; the square footage of college facilities had almost tripled; and the student body had grown by fifty percent. The faculty had increased too, and the administration and staff of the college had begun to register major advances.

The frenetic pace of the nineteen sixties created a momentum that brought the college well into the decade of the seventies. But there were signs already that the enthusiasm might tend to dissipate. The enrollment struggles of the early seventies were only the foreshadowing of some major reversals by mid-decade. The tidal wave of the 60s would crash by 1975.

Registration seemed to be getting worse in the late seventies!

As the new president would soon learn, having a bigger college could often mean having bigger problems. And the first major obstacle that Fintel would confront was the steady decline in enrollment. Few campus officials present in the sixties when the boom in residence hall construction occurred could have imagined that between 1972 and 1982, the dormitories were never full. The student body had climbed back over the 1,250 mark in 1975, but then the bottom fell out. In America's Bicentennial year, the numbers plummeted by over twenty percent with only 1,002 student registered for fall classes. College officials had revised the budget figure downward, but even the 1,025 mark could not be held, starting the college $132,000 in the red. Between 1977 and 1980, the college slowly rebuilt its numbers. In the fall of 1977, 1,046 students were present, 1978 saw 1,123 enrolled, and in the following year, 1,153 students signed up for courses. The college also struggled in attracting large numbers of applications. As a result of the increased demand for students, freshmen rejections reached dangerously low levels. Only 82 students were rejected in 1977 and 138 more in 1978. Clearly, the college needed to do better. Not only increased enrollment but an expansion of the applicant pool were established as major college priorities. A 1980 projection called for a stable enrollment profile of 1,120 students by 1986 but with an ever-increasing list of applicants to make that number more academically fit.

The key word for the college by the late seventies had become retrenchment. Given the national prognostications of decreasing numbers of students and the increasing economic uncertainty of inflation, the college faced some grim prospects. President Fintel had to steer a careful course between zero growth on the one hand and continued expansion on the other. A kind of formula was soon identified that would become the hallmark of the Fintel years: a demonstrated need would be met by a measured response. The times demanded caution and Norm Fintel could be as careful as anyone.

Step one for the new president was study and review. Consultants were hired to assess the state of the college by 1976; their findings indicated that the school's administrative management could be tightened, that planning be done on a stronger basis, and finally that the college's Statement of Purpose be redrafted to be brought into step with the college's academic program and mission.

Assisted by a sixty thousand dollar grant from the Exxon Corporation for a "resource allocation management program," the college administration prepared to move into the eighties. The year 1976 marked major changes in college personnel. With Dean Edward Lautenschlager's resignation, C. Freeman Sleeper became the college's seventh dean since the post had been created in 1920. David Thornton's decision to move on to Harvard University and its development office opened the door for Jack Hills to be named as new Vice President for Development. Don Sutton, for twenty years a principal in the student affairs arena, shifted his expertise into Chalmers Hall to become Director of Alumni Affairs. Bill Miller was promoted to succeed Sutton as Dean of Students, and Mac Johnson returned to campus as Associate Dean for Student Affairs.

A new college "Statement of Purpose" was adopted in 1977, and institutional planning was further highlighted. The college operations budget approached a million dollars annually by the late seventies, and given the expanded campus physical plant and the loss of revenue caused by declining enrollments, the college was faced with hard choices. To maintain the overall balanced budget, the percentage of the budget that was designated for academic programs or "instructional support" was cut from 47% to 34% over a several year period. These were to be lean times for everyone involved.

If enrollment and applications were a problem, money in the form of financial aid might be a solution. As a result, the college allocated more and more resources to student aid; in 1977 alone, 435 new students were added to the list of those receiving assistance, and by 1979, the financial aid budget of 1.6 million dollars would have shocked college officials of only a decade before. The Bittle Scholarship program was expanded, and a $75,000 scholarship fund was established for minority recruitment.

With the strain on college resources, eyes increasingly looked toward the college development office as the means not only to make up the difference between revenues and expenditures but indeed to get the college ahead. Jack Hills and his staff were prepared to do exactly that. One target was the college's endowment, not quite five million dollars in 1976; by 1983, that figure had doubled. New guidelines, adopted by the board in 1982, liberalized the investment policies of the endowment fund. Another aspect of the development strategy was the college's first "deferred giving" program outlined in 1977. In the following year, the percentage of friends giving to the annual fund shot up by 22%, compared to the six percent national average.

Major gifts continued to come the college's way. Corporate awards from the Olin Foundation, Kresge, and the Dana Foundation all were put to good use. The VFIC, the Virginia Foundation of Independent Colleges, became an important source of revenue, annually contributing over a hundred thousand dollars. The major campaign of the period was announced in 1982 as the Sesquicentennial Campaign, marking the ten year point before the college's 150th anniversary in 1992. The twenty-five million dollar goal was easily the largest in college history. Within a year, the school had doubtless surprised itself by realizing ten million dollars of its campaign. The board alone had contributed two and a half million dollars, and a special campus drive netted over a hundred thousand more, with over ninety percent of the faculty and staff participating. By the 1980s, record bounties would continue to be reaped.

The annual Elizabeth College alumnae reunion met on campus from the mid-fifties until 1990. It was always a weekend to catch up with friends and recall fond memories.

Even though the college's physical plant had been transformed by the early seventies, there were still a couple of needs and some long-standing plans which required attention. Since the early sixties, a fine arts facility had been a dream; by the mid-seventies, the Olin Foundation made it a reality. Opened in 1977, Olin Hall became an instant campus and community showpiece. It housed classroom, studio, and rehearsal space for the music, art, and theatre faculties and featured a state-of-the-art 400 seat theatre. By 1982, the Olin Foundation announced an additional two million dollar grant for the expansion of the facility to its present size and composition.

Another major project also got under way in 1976: the renovation of the old Lab-Theatre and the Commons complex. Construction added a new entrance in front of the original gymnasium which

then connected to the Commons. To prepare the way, a part of the old Lab-Theatre was taken down and for a dollar a piece, faculty, students, and friends carted off the old brick as souvenirs. Financed in part by a grant from the Kresge Company, the new building opened in the fall of 1977 as the Student Center. The old gym-Lab-Theatre was rechristened the Ballroom, and the building offered an expanded bookstore and post office, student lounges, offices for student publications and government, and a new meeting room for the board of trustees, dedicated that same year as the Kime Conference Room, in honor of Robert S. Kime and his son R. Sagen Kime. The father and son had served consecutively as secretaries of the board since 1900.

Theatre professor George Arthur demonstrates some of the finer points of life behind the scenes. (David Garcia '85 photo)

The board of trustees meets in the Kime Conference Room in 1982 and listens to a presentation.

A capacity crowd was on hand, along with Lady Bird Johnson, for the formal dedication of Olin Hall in 1977. (Tim Ribar '74 photo)

There were other campus plans that proved controversial, and one was downright unpopular. In 1975, the administration recommended that the Sections be razed; the student response brought back memories of the sixties as an afternoon rally was staged to protest the closing. With banners flying and the media assembling, the students presented their case. For the college, the Sections represented a decaying old structure which would take hundreds of thousands of dollars to renovate; moreover, the college had too many dorm rooms anyway, and the federal grants signed in the 1960s for the construction of the various residence halls stipulated that unless the buildings were filled to within 95% of capacity, penalty charges would be assessed. If the college decision made sense economically, it failed historically and in terms of public opinion. The Sections were spared, and a 1983 matching gift of $930,000 by college trustee and benefactor John Mulheren insured their renovation and survival. Incredibly, another campus committee recommended the destruction in 1980 of most of the historic front range of campus buildings—the Administration Building, Trout, and Bittle Hall—as not being "cost efficient." A new structure was to be erected which would consolidate those offices and functions; luckily, those plans were never implemented.

Happy times with John Mulheren, center, and Don Sutton, left, and Homer Bast, right. Mulheren's gifts in honor of his two favorite mentors resulted in the naming of the student center for Sutton and the new gym for Bast.

Bittle Hall was renovated twice during the period, once in 1978 to modernize the student affairs operation, and again four years later when the Virginia Synod of the Lutheran Church moved its headquarters and the office of the Bishop onto campus. The move symbolized a growing closeness between the college and the church, and reflected the spirit embodied in the "Statement of Partnership" signed by both parties in 1979.

The campus saw other change too. The City of Salem was approached regarding the closing of High Street between Clay Street and Peery Drive at the north edge of campus. The college, in fact, had donated the land through which Peery Drive had been constructed and "an understanding" had developed between the college and the town about the eventual closing of High Street. But when President Fintel appeared before the town council, it soon became apparent that not a lot was fully "understood." The city turned down the college's request.

The final construction project of the period focused on the athletic needs of the college. Even by the 1960s, tiny Alumni Gym was feeling the pressures of the rapidly expanding campus. But before the situation grew out of hand, Salem opened its Civic Center by mid-decade, and the Maroons gladly

moved across town to hold their home games there. The glory teams of the late sixties and early seventies hardly scored a basket on campus. By 1976, the decision had been made to deemphasize athletic competition by dropping from Division II to Division III in NCAA sponsored events. Hand-in-hand with that change was the return of basketball to campus to make it more visible and more easily accessible to the students. Alumni Gym proved cozy, but with the Maroon's increasing success by the end of the seventies and the early eighties coupled with the ever-increasing crowds, the facility was simply inadequate. Consequently, the trustees approved the construction of a new physical education building dedicated in 1982 as the C. Homer Bast Physical Education and Recreation Center.

Other campus buildings got their names during the times. A gift from Duke Trexler, class of 1913, resulted in the dedication of the physical science building in 1977 as Trexler Hall. John Mulheren donated a half a million dollars each for the privilege of naming two campus structures for his most favored mentors: Homer Bast and Don Sutton. Having named the new gym for Professor Bast, Mulheren had the newly constructed student center christened as the Donald M. Sutton Student Center in 1982.

A few final campus additions also appeared. Art officially made its way on campus in 1982 as two competition winning pieces were dedicated. Alice Aycock's "Solar Wind" was erected in the grassy area between Miller Hall and the Alumni Gym, and "The Reading Garden" was constructed first in front of Olin Hall and later relocated across the street under the trees next to Bittle Hall. With the completion of the Bast Center, the college found itself down to just one athletic field and the stadium. Consequently, by the summer of 1983, the college regraded much of its property to add two additional practice fields, place more of the creek in a conduit, and construct six new tennis courts.

Academically, the faculty was prepared to review and revise the existing curriculum and calendar. Required courses in the "distribution system" were always subject to discussion and, in 1976, to change when foreign languages lost out in a major faculty battle. Interdisciplinary courses were scaled back from two to one, and in the following year, the ill-fated Bachelor of Liberal Arts degree was resuscitated one more time. By 1979, the BLA had seen its last new candidate as the faculty voted to phase out the degree by 1983. A few majors went by the boards too: radiologic technology was curtailed in 1982 along with nursing, and the philosophy major was never offered after 1983. There were always new fields of study to replace the older ones. International relations appeared in 1976, and with a new Olin Hall, music and art were added in 1977 with theatre following in 1982. A major in early education debuted in 1979, and statistics and computer science in 1982.

The newest of the college's three gyms. Opened in 1982, the Homer Bast Physical Education and Recreation Center offers seating for 2,200 and facilities that should see the college well into the next century.

The campus was the recipient of pieces of art in the eighties. Solar Wind, pictured here, has always been controversial. The Reading Garden started out in front of Olin Hall but is now in the woods to the east of Bittle Hall. (David Garcia '85 photo)

Calendar discussions routinely focused on the much beleaguered Interterm. To be sure, there were always some courses that were tailor-made for the January setting; travel courses to Europe and beyond were never more popular. There were exciting options for those left behind too. The 1976 "Insearch Program" featured meditation, biofeedback, and yoga for those so inclined. The English Department demonstrated the Interterm's potential as well as anyone; Professor Bob Coulter headed off to Hollywood to study "Literature and Film," Bob Walter ascended the hills of Franklin County with his students to conduct interviews on folklore, and Denis Lape actually moved into Sections one January to "do Southern literature" with his students. Denis has never been the same since. But in spite of its successes, the Interterm still labored and for most students and faculty, it represented a time of drudgery and exhaustion.

Improving the quality of the incoming students became an increasing concern of the faculty. As the pool of applicants began to dry up, college standards dropped to maintain essential enrollment numbers. Once the students were admitted, the faculty worked hard to maintain academic standards; one result of that was a crisis in "retention" by the early eighties. Many students who were getting in were having trouble staying in. The faculty identified better advising as a key and the establishment of new study areas on campus as a means of support. Academic living space also appeared to better ensure success.

Sam Good poses with a group of students in London for an Interterm theatre trip. Off-Campus Studies offered increasing opportunities for travel and study from the seventies into the eighties.

New academic policies dotted the landscape. "Concentrations" and double majors appeared in 1981; pass/fail courses were cut back to one in 1982; and honor roll and graduation honor requirements were both raised by the faculty. The professors had been shocked in 1977 when nineteen seniors graduated with cumulative grade point averages under a 2.0; that situation was promptly rectified.

The Lilly Foundation rewarded faculty efforts with a $135,000 grant for faculty development in 1977. The award funded the "New Dimensions in Total Teaching" program which offered faculty stipends for course development, featured a collection of "clusters" for discussion, and helped finance the renovation of the former president's home, Roselawn, into the "Center for Creative Interaction" where faculty and students could meet to ponder significant issues. The program also inaugurated a series of faculty internships which took the faculty, for instance professors Bill Hill and Gene Grubitz respectively, into the jails and zoos of Southwestern Virginia for a first-hand look.

PRESENTED BY THE CLASS OF 1939 IN MEMORY OF "DAD" STRUDWICK

Memories of Dad Strudwick might have begun to fade, but his bench is still appreciated; a campus pooch takes a little break underneath.

An academic computer came on line in 1980, the faculty restructured their committee system in 1978, and the college engaged in yet another self-study in 1979. A new faculty lounge was added in 1982, and in the same year, the first of a series of annual weekend faculty retreats was instituted. The faculty bade farewell to numerous colleagues including Homer Bast, the Snows, long-time athletic stalwarts Elwood Fox and Fran Ramser, and after almost thirty years as chairman of the English Department, Matt Wise. Key administrators Clarence Caldwell and Don Sutton both retired with Professor Wise in 1983, and the college honored them all with a special dinner in the Bast Center. Their combined 93 years of dedicated service prompted John Mulheren to add a few zeros and to present a check for $930,000 for the Sections renovation.

Increasingly, the college paid more attention to the community as a whole. Starting with the "Public Forum" series in 1975, the college hosted numerous events which incorporated people in the community as an important constituency. Symposia featured Blue Ridge culture, the free enterprize system, and life in the sixties. Olin Hall debuted its performing arts subscription series in 1983, and other annual events included Women's Weekend and the Science Olympics for area high school students. With Henry Fowler's retirement as Chairman of the Roanoke College Board of Trustees, Goldman, Sachs & Co., of New York City, where Fowler was a partner, and The Brown Foundation, Inc., of Houston, each presented the college with a check for $250,000 to establish the Henry H. Fowler Public Affairs Lecture Series. For the initial event in the spring of 1983, former Secretary of State Henry Kissinger met with students and faculty on campus and then addressed over 5,000 onlookers in the Salem Civic Center. By the early eighties, the college had spawned a number of "centers" to underscore the commitment to the larger community. The Center for Continuing Education served as a clearinghouse for an increasing number of courses designed for the "non-traditional" student; the Center for Community Research undertook numerous studies for local organizations and

conducted an annual poll on community opinions and attitudes for the Roanoke newspaper; the Center for Church and Society sponsored programs and workshops designed to investigate the relationship of those bodies.

"A 'TOWNIE' TALKS"

It would seem that since I've lived in Roanoke all my life (yes, it is possible), and am presently a non-resident student at R. C., I should at least have something to say about what it's like to be a "townie". Well, even if I don't have anything to say I plan on making something up.

After all, it's not often that the day camp crowd gets noticed at all, and we really haven't done much to dispel the numerous myths that have arisen about the Roanoke Valley in general.

So lets take this time to blast a few of the misconceptions about good old Roanoke. Believe me, this is a meager sample:

Myth number one: The Roanoke Symphony Orchestra is not a bluegrass quartet folks, it never has been.

Myth number two: No matter what you might hear whispered in some deep, dark corner, Salem is not still on a pony express route. We get our mail on the stage coach run like everybody else.

Myth number three, four, five, and six (respectively): not everyone in Roanoke grows up to work in a gas station, Woodrum Airport was not designed to service hot air balloons, the Roanoke Star is not lit by torch, and I have never in my life milked a cow, never even once. Don't plan to either, I've got shaky hands.

Beginning to see the light? Starting to perceive the error in your judgement? People have to understand that Roanoke is much smaller in scale than what they might be used to. Folks in the valley don't really live any differently from anyone else, they just take it a little slower, and a little smaller dosage.

The differences in sports backgrounds also presents a problem to many of the locals. Bruce the lacrosse player almost killed me when, ignorant of my inexperience, he fired a ball at an alarming rate of speed in the general direction of my body. Put me and a lacrosse stick together and you have a totally useless combination. The ball glanced off in a rather compromising place. Thus endeth another brilliant career in sports. (I'm lucky it didn't end something else.)

I, and many of my peers have just never had any contact with northern pastimes whatsoever. Can you expect much more from someone who thought backgammon was something used to clean unsightly denture stains?

You can't really expect non-resident students to be up on the ins and outs of campus life. Just think of all we miss: The primitive wonder of a new motorcycle at the K. A. house, the semi-annual Bowman Hall Shaving Cream Orgy, and sleeping under a bush when your roommate's "entertaining."

Just remember that a townie is a valuable source of local information, a priceless form of taxi service, and a good friend to have if you're talking your way out of a public hanging.

And as a closing note I want to suggest you all go to see the Roanoke Symphony Orchestra play at Olin Hall this spring. They'll be opening with Tchaikovsky's Peer Gynt Suite, following up with Saint-Saen's Piano concerto number one, and finishing up with a bit of Foggy Mountain Breakdown. Ya'll come.

Excerpts from an article by Robert Bess, *Brackety-Ack,* 21 October 1977.

The Henry Fowler Public Affairs Lecture Series debuted in 1983 with this overflow crowd of 6,000 at the Salem Civic Center to hear former Secretary of State Henry Kissinger.

Some of the gang from Bartlett Hall exchanging pleasantries for the camera.

Student life by the late seventies and early eighties was enjoying the more leisurely pace of the post-sixties generation. The level of activism was down but not entirely dead; Clarence Caldwell still had to confront a student gathering in 1977 to explain "where the money goes." The SGA continued its struggle for student rights, but much of the fervor had dissipated. Of the 11 students eligible to witness faculty meetings by 1979, only one was in regular attendance. The Iranian crisis of 1979 irked more than a few students, and many contributed to a Cambodian relief drive in 1980. Yet more of the student tone seemed less concerned about challenging society and more interested in getting ahead in it. By far, the major of the period was business, and Miller Hall almost burst at the seams trying to accommodate the demand.

The campus had its share of visitors; Lady Bird Johnson was on hand to help dedicate Olin Hall in 1977, and soon thereafter, the likes of Count Basie and Elizabeth Taylor helped entertain. The rock band "Night Hawks" also performed in the theatre in 1981, but given the state of Olin Hall on the morning after, no rock group has appeared in the building since. Outside, the various festival weekends featured Little Feat, Jesse Collin Young, and Livingston Taylor to name a few. The most popular weekly event of the late seventies had to be "Wednesday Night Live" in the Cavern; when the faculty began complaining about "Thursday Morning Dead" in the various classes that they had to teach, things began to change. In 1981, the Program Board was born to coordinate all aspects of campus entertainment. By 1980, a new campus landmark opened on East Main Street—Mac 'n Bobs— which has been the most popular night spot ever since.

The college introduced the housing lottery in 1977 and refined it two years later with the advent of "squatters rights," whereby a student in a dorm room could reserve it for the next year. Bunk beds had to be "officially" approved by 1982, the same year Bowman went co-ed and the old KA House was rededicated as "Mt. Tabor," a co-ed academic living space. The KAs had amassed such an incriminating record that the college revoked their charter and placed them on a five-year suspended status.

The attempted milk cut back prompted a campus sit-in in the Ad Building. President Fintel ordered the milk restored.

Dorm life was never quite this refined, despite the college's best efforts with this publicity still from the early eighties.

"Mac & Bob's Sub Shop is 'The Place To Be'"

Roanoke College students have recently discovered a new escape from the drudgery of Commons food and Cavern beers. Simply step across Main street to Mac & Bob's Sub & Pub, where good times spill out on tap. Don't let the smallness of this quaint pub throw you; its intimate size adds a homey and friendly touch to the Long Island atmosphere. Good food, free peanuts, color television, good friends and tunes are all part of Mac & Bob's success story, but it's more like a small spontaneous party rather than your average beer and sandwich joint.

James McEnerney (Mac) and Bob Rotanz were two R. C. students with a dream. They met playing lacrosse and quickly became friends but confided that life in Salem wasn't quite up to their expectations. Salem needed a place for students to meet and relax off-campus; a place with beer and sandwiches at a price they could afford. They dreamed of opening a small pub that would cater to the student's needs, and they knew those needs well.

Mac and Bob graduated in '78 and went their separate ways, but their dream stayed alive. Mac, to get some needed experience, opened a wholesale seafood business in Long Island. Bob

was successful at Allstate for two years. But when they heard that a spot was for sale across the street from the college, they couldn't resist. Mac & Bob's Sub & Pub was born.

The pub's success formula is simple. They were R. C. students once and they know what the students want. By making this job their social life, they not only build a good rapor [sic] with their customers but also have a hell of a good time themselves.

Mac & Bob's is quickly becoming 'the place to be' on Monday nights. The Monday night beer special at $.40 a draft, which runs the length of the football game, is hard to resist. Moreover, the $.7 draft special at every touchdown is a clever and original touch.

The students of R. C. also are invited to give a hand in the decor of Mac & Bob's. They will blow up and frame any photograph or trivial picture and hang it up for a month. After that, the picture is up for sale and another student gets a chance of being "photographer of the month".

Many students have already agreed that Mac & Bob's Sub & Pub will be "The Great Escape" from the pressure and papers of the 1980–81 school year.

Excerpts from an article by Julie Ison in the *Brackety-Ack*, 19 September 1980.

The *Brackety-Ack* survived the age with its popular back page "And so they say" and various articles on the seasonal appearance of "Crawford Beach" and pool-shark Jack White. Ice sculpting became a popular winter-time activity, and people around these parts still talk about the eighteen and a half inch snow fall in February, 1983. Taj Mahal was on hand to help entertain as were a few spring folk fests. The annual "Jungle Weekend" always helped to thin out Tex Ritter's supply of bamboo, and the costume party packed the Cavern each Halloween. The campus was saddened by the loss of a student, Todd Faw, in the fall of 1982 and vowed to remember him through a memorial run staged ever since. The school could celebrate the accomplishments of its "Marathon Man," biology professor Bob Jenkins, as he was top ranked in the nation in his age division in the early eighties.

Greek life rebounded from the leaner days of the early seventies. The administration imposed a mandatory 2.0 GPA in order to pick up a bid, a move the *Brackety-Ack* announced would result in the "demise of the frats." The Greeks did survive the crisis and asked that rush be moved to the fall to help ensure the eligibility of the freshmen. By 1981, the faculty agreed. The KAs still "seceded" from the college each Old South Week—at least until the college declared its own disunion in 1982. The Pi Lams offered their first Florida Fly weekend in 1978 when the winner of the raffle and a guest were whisked off to the airport directly from the party at 6 P.M. Friday to return by Sunday evening. The biggest Greek event of the spring continued to be Derby Week, replete with the chase, the scavenger hunt, and games day.

The sororities increased in popularity by an even greater extent than did the fraternities. Numbers swelled to the maximum limit set by the college, and the sorority sponsored events like Chi Omega's *Mad Hatter,* the Phi Mu's "Mister Legs Contest," and the Delta Gamma's folk festival were enjoyed by the entire campus. Cabin parties and thumper matches were still the rage.

Academic groups offered alternative programming. Pi Sigma Alpha and Phi Alpha Theta were chartered as political science and history honor societies respectively. Alpha Chi was established for freshmen who amassed a 3.5 or higher grade point average. A model United Nations organization also sprang up and marched off to Harvard University in the winter of 1980 as the PLO.

The Circle K was first formed in 1975 as the student arm of the Kiwanis International. Students organized an Outing Club which sponsored various hikes and excursions. A First-Aid Crew was ready for campus emergencies and the radio station, WRCR, signed off for the last time. Black Students continued their Union, and the Foreign Students Union also appeared for a couple of years with its newsletter "Far Away From Home." The Legal Aid Society first defended students charged with academic or social offenses in 1981.

Sigma Chi's Derby Week always featured exciting events on Games Day.

A swarm swoops down the Science steps headed toward the fraternities across Market Street for the annual Bids Day festivities.

There just wasn't anything quite like Bids Day. The lawn of the Fraternity Quad resembled more a sea than terra firma *when all was done.* (Tim Ribar '74 photo)

Artistically, a student Instrumental Ensemble performed in 1977 and, because of increased popularity, split into two groups the next year: the Wind Ensemble and the Jazz Ensemble. Less traditional was the Music Guild organized by 1979. The college choir continued its success and even accompanied Barry Manilow during an appearance in Roanoke. The literary students of the "Grubb Street Tribe" and other avenues continued to publish their works, and a new magazine *Just a Little Green* first was printed in 1980.

On the sporting front, the college picked up its second national championship in six years with a 1978 NCAA Division II title in lacrosse. The men's lax record was impressive throughout the period with number one ranking in 1976 and a third place national finish in 1979. The women's lacrosse team enjoyed its first post-season bid in 1979. Maroon golfers did nearly as well with either state or Old Dominion Athletic Conference titles in 1978, 1980, and 1981. The Roanoke cross country team also amassed three straight championships for good measure.

Lacrosse champions for 1978. Roanoke stopped Hobart 14-13 for the crown.

The score was tied 13-13 with 50 seconds left. Roanoke College had the ball and called time out. Coach Paul Griffin then asked Robert Rotanz if he wanted to win the game. Without waiting for an answer, he diagrammed a play that sent the All-American defenseman streaming down the sideline to score the winning goal of the 1978 National Lacrosse Championship against Hobart College.

That was the end to the most breathtaking, emotionally charged and consequential game in the history of Roanoke College.

The Maroons came into the game as a big underdog to the Hobart Statesmen, who were two-time defending National Champions. It was figured that Roanoke would just be another hurdle in Hobart's vault to a 3rd straight championship.

The game started like everyone thought it would, with the Statesmen scoring in the first 22 seconds. Roanoke came right back as Joe Brown scored seconds later to tie it up.

Hobart scored the next three goals, and the 5000 obviously biassed Hobart fans started getting ready for a huge celebration in Geneva that night. To their dismay Roanoke answered back with four consecutive goals of their own to pull ahead 5-4 . . . the teams went into the lockerroom with Hobart on top 11-9.

During half time the Roanoke team was still confident that the outcome would be positive. The adrenalin was still flowing, and even 5000 crazies couldn't convince the Roanoke team they were out of the game.

As the second half started, early goals by Joe Dishaw and George Parks tied the score and made a close game even closer.

The fourth quarter was the climactic build up to the dreams ending for the Maroons. Miky "Bird" Rowley and Scott Allison scored to put Roanoke ahead 13-12. The fans were in disbelief that their team was losing. An extra-man goal with 2:13 remaining tied things up, and the fans were again in a deafening frenzy. Roanoke finally ended up with the ball with 50 seconds left and the rest is history (Roanoke history).

Excerpts from an article by Bruce Solomon in the *Brackety-Ack, 22 September 1978.*

On campus, there was always lots of excitement too. In 1977, an Equestrian Club was formed, and by 1980, a Fencing Club offered a different kind of competition. The following year, other students tried with some success to resurrect a baseball club. Intramurals continued in popularity, and a championship speedball game could attract as big a crowd as any sport at the college.

But if lacrosse was impressive, men's basketball was positively incredible. The record of victories from 1978 through 1983 boosted Coach Ed Green's winning percentage to the best in the nation, of any coach in any division. Roanoke captured every ODAC crown in sight and made the NCAA playoffs each time it was eligible. By 1983, the Maroons reached the Division III final four only to finish third. Among a host of quality players, no one stood out more than Gerald Holmes, twice the division's National Player of the Year. The sports legacy of the period 1975–1983 is perhaps unsurpassed by any other in Maroon annals.

Rugged action with the field hockey players. No weak knees or shins out here. (Tim Ribar '74 photo)

Captains Bruce Hembrick (left) and Ken Belton guided the Maroons in their 27-2 season in 1980/81. (Courtesy Salem Times-Register)

In the space below, write an essay of not more than 300 words describing your most important experience in the last five years. Explain how that experience has affected you and helped to shape your personality.

My present interest in Biology, Business, and Theatre developed when, after my sophomore year at Roanoke, I took an internship at the Veteran's Hospital in the rehabilitation center. . . .

It's 2:30 in the morning and I've just about had it with applications and resumes. How can I put into words what these past few years have meant to me, how I have grown and what I have gained? What will I have on May 23, 1982 besides a diploma? I'll have picnics on the Back Quad, Halloween parties, Wednesday Night Live, and concerts in Olin. I'll have Dunkin' Donuts, Frosties from Wendy's and bagels with cream cheese. Forgotten ID's, pizza for breakfast, Friday afternoon Lacrosse, NCAA finals, the Brackety-Ack, secret mixers, Mac & Bob's, and London in January. Blanket movies, snow, sweatshirts, rain slickers, squirrels, frisbees, duck shoes, empty beer cans, mud and wind. I've talked for hours with my roommate, survived QM, had firedrills at 3 am and pulled a 10 in the lottery. Spent the night cramming, spent the night at rehearsal, spent the night at the Cavern, and spent the night. I've gone through rush—I never thought I'd get a date for the inaugural. I was packed for Pi Lambda Fly, cleaned up garbage for Green Up, broke my finger for a Derby, and saw the South rise again. I've suffered the bookstore blues and registration panic, made road trips, ABC runs, Hop In runs, or better yet, "Let's go Krogering." I've laughed, I've cried, I've shared, I've contemplated, I've been lonely, I've been happy and I've been scared . . . but I've survived. Roanoke has given me a lot in the past four years, both good and bad. Most of my experience cannot be described in a personal statement. But years from now, when I smell popcorn or find a tattered ticket or a faded picture of a dorm party, I'll pause and smile as laughing images of faces, places, and times well spent come rushing back to the rising beat of "Candy Apple Red." . . .

I hereby certify that to the best of my knowledge the information given by me on this application is complete and I understand that any misrepresentation may be the cause for denial or cancellation of admission.

Signature _____   Date _____

Rawenoch, 1982

CHAPTER 21

"The pursuit
of excellence,"
1983–1990

President Norm Fintel oversaw a second major campus transformation—both in physical terms and in enrollment numbers.

Pursuing excellence became a favorite pastime of the 1980s; institutions across the country, colleges and corporations alike, adopted the challenge in bewildering numbers. For most, "excellence" was a slogan or buzz word which amounted to a goal but typically lacked any means to achieve that desired state. But at Roanoke in the years from 1983 to 1990, there was a remarkable degree of dedication and commitment to the professed excellence. Although at times the campaign seemed a big slangy or trite— even the faculty softball team was named "The Pursuit of Eksellance"—in the end, the Roanoke College moving into the new decade of the nineties was a far more excellent college than it had been ten years earlier. By every measure—students, faculty and staff, financial resources, and general reputation— the college had improved dramatically.

When President Norm Fintel arrived in 1975, enrollment had been principally a quantitative problem. By the early eighties, applications and enrollments had risen to provide a fairly stable and dependable level of students. By 1985, the college raised its ante and made enrollment principally a qualitative challenge.

The way Roanoke transformed itself could serve as a case study for any college in the nation. It required a rededication to academic principles, a dynamic strategy for admissions, and critically, the financial support to enable it all to succeed. First, the faculty reaffirmed the college's academic standards by setting higher admission requirements and by raising the academic bar for those students already enrolled. As one illustration, the faculty adopted a minimum grade point average of 1.0 for all freshmen after their first semester at Roanoke; if they failed, they would be suspended until the following year. In comparison to the previous years, the impact was positively brutish; in 1983, sixteen students had been suspended and in 1984, a mere seven. But in 1985, seventy freshmen were sacrificed in the execution of the new policy. Although the college paid an immediate financial price for the lost students and their revenues, in the long run it foreshadowed the tougher policies of the new Roanoke.

Imposing loftier standards made little sense unless the college was prepared to assist students to some extent in that quest. If retention was mentioned during the seventies, it became a passion during the 1980s. By mid-decade, the Learning Center was dedicated as a means of ensuring freshman survival, and almost from the outset, it had marked success. With its network of freshman advisors, tutors, and study skills courses, it had all but eliminated the long-standing crisis over retention.

The second piece of the plan called for a more aggressive posture in admissions. It demanded an expansion of the pool of applicants whereby the college could become increasingly selective, and also sought to identify more sources for financial aid and the adoption of new awarding criteria. As far as applications were concerned, the college had received from between 1,300 to 1,500 yearly since the late 1960s. By 1985, a record number of 1,589 completed forms made their way to Roanoke. But that was only the beginning. By increasing the number of mailings, from fewer than 10,000 in 1980 to 14,500 by 1987 and 18,000 by 1988, the applicant pool increased accordingly; by 1987, over 2,000 applications materialized, and by 1989, the three thousand plateau had been achieved.

Graduation under the trees is always a festive affair; the annual wait for the weather is a nervous time for all. (David Garcia '85 photo)

Once the pool had reached that breadth the college could afford to become more selective. In 1980, the college accepted fully ninety percent of those students who applied; by 1988, the acceptance percentage had been dramatically cut in half. Another key ingredient was the promotion of campus visits as a means of recruitment. In 1985, 66% of all those prospective students taking a campus tour elected to apply at Roanoke. By 1987, the percentage reached 83%.

The third feature of the college's strategy was a restructuring of its financial aid program. First, need-based financial assistance was replaced in large part by a merit scholarship system. Before, the college could offer assistance to outstanding student prospects only if there was financial need; if the principle was a noble one, the practical result often meant that the college lost out on some of its most promising applicants. The change allowed Roanoke to go head-to-head with the best of the competition. A second part of the plan focused on the need for more financial assistance, a need made even greater by federal cutbacks in the early eighties. The college redoubled its efforts, and additional funds were raised to fuel the demand. The Bittle Scholar program was expanded; Faculty Scholars were established, as were Morehead Scholars by 1986. In the following year, a million-dollar gift funded the Fintel Scholars endowment. In general, financial aid increased substantially by the end of the decade. Where only twenty years before, a few students received a few hundred dollars, by 1987 the college administered 4.8 million dollars in aid including 1.6 million of Roanoke's own assistance. Over eighty percent of the student body averaged $3,115 each in support. By 1990, the total had reached 7.1 million dollars including 3.6 million of Roanoke's funds, with seventy-four percent of the student body receiving an average of $6,725 each.

As the capstone to Roanoke's "Pursuit of Excellence," the faculty and administration designed and implemented a new honors program by 1986. Accepting twenty-five new students each fall, the program has its own integrative curriculum and offers the students a variety of other enrichment opportunities.

The impact upon the college of all of this planning and dedication was truly astonishing. The college could not have dreamt of the immediate return and response to its strategy; between 1985 and 1987, the Scholastic Aptitude Test scores of the incoming freshman vaulted eighty points—the highest such increase by any college in the eastern United States. Roanoke was not only getting significantly better students; the improvement in the retention rate ensured that the college was keeping them as well.

With all of their good fortune, college officials failed to predict one of the more taxing side-effects of stronger enrollments and better retention: overcrowding. Ironically, the student body had grown so quickly because of increasing retention that college planning was caught off guard. Roanoke got almost too much of a good thing. Between 1980 and 1985, enrollment hovered between 1,150 and 1,200 students; but by 1986, the figure had risen to 1,262; by 1987 to 1,303, and by 1987, to 1,402. By 1990, the enrollment count was 1,472, the highest in the history of the college.

Physically, the campus was challenged to respond to the added numbers of students needing space for living and for taking classes. The crunch was made even worse during the 1985–86 school year when the Sections were closed for their three million dollar renovation. When the college acquired the Lutheran Children's Home property for 1.5 million dollars in 1985, it had no idea how quickly its buildings would be pressed into service. The property, the former site of Elizabeth College until it closed in the early 1920s, became the "Elizabeth Campus" and by the fall of 1986, had two dormitories full of Roanoke students. By 1989, a third residence hall would come on line.

The other major acquisition during the period was the purchasing of the old Roanoke County Courthouse for half a million dollars. Built in 1910, the massive old structure cost the college $500,000 to renovate the building. The Courthouse became home to the Department of Economics and Business Administration.

For the third year in a row, Roanoke College students and faculty descended on the Hotel Carlton and the hospitality of Johnny and Schteck for Interterm 1985 Luxembourg. Leading the caravan of 44 eager-minded students was Dr. Mark Miller, Dr. Bobbye Au, Dr. Jan Heyn, Professor Larry Lynch, and Dr. Greg Weiss. . . .

Of course the highlight of any academic setting is the time spent outside the classroom. Three free week-ends provided ample opportunity for both students and faculty to develop that sense of adventure and brutal pleasure which yearns in every good Roanoke College Person. . . . Each of the faculty members in Luxembourg were quick to emphasize that being in Europe is a learning experience in and of itself, both for students and faculty. . . .

In an attempt to exchange intellectual enlightenments with the Middle East travelers a majority of the group headed to Rome on the longest of the free week-ends. Half the group made it as far as Milan, the other half to Florence, and a few actually ended up in Rome. Only a Roanoke College group could find themselves in Italy during the worst snow storm in 40 years! For the Florence group, a normally two hour train trip between Florence and Milan lasted 12 hours. . . .

It is important to point out that interterm in Luxembourg did not consist solely of nights at Pub 13 and the Trocadero. Not only were the courses demanding, but being in a foreign country forces one to learn every minute! The trip also offers both students and faculty the opportunity to interact with one another, eliminating often false impressions each group holds of the other. Thanks to all the Roanoke residents of Hotel Carlton for making this trip a great month!

Excerpts from an article by Carol Bernick in the *Brackety-Ack*, 8 February 1985.

Mary Evans Lott and Jeff Walker share a scene in "Hedda Gabler."

Professor Mamie Patterson was frequently abroad for interterm; here a group of her students pose on a hillside in Spain.

The college acquired the former Elizabeth College property, recently the Lutheran Children's Home, in 1984. Today, the college maintains several residence halls there, the Cabell Brand Research Center, several athletic fields, and leases other facilities to community groups. (David Garcia '85 photo)

Two principle construction projects kept things from ever getting too quiet on campus. First was a significant addition to the rear of Olin Hall. Finished in 1985, the annex almost doubled the amount of classroom and studio space, and also featured a new fine arts library and rehearsal hall. Second, the college witnessed the expansion and total renovation of the library. The eight million dollar undertaking, raised by the college in little more than a year and led by a 2.2 million dollar anonymous gift, produced a structure named in honor of the college's "first family," Norm and Jo Fintel. The new structure expanded the square footage from 28,000 to over 70,000 and featured state of the art automation for the library's holdings. The new facility has classrooms, audio-visual production studios, ample study and work space, a boardroom for the trustees, and a special collections area for the college archives and the Henry H. Fowler Collection. To facilitate the construction, the old library was closed for two years, from the spring of 1989 to the spring of 1991, and its collections were housed in two locations on campus: in the basement of Bowman Hall and on three separate levels of the Courthouse. The former county headquarters had proved invaluable within a couple of years of its purchase.

By 1988, campus beautification was in full swing. The venerable historic front range of buildings—Administration, Miller, Trout, and Bittle—were all carefully hand-sanded and had their mortar repointed. If Miller and Trout had cost two thousand dollars each to construct in the nineteenth century, by the end of the twentieth century it cost $230,000 just to clean them. Red brick paths soon began to appear on campus too, and the old roadway up to the front steps of the Ad Building was replaced by a center brick path, replete with benches and flower beds.

A new campus master plan was developed, which took into account the fact that, with the new interstate exit located north of campus along Thompson Memorial Drive, what had historically been the rear of campus had suddenly been made the front. The vast majority of campus visitors now approached the campus from Peery Drive and encountered the rear parking lots and the back of Sections. Steps were identified to reorient the campus to some extent in that direction, and the "rear" of the Fintel Library was especially designed to welcome guests to campus. The college again approached the city about the closing of High Street, but again to no avail.

The college came to Main Street in 1986 with the purchase of the old Roanoke County Courthouse. It became home to the Business and Economics Department as well as temporary headquarters of the library when it was being renovated.

The new Norm and Jo Fintel Library comes on-line in the summer of 1991. The expanded library almost triples the size of the original 1962 structure.

Life in the Back Quad has always been fun.

Building renovations were endemic during the period. One by one, every residence hall on campus was refurbished and brought up to code. The Cavern was remodeled, and the darker pub atmosphere was brightened to create more of a snack bar atmosphere than a late night gathering place. Roselawn became home to admissions in 1985, but the displaced faculty were made content again a few years later with the opening of the Faculty House in the old Deanery next to Chalmers Hall. The college continued to add property to its holdings, along High and Market streets, and maintained "Walden House" for a couple of years as an academic living space for a number of students. The athletic fields were redesigned during the summer of 1986 with the construction of a large storage building to serve both athletic and maintenance needs.

It goes without saying that the academic success and the physical plant renewal did not come cheaply. A prerequisite to any of the developments of the eighties was having the financial resources available to undertake the challenge. Fortunately for all concerned, the teams assembled by Jack Hills and, after his departure in 1986, by Ben Case provided the funds in record amounts.

By 1990, the fifty-million-dollar goal of the Sesquicentennial campaign was well within sight with additional endowments in Business, a John P. Fishwick Chair in English, numerous corporate gifts and matches, and ever-increasing numbers of college "Associates." Faculty and staff contributed over a million dollars to the campaign chest, and students helped through various drives and the annual Senior Class gift. One phonethon in 1985 involved two hundred students calling over 5,800 alumni over nine nights and raising $125,000. The money kept rolling in.

Academically, the faculty and new Vice President-Dean of the College Gerald Gibson took the eighties right in stride. The faculty advanced both in quantity and quality; in 1980, the faculty numbered 72, yet by the beginning of the next decade, there were ninety full-time professors. During the same period, the percentage of faculty with terminal degrees improved from 70% to 85%. Moreover, professional development among faculty was encouraged and supported like never before. A new faculty research committee was organized, and new programs of grants and leaves gave faculty additional time and ability to engage in professional pursuits.

Students staff the phones for the annual college phon-a-thon; students raise thousands of dollars each year calling alumni and friends. (David Garcia '85 photo)

Major faculty concerns of the late eighties focused on the curriculum and the calendar. In 1988, the faculty voted to adopt a new course of academic study which replaced the older, more flexible curriculum with a new structured one, complete with general education requirements, a year-long English writing course, an ethics course, and a required foreign language. The old 4:1:4 calendar was revamped in 1986, and a new semester system was soon in place to supplant the old Interterm.

Faculty reintroduced minors to the academic market place, ended majors in elementary education and urban studies, adopted a plus/minus system to be added to letter grades, and participated in yet another self-study. The faculty rewrote its *Handbook*, restructured requirements for tenure and promotion, and pursued studies concerning workload and "outcomes assessment."

Class schedules were adjusted to allow more free time in the middle of the day to accommodate meetings

A smiling Dr. Dan Richardson is off to class to set another group of students right about the Cold War. (David Garcia '85 photo)

and the college's new convocation series every Thursday; students welcomed the lunch time option but were less than delighted to learn that classes now started at 8:00 A.M. instead of 8:30. Fall Break reappeared in 1987; students had new evaluation forms to grade their instructors, and the faculty welcomed their first mainframe computer, the Data General MV-100 Super-minicomputer, in 1984.

The campus had numerous visitors through the decade, many sponsored by the Henry H. Fowler Public Affairs Lecture Series. Former Presidents Jimmy Carter and Gerald Ford, UN Ambassador Jean Kirkpatrick, and former German Chancellor Helmut Schmidt all addressed capacity crowds in the Homer Bast Center. *Roots* author Alex Haley, Betty Friedan, Benjamin Hooks, homeless advocate Mitch Snider,

and Billy Hayes of the "Midnight Express" all engaged campus and community audiences. The college's Center for Community Education hosted thousands on campus each summer with programs ranging from youth sports camps to the Elderhostel program, a nationally sanctioned institutional program for senior citizens. The college bade farewell to a host of dedicated faculty and staff and was particularly saddened in the summer of 1985 with deaths of Harry Poindexter, Ron Walpole, Charlie Bondurant, and Jimmy Rikard. The college had lost its former president and friend Perry Kendig the year before.

Socially, the campus had changed about as much between 1985 and 1990 as it had improved academically. The administration and the

The Preparatory Division in Olin Hall offers instruction to even the youngest learner.

Life-long learning is the object of the International Elderhostel program. Roanoke has had greatest success with its summer offerings.

Commonwealth of Virginia had seen to that. With the state raising the minimum drinking age to twenty-one coupled with two alcohol-related deaths on campus, the president appointed a task force to review the college alcohol policy. Its report, issued in the spring of 1985, brought significant change to the campus. It rewrote most of the party rules for the students, ended the use of keg beer, and had the effect of moving most social functions off campus. Alumni are shocked to learn today that the busiest place on campus each Friday and Saturday night is the Bowman parking lot—where the buses arrive to take the students away.

Symbolizing the shift from the old Roanoke of the seventies to the new Roanoke of the eighties is the Sections. Once the home of the hippies and Bohemians—the *Brackety-Ack* called the Sectionites "Homo Dead Headus"—where the walls were thin, the plaster loose, and the plumbing irregular, the Sections' renovation of the mid-eighties created a home, not for the hippies, but for the preppies. The Sections today is air conditioned, fully carpeted, and comes complete with spiral stair cases and skylights.

Student Government was new and improved during the period and introduced an Interhall Council which served to channel and direct student comment and concern. Students survived the great flood of November 1985, twenty-seven inches of snow during

a couple of days in January 1987, the Taiwan Flu, and the biggest crisis: the end to college summer storage of dorm belongings. Mac and Bob's moved down the road a few doors and expanded twice since then. The Malibu always offered an economical alternative until it closed its doors in the spring of 1990. Not all fun and games took place off campus; there was a never-ending supply of acts and shows to keep the students entertained. May Daze, Marooned 84, comedian Rich Hall, Winter Fest, and a new Homecoming all attracted crowds. Annual visits from hypnotist Tom Deluca and Billy Wertz had their followings, and Halloween was never complete without a viewing of "The Rocky Horror Picture Show."

AND SO THEY SAY

For much of the 1980s, one of the most popular sections of *The Brackety-Ack* was the column "And So They Say." Members of the College community (mostly the students) were asked "the question of the week." Hopefully, your response was quick and clever. But if not, you could at least have your picture in the paper. Here is a sample of the questions of the decade.
•What excites you the most about the upcoming school year?
•What is the meanest thing you have ever done?
•Who would you pick for the first woman president?
•What is your favorite facial expression?
•If you were an escapee where would you run to?
•What do you think people do behind closed doors?
•If you could have a date with anyone, who would it be?
•What do you want to be when you grow up?
•What does Roanoke College do with its money?
•What don't you want to be in life?
•What would you do if your parents came for an unexpected visit?

A fallen, but happy warrior. Jimm MacGregor, a student in Professor Susan Millinger's "Reliving the Past" course, recovered from this class-related battle. (Roanoke Times & World-News photo)

In 1983/84, Annie Nutter, much-loved member of the Commons staff, offered her advice to students in the *Brackety-Ack*. The problems varied.

Dear Annie,

You know this is parents weekend. Well, I told my boyfriend that I'd like to spend it with my parents, but he said "What about me?" You see, his parents are not coming, so he'd like to spend the weekend with us. This will be the first time I've seen my parents since I left home, and I don't think they will appreciate him being around the whole time. Besides that, I have a lot of things I'd like to talk with them privately about. He could go out with us to dinner one night, but don't you think he should go out with his friends the rest of the time?

Signed,
A Sad Freshman

Dear Sad,

I think you should sit down with your boyfriend and tell him how things are. If he can't understand your wanting to be with your parents, that's tough. You only get one mommy and daddy in life, so you should spend all the time you can with them. Three days with your parents is not asking too much! So yes, I think your boyfriend should go out with his friends. If he's acting this selfish now, what would he be like if something really big came up? Think about it.

Annie

Dear Annie,

I will be graduating in May. I owe college loans, a car loan, and beginning next year, it'll be "me against the world," (with no job prospects in sight).

I'm so afraid that I'm going to be poverty-stricken when I leave this "institution of higher learning." What can I do??

Signed,
Up the Creek Without a Paddle
P.S. I haven't finished my resume yet!

Dear Up the Creek,

Listen to what you are saying! You are not acting like a mature college senior. Sit down and take one day at a time. Finish your resume, go fill out some job applications, sell yourself at any job interviews you have, and hope and pray for the best. For all you know, you might just find something. I've found through experience that "where there's a will, there's a way."

Ha! Ha! I'm still around and if you get too far poverty-stricken, I'm always good for a meal or two or a night or two at my house (on a helpful basis, that is!). You'll make it!

Annie

"A Celebration of Sections" took place at Alumni Weekend, 1985, when the renovation of the aging dormitories was announced. The Sections were closed for a year and a half and reopened in the fall of 1986, fully air-conditioned and carpeted. (Tim Ribar '74 photo)

November of 1985 brought record floods to the Roanoke Valley; the campus was hit hard too, wiping out cars in the Market Street parking lot and flooding the fraternity houses.

The decade spawned a number of musical groups. Some of the music faculty in Olin Hall formed first the Olin Trio, later the Kandinsky Trio, to entertain at recitals and special college events. Several other faculty pooled their rock and roll talents to form "Time is Tight." It was always worth the price of admission just to see Professor Howard Warshawsky serve as the band's "roadie." A popular local band, "Echoes Farm," was organized in 1985 by a number of Roanoke students.

Parents Weekend remained a popular tradition, and Alumni Weekend grew to such an extent that it outgrew its name to become the "Alumni Festival." A new Alumni magazine, *Roanoke College*, first came off the press in 1985, and alumni chapters around the country were more active than ever.

Greek life rebounded in the eighties. The traditions and ritual of the fraternities and sororities, the subject of some scorn and dwindling numbers in the seventies, proved more appealing in the conservative atmosphere of Ronald Reagan's America. In 1982, only 37% of the campus male population was Greek; by 1987, the figure stood at 66%. The sorority population grew as well, with the percentage close to fifty percent. Although still without houses, the three sororities have suites in the basement of Crawford Hall and since 1984, two quads each in Bowman Hall.

Halloween was always costume night in the Cavern. (William G. Kendig photo)

Student academic pursuits reflected the general mood of the campus. Almost every department and discipline had its separate honor society, and most sponsored another group as well to hold meetings, host a film or a speaker, or have a social get-together. Pi Gamma Mu, a social science honor society, sponsored monthly forums which featured faculty and student presentations. Echoing the popular game of the early eighties, the group organized a campus "Trivial Pursuit" contest to a packed Cavern.

Outstanding students were annually elected to "Who's Who Among College Students," and many participated in the fall and spring leadership banquets and the annual honors recognition banquet each April. The Biology honor society, Tri Beta, relabeled the trees on campus, and the Model UN Club headed north to New York City each Easter week to participate in the conference hosted by the United Nations itself. The Black Student Union became the Black Alliance and the Fandom Federation was a group dedicated to life between science and fiction. A new literary magazine debuted too: "On Concepts Edge."

Athletic success was excellent during the decade as well. Between 1983 and 1987, Roanoke won more titles than any other college in the Old Dominion Athletic Conference. In 1987 alone, Roanoke's men's and women's teams won five championships and finished either first or second in eight of the thirteen sports in which the college participated.

Basketball continued its winning ways by capturing the ODAC crown in the first seven years that the college was in the league. Our string of conference play-off victories was finally snapped at twenty-two. Women's basketball compiled a record almost as good with several league titles and a first visit to the NCAA playoffs in 1990.

Lacrosse still ranks as the most popular sport at Roanoke, and the men's team has consistently won the ODAC title and is perennially ranked among the best in the nation. Coming on strong are the Lady Maroons who finished the seasons from 1986-1990 ranked among the top few teams in the county as well.

Soccer continued its winning tradition and captured its first ODAC crown in 1984, with several added since. Women's soccer became a club sport in 1983, an intercollegiate team in 1985, and brought home its first conference title just two years later.

The cross country team did not lose a dual meet for two years in the mid-eighties and placed several runners in national competition. A women's team

The Maroons enjoyed great success in the new Bast Center; Coach Ed Green's cagers gave him the best record of any coach in America.

debuted in 1988. Baseball has recently returned again as a club sport, and the students supported an ice hockey team for a couple of seasons. Intramurals continued to attract scores of students, and no event was more amusing than co-ed innertube water polo. Rollerskating and skateboarding made reappearances on campus by 1986, and hackeysack is still played on the Back Quad.

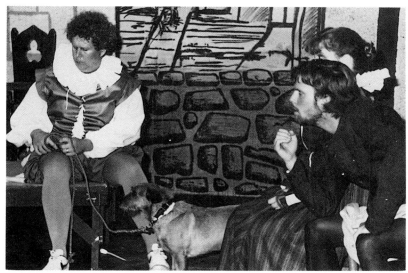

A strikingly handsome dog gets ready for his line in the rehearsal of "Knight of the Burning Pestle" in 1985.

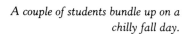

A couple of students bundle up on a chilly fall day.

Norm and Jo dashing off to where or sneaking away from what on Alumni Weekend in 1988.

In the spring of 1988, President Norm Fintel announced his intention to step down by the summer of 1989. The college and community were saddened upon hearing the news but comforted upon learning that the Fintel's would stay in town. Most of all, the college felt appreciative of the dedication that the couple together had brought to the assignment. Fittingly, the Board of Trustees honored both Norm and Jo Fintel with honorary degrees at the commencement in April 1989.

The college would miss the Fintels, the dinners and receptions they hosted and the practice of letting the graduating seniors carve their names in the downstairs shelves and woodwork in the President's Home on Market Street. The "gauntlet" would continue—the commencement custom begun by Fintel whereby faculty would form two lines through which the graduates would recess to accept the congratulations and good wishes of their former teachers. The best experiences and memories are soon transformed into traditions.

By the summer of 1989, Norm Fintel left the college not only better than he had found it but, in terms of academic reputation and physical and financial shape,

The Drs. Fintel.

arguably better than it had ever been in its history. The college was poised and in a position to embrace the future with a confidence and an optimism rarely matched.

Local restauranteur Bob Rotanz gives college head chef Bill Nutter a hand at an alumni cookout. Bill and his wife Annie, were fixtures in the Commons for years; the college was saddened by his death in the summer of 1990. (David Garcia '85 photo)

You couldn't believe that you were in a gym the night the Bast Center hosted the Inaugural Ball. (Tim Ribar '74 photo)

The board of trustees named David M. Gring as the ninth president of the college, and he and his wife Susan made their way to Salem as eight predecessors had in the previous 147 years. By the fall of 1989, the college was prepared to celebrate the present, to honor its past, and to anticipate its future with an eagerness that was contagious. At President Gring's inauguration, the constituencies of college and community came together both to honor this man and to remember the vision and strength of others who had gone before. In his inaugural address, David Gring announced that Roanoke was a college of "considerable strength" and that with continued effort and dedication, it was soon destined to become a college of "significant distinction."

The students offered a special tribute to the new president and his wife by staging an "illumination" ceremony during the inaugural festivities. The historical reenactment, set in the early evening, was constructed from the sole description of David Bittle's inauguration in 1854—from a student writing his mother about that grand event. From the Presbyterian Church where Bittle had been inaugurated, the Grings were transported in a horse-drawn carriage escorted down Main Street by a town honor guard dressed as militia, and marching students and faculty. As the little band turned up College Avenue, the sight in the Front Quad was remarkable. A thousand friends of Roanoke had appeared, each holding a single candle to provide the illumination.

The scene was as silent as it was simple. For the new president, it must have seemed an auspicious occasion, but in viewing the crowd of well-wishers, he might too have sensed their strength and dedication and knew that with their help, he could not fail. Roanoke awaits its Sesquicentennial of 1992 with the assurance that the likes of Bittle, Dreher, Smith, Kendig and all of the others—presidents, students, faculty and staff alike—would be heartily proud of the college which they helped fashion.

President and Mrs. Gring reenact the 1854 inauguration of David Bittle with horse and carriage, an honor guard, a musket salute, and a thousand on-lookers holding candles. The "illumination" was a grand success. (Tim Ribar '74 photo)

The passing of the guard; Norm and Jo Fintel greet David and Susan Gring.

Index